HEALTHY
SOUTH INDIAN
COOKING

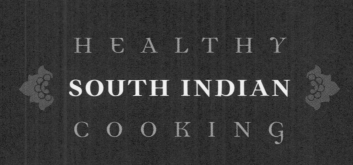

HEALTHY SOUTH INDIAN COOKING

EXPANDED EDITION

ALAMELU VAIRAVAN

AND

PATRICIA MARQUARDT

HIPPOCRENE BOOKS

NEW YORK

This book is dedicated to Dr. K. Vairavan, our dear
friend and mentor, for his unending patience,
optimism, inspiration, and love.

For information, address:
HIPPOCRENE BOOKS, INC.
171 Madison Avenue
New York, NY 10016
www.hippocrenebooks.com

Principal Photography by Kevin J. Miyazaki.
Book and jacket design, interior black & white photographs by Brad Rickman.

Library of Congress Cataloging-in-Publication Data

Vairavan, Alamelu.
    Healthy South Indian cooking / Alamelu Vairavan and Patricia Marquardt. -- Expanded ed.
        p. cm.
    Includes index.
    ISBN-13: 978-0-7818-1189-7
    ISBN-10: 0-7818-1189-9
  1. Cookery, Indic. 2. Low-cholesterol diet--Recipes. I. Marquardt, Patricia. II. Title.
    TX724.5.I4V175 2008
    641.598--dc22
                            2008007477

Printed in the United States of America.

contents

ACKNOWLEDGMENTS

We would like to express our deep appreciation to Alamelu's husband, Dr. K. Vairavan (KV), for his unfailing encouragement and guidance throughout the writing of this book. Despite his extremely busy professional life, he tested many of the recipes himself, suggested revisions, and truly provided the inspiration, love, and support that kept the project progressing. It is no exaggeration to say that KV is the muse who sparked our creativity.

Expressions of gratitude are also in order for Valli and Atul Gupta, and Ashok Vairavan for all their creative ideas, encouragement, and support. Alamelu would like to thank her mother, Umayal Palaniappan, and sister, PL. Lakshmi, for their constant encouragement, and would also like to thank her aunt, Visalakshi Alagappan, in whose home she originally learned to cook from chef Nedungudi Natesan, who is now widely known in Chettinad, South India.

Patricia would specifically like to thank her sister, Lolita Lukach, and dear friend Dr. James Shey for their loving support. She dedicates this book to the memory of her beloved mother, Ruth Hovde.

The authors also express appreciation to registered dietitian Suzie Dunn, who provided nutritional analysis for the recipes included in this book. Her enterprising attitude and practical contributions have been invaluable.

The authors would like to thank Kevin J. Miyazaki, the photographer for most of the pictures in the book including the jacket picture. Thanks are also due to Ken Schwacher (vitabella photography) and K. Vairavan for their additional photographic help. We would also like to thank Dr. Leonard Levine for his valuable computer support. Acknowledgment is also in order for Web-site designer Cliff Peters for his excellent work in designing Alamelu's Web site www.curryonwheels.com which highlights this book and her culinary activities.

We are grateful for the numerous useful comments from students in Alamelu's cooking classes offered at various locations including Froedtert Hospital, Waukesha County Technical College, Waukesha Culinary Arts Program, Wisconsin Kitchen Mark, University of Wisconsin-Milwaukee (Continuing Education), and many suburban recreation departments. We should not forget to acknowledge the countless e-mail messages and telephone calls received from people with comments and questions related to our books. These encouraging contacts were very helpful and resulted in improved presentations of many recipes.

We would like to express our sincere appreciation to our editor, Priti Chitnis Gress, for her timely help and guidance throughout our cookbook projects. More importantly, Priti understood our vision for the book and provided the essential advice, and for that we are also grateful to copyeditor Barbara Keane-Pigeon for her extraordinarily thorough proofreading. Thanks are also in order to Monica Bentley, Senior Editor, Tracy Liaw, Editorial Assistant, and Brad Rickman for cover and art design.

Finally, our acknowledgments would not be complete without thanking George Blagowidow, the publisher of Hippocrene Books, New York. We are very grateful for the enormous confidence and support that this learned gentleman has shown us.

A NOTE FROM ALAMELU

Max, my late adorable West Highland Terrier, sitting near my feet in the kitchen, savoring the aromas from the cooking, and being present throughout the writing of this book, will always be a cherished memory.

preface

Our cookbooks are the result of a long-standing friendship between two neighbors who enjoy cooking together and sharing food with their families. We regard our cookbooks as a tribute to our treasured friendship. We hope this book will help you also discover a special joy in cooking and sharing.

In our first cookbook, *Art of South Indian Cooking* (1997), we presented a simple introduction to South Indian cuisine with over 100 recipes. In our second book, *Healthy South Indian Cooking* (2001), we aspired to far more. We expanded the explanations of our recipes, refined the recipes themselves, and added new ones. We also included new features, notably nutritional analysis and photographs of the spices and dishes. An important aspect of the second book is that it reflects the suggestions and comments we received from many people who used our recipes. What an amazing experience it has been to learn that our cookbooks have encouraged so many people to enjoy new foods and a new approach to healthful eating!

In this Expanded Edition of *Healthy South Indian Cooking*, we have added over forty new recipes. These additions reflect the fact that South Indian cuisine is itself evolving. The additions are also a result of our desire to include recipes featuring foods not considered traditionally South Indian, such as asparagus and avocado, that are popular in the U.S. As in our previous books, the cooking techniques presented in this book reflect authentic methods from South India. Most of our recipes have their roots in the rich cooking traditions of Tamil Nadu and, in particular, its Chettinad region. These foods, however, are also commonly enjoyed in other regions of South India, including the famous high-tech cities of Bangalore and Hyderabad.

We believe that this book will be useful to both novice and experienced cooks. We added a shopping list for spices. We also included healthful suggestions for assembling a spice pantry. In order to encourage people unfamiliar with Indian cooking,

we set forth a list of recipes for beginners that are particularly easy to follow. We further expanded the section on fusion meals, and even included recipes for a festive Thanksgiving dinner that unites American and South Indian flavors!

Since the publication of our previous books, there is even more scientific evidence and appreciation for the remarkable health benefits of spices. In fact, some people use spices, such as turmeric and cayenne, primary ingredients in South Indian foods, by themselves as health supplements. Thus we are all the more motivated to reach a wider audience through our recipes.

It is our hope that the reader will find in this book an easy-to-follow guide to discovering the joy of South Indian cuisine and cooking. The chapter "A Glimpse of South India" provides an introduction to this extremely interesting part of India with a focus on its cuisine. Following this introduction are useful sections on spices, dals, and other ingredients; a glossary of South Indian dishes; and an expanded list of general cooking tips. Those who are eager to try the recipes may read these preliminary sections selectively and go on directly to the main recipe chapters. You will find the Vegetables chapter to be the largest in this book, since vegetables are predominant in the South Indian diet. South Indian vegetarian cuisine is unmatched for the variety of its dishes, methods of cooking, and exquisite tastes.

Finally the reader will also find sections on sample menus for preparing complete South Indian meals as well as suggestions for integrating South Indian dishes into traditional western meals. Explore and enjoy!

Alamelu Vairavan and Patricia Marquardt
www.curryonwheels.com

remarks BY ALAMELU VAIRAVAN

The Chettinad region of Tamil Nadu, South India, is where I was born and raised. I grew up in a large household with a professional cook and regularly shared in an abundance of delicious foods. Although I knew nothing about cooking itself, I did enjoy good food. In 1967, I accompanied my husband to the United States as a young bride. While my husband was finishing his doctoral studies at the University of Notre Dame, I was in New York learning how to cook from professional Chettinad chef Nedungudi Natesan under a most disciplined but enjoyable regime, imposed by my aunt Visalakshi Alagappan in her home. Necessity, as they say, is the mother of invention. Following my cooking lessons and orientation to American life in New York, I joined my husband at Notre Dame.

To my surprise, I found immediate joy in cooking. I am people-oriented and love to entertain. My husband and I entertained numerous friends and family from all over the world. Frequently, when friends dined with us, they indicated how much they enjoyed the food. Many even asked me for the recipes. These compliments not only gave me joy but inspired me greatly. I also gave numerous cooking demonstrations in the community, participated in block party contributions for neighbors and friends, and conducted cooking classes. All these activities greatly encouraged my interest in cooking.

As my interest grew, I discovered that there were very few books on South Indian cooking written in English. This fact, plus repeated requests for recipes from friends and my own growing interest in cooking, led me to write a South Indian cookbook. Another motivating factor was my desire to pass on my recipes to our children and to the generations to come.

My co-author, my dearest friend and neighbor Dr. Patricia Marquardt, and I set out on the exciting adventure of writing our first cookbook. I was thrilled to have Pat observe my cooking, ask questions, request precise measurements of the ingredients, and help write the recipes in an organized manner. My dear husband KV, Pat's late husband Bill, and my children, Valli and Ashok, provided the ongoing inspiration that kept the project alive despite many lengthy interruptions. Our collaboration, that began with a vision of a good South Indian cookbook accessible to today's cooks, culminated in our first publication, *Art of South Indian Cooking*. The goodwill that surrounded that book from the beginning has truly been a blessing.

As I reflect on the publication and the favorable reception of our first cookbook, I am filled with the deepest gratitude to the many people whose helpful suggestions and encouragement sustained my continued work with the recipes. The participants in various cooking classes conducted at community centers, hospitals, and gourmet clubs over the past three years inspired me greatly. The continued collaboration of my co-author was invaluable in writing this new book. Pat is not only a scholar but a natural cook who devoted many months to refining our recipes and perfecting her own South Indian cooking skills. Pat tested a wide variety of exquisite South Indian dishes on her own. My husband has observed that he has not found a match anywhere for Pat's coconut rice dish. Pat's crowning achievement as a South Indian cook came when she prepared dosais to perfection together with truly authentic sambhar and kosamalli. I felt very

much like a proud teacher who wanted to show off her pupil to the world. The more Pat and I worked together, the more we found the bonds of love and admiration between us grow.

I feel gratitude beyond words towards my beloved father, AV.M. Palaniappa Chettiar, who before his death in the spring of 1999 expressed enormous joy and pride in seeing our first cookbook in print. I remember during my childhood my dad fondly arranging for a broad array of delicious foods and skilled cooks who would indulge my every whim.

Most importantly, I would like to acknowledge the divine source of guidance and strength, which truly gave this project its wings and enabled me to accomplish an important goal.

I would like to suggest that readers approach South Indian cooking with an attitude of relaxation and enjoyment. Don't allow yourself to be burdened with concerns about the exactness of measurements or the lack of certain ingredients. Your dishes will be delicious and family and guests will be delighted with your efforts. There is great joy to be found in sharing with others the food one has prepared. I hope that your cooking experiences will bring you much happiness that will extend to all areas of your life.

Alamelu Vairavan
Milwaukee, Wisconsin

remarks BY PATRICIA MARQUARDT

The tantalizing aromas of Indian cooking emanating from the kitchen windows of my dear next-door neighbor Alamelu over twenty years ago beckoned me to a culinary journey and a treasured friendship. The first delicious tastes of lemon rice and beet vadas over the side fence led to years of informal cooking sessions in Alamelu's kitchen, during which she generously shared with me not only her South Indian recipes but also her philosophy of cooking. Copious notes from our cooking sessions were incorporated in the text of our first book, *Art of South Indian Cooking*, which was published in November 1997. The enthusiastic reception of that book was most gratifying, and our cooking sessions continued with the testing of additional delicious recipes from the culinary tradition of South India. These sessions were enriched by the many comments we received from the readers of the first book and from participants in Alamelu's cooking demonstrations and our joint book-signing events.

Alamelu and I worked intensively on the second book during the summer of 2000, retesting and refining the recipes from the first book and adding numerous others. Always Alamelu was energized by a zeal to share her glorious culinary tradition through recipes that are as authentic as possible, clearly written, and accessible to everyone. The summer of 2000 proved to be a real learning experience for me as I cooked more South Indian dishes than ever before and read widely about the nutritional science that underlies the use of particular ingredients and spices in Indian dishes. The reward for my efforts came when KV, Alamelu's husband, commented that even a native of South India would believe that my cooking was the work of a true South Indian cook! That was rare praise, indeed, for one who has come to admire much about that rich culture.

Alamelu's enthusiasm for sharing her culinary tradition and for guiding others to a varied and healthful diet has been most inspirational. I learned from Alamelu not only techniques of food preparation and many delicious South Indian recipes, but also something of a true reverence for the act of cooking itself and the satisfaction one can find in serving the food to others. Alamelu and I visited South India in the winter of 1996, and there I personally experienced the cultural roots of that gracious hospitality that Alamelu embodies so beautifully. I am grateful that Alamelu has been my dearest friend and mentor for many years. How far I have traveled on my culinary journey!

I hope you, too, will begin a journey to a more varied and exciting cuisine, by way of South Indian cooking. I know that I shall continue on the cultural journey I began more than two decades ago with return trips to India, continued cooking sessions with Alamelu, and the inclusion of these extraordinarily delicious South Indian foods into my diet forever. I am equally certain that the treasured friendship with Alamelu will also be forever.

Patricia Marquardt
Milwaukee, Wisconsin

a glimpse of south india

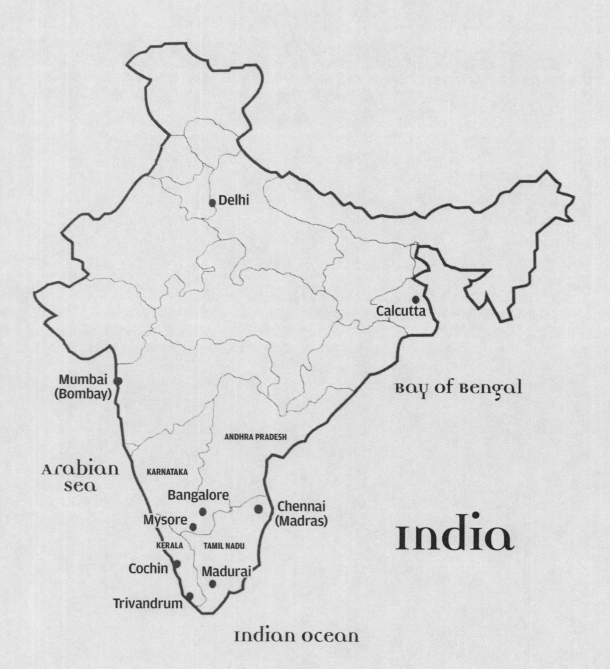

Delhi

Calcutta

BAY OF BENGAL

Mumbai
(Bombay)

ANDHRA PRADESH

ARABIAN
SEA

KARNATAKA

Bangalore

Mysore

Chennai
(Madras)

INDIA

KERALA

TAMIL NADU

Cochin

Madurai

Trivandrum

INDIAN OCEAN

The term "South India" usually refers to the southern peninsula of the vast Indian subcontinent made up of four states: Tamil Nadu and Andhra Pradesh on the east coast; and Karnataka and Kerala on the west coast. South Indian people from these states have distinct cultural character-istics and speak different languages: Tamil, Telugu, Kannada, and Malayalam respectively. These languages have rich and well-established literatures. Tamil is the most ancient of them with a great literature that dates back more than 2,000 years. An important common feature of the South Indians is their Dravidian origin, in contrast to the predominantly Aryan origin of the people of the North. The vast majority of South Indians are Hindus, but Muslims and Christians form sizeable minorities and have also made significant contributions in the South. Since historically the northern part of India bore the brunt of foreign invasions, South India has been affected less by outside influences. Thus the culture and religious practices, as well as the food, of the South tend to reflect long-standing traditions.

South India is known for its magnificent Hindu temples, some of which date back to ancient times. This region of India is also known for classical arts such as the Bhara-thanatyam dance and Carnatic music, each with long, rich traditions. Also, some of the most ancient and beautiful sculptures in India can be found in this region.

South Indian geographical features include hill ranges, beautiful plateaus, dusty hot plains, rivers, and seacoasts populated by a large number of villages, towns, and many cosmopolitan cities. Two of the premier cities of South India are Chennai (for-merly known as Madras) in Tamil Nadu and Bangalore in Karnataka. Both of these cities have large industrial complexes, extensive cultural activities, centers of state governments, and highly regarded academic institutions. Because of its high-tech industries, Bangalore has come to be known as the Silicon Valley of India, and has attracted numerous multinational corporations. Chennai is on the east coast and has a tropical climate, while Bangalore is located about 200 miles to the west on the Deccan plateau and has a moderate climate. Interestingly, from the perspective

15

of our cookbook, both cities boast of an exquisite variety of South Indian foods. Each of these cities offers a remarkably broad and wonderful array of restaurants that serve some of the best South Indian foods anywhere.

Other areas in the South noted for their outstanding cuisines include the Chettinad region and the ancient cities of Tanjore and Madurai in Tamil Nadu; Udupi and Mysore in Karnataka; Cochin and Trivandrum in Kerala; and Hyderabad in Andhra Pradesh. Chettinad, the land of Chettiars, is a region located about 250 miles south of Chennai. The Chettiar community was historically known for its banking and business achievements, wealth, charitable pursuits, and hospitality. Chettinad cooking has always been distinctive, and recently has become especially popular in Chennai and in many other cities in India. Chettinad cuisine is characterized by thick delicious sauces, such as *kulambu*, and a dry stir-fry style of cooking vegetarian and nonvegetarian dishes called *poriyal*. This cuisine is also known for a wide variety of unique savories and sweets called *palakaram*, usually served at breakfast, teatime, and the evening meal. Chettinad cooking techniques have influenced the cuisines of many other parts of South India. Conversely, other parts of South India, in particular Kerala and Karnataka, have influenced Chettinad cooking.

South India is known for the hospitality of its people. Guests at a private home are treated with much warmth and respect and are welcome almost anytime. For example, it is not uncommon for people to drop by the homes of their friends and relatives, or even neighbors, informally and without invitation. Whether the visit is casual or is in response to a formal invitation, guests are received graciously and with eagerness and offered snacks and soft drinks or coffee. If the visit is close to a mealtime, the guests are often persuaded to stay on and have the meal with the hosts. During a meal it is very common for the host to focus attention on the guests' comfort and satisfaction. This special treatment of guests is a heartwarming and sometimes even an overwhelming experience.

A typical South Indian breakfast may include white fluffy idlis (steamed rice cakes) or crisp dosais (thin pancakes made with rice and urad dal) served with a chutney (savory accompaniment) or sambhar (a vegetable stew). Other possible breakfast items include uppuma (cream of wheat or rice cooked with spices), vadas (doughnut-shaped fritters made with lentils), and pongal (creamy spiced rice). A beverage often served with breakfast is a latte-like coffee made with steamed milk and sugar called Madras coffee or Mysore coffee. For lunch, plain rice is a staple food and is usually served in at least three courses. First, rice is served with sambhar or kulambu, then with rasam (a thin peppery soup), followed by plain yogurt or buttermilk to be mixed with rice. A variety of vegetable dishes, such as kootu and poriyal, are served with all three courses. If the meal is nonvegetarian, meat is served as a side dish or as a sauce served over plain rice.

Pappadum, a crispy wafer-like accompaniment made from urad dal and spices, often enhances a meal. A South Indian dinner is usually a light meal and may consist of rice with vegetables, or idlis or dosasi served with sambhar or chutney. During meals people habitually drink plenty of water. Coffee or tea is not served with lunch or dinner. On special occasions, a dessert such as payasam (rice, tapioca, or vermicelli cooked in milk with saffron and cardamom) is served with a main meal.

It is interesting to note that a traditional way to eat a meal in South India is to use the right hand. Eating with the hand allows one to feel more connected to the food. Also a traditional South Indian way to serve meals is on a banana leaf rather than a plate.

Foods play an important role in the South Indian life. Even most Hindu temples have kitchens associated with them, where only pure vegetarian foods are prepared and are used in religious ceremonies and then served to the devotees. In South India, many Hindus, as they get older, tend to become vegetarians for religious reasons and for health benefits.

South India is a remarkably interesting region of India with a wide range of characteristics that include ancient arts, textiles and high-tech industries, many languages with rich literatures, and a cuisine that is among the best in the world.

NUTRITIONAL INTRODUCTION

Study after study of people's diets show that there is great benefit from eating a wide variety of foods in moderate amounts. Emphasis has been on increasing vegetables and legumes and decreasing total fat and sodium. The terms "phytochemical" and "functional foods" have become part of our language. We are learning that the foods we choose can make a difference in susceptibility to chronic disease or to the degree of genetic expression of disease or aging in our bodies.

The South Indian recipes in this book offer us a rich array of foods that include such phytochemicals as allium compounds, carotenoids, coumarins, and flavonoids. Examples of these are found in, but not limited to, garlic, onions, ginger, bell peppers, chili peppers, tomatoes and tomato products, broccoli and other cruciferous vegetables, nuts, eggplants, fenugreek, potatoes, and turmeric. The South Indian recipes also afford us functional foods such as wonderful sources of increased fiber, vitamins, and minerals. Minimal cooking oil, reduced salt, use of lean meats, and short cooking times round out the means to maintain good health through diet.

The authors include a nutritional analysis with each recipe in this book. Though it is good to be aware of the nutrients in each recipe, exclusive attention to particular nutrients can lead to an incomplete picture of the overall health benefits and enjoyment of food. For example, some vegetables by nature have a significant sodium content, but the overall nutritional value of vegetables in general is well understood.

If readers have concerns about sodium content, the amount of salt can be reduced or eliminated altogether, without sacrificing to any great extent the delicious flavors of these recipes. Do not lose sight of the fact that the recipes as written are authentic, delectable, and, once tried, will be forever remembered as truly wonderful. South Indian food affects you in a good way. I hope you appreciate the good nutrition as well as the sumptuous aromas and tastes.

Nutritional analysis in this book was performed using data found in *Bowes and Church's Food Values of Portions Commonly Used*, Jean A.T. Pennington, 17th Edition, Lippincott, 1998; United States Department of Agriculture (USDA) research publications; and the nutrition labels on some food products. The nutritional analysis for each recipe in this book is for a single serving unless the number of servings is unspecified as, for example, in the various appetizers and most bread items. In such cases, the nutritional analysis provided is for each food item.

Susan Sharer Dunn (Suzie)
Registered Dietitian
Sedona, Arizona

MULTILINGUAL GLOSSARY OF
SPICES, DALS, AND FLOURS

This glossary will be helpful in shopping for spices, lentils, and flours from Indian stores. Because spices are commonly labeled in Hindi in Indian groceries, the Hindi term is provided here. The Tamil term is also provided, as Tamil is one of the four major languages of South India.

ENGLISH	HINDI	TAMIL
Asafoetida	Hing	Perungayam
Bay leaf	Tez Patta	Lavangilai
Black pepper	Kalimirch	Milagu
Cardamom	Elachi	Ellakkai
Cinnamon	Dal Chini	Pattai
Chickpeas (roasted)	Chana Dalia	Pottukadalai
Chili peppers (red)	Mirch	Milagaai
Cloves	Lavang	Krambu
Coriander seeds	Dhaniya	Kothamallivedai
Cumin seeds	Jeera	Jeerakam
Fennel (aniseed)	Saunf (Sonf)	Perunjeeragam
Fenugreek seeds	Methi	Venthayam
Mustard seeds	Rai (Sarson)	Kadugu
Poppy seeds (white)	Khus Khus	Kus Kus
Saffron	Zaffran (Kesar)	Kungumappu
Tamarind	Imli	Puli
Turmeric	Haldi	Manjal

DALS AND FLOURS

ENGLISH	HINDI	TAMIL
All-purpose flour	Maida	Maida mavu
Almonds	Badam	Badam
Bengal gram dal	Channe-ki-dal	Kadalai paruppu
Bengal gram flour (Chickpea flour)	Besan (Gram flour)	Kadalai mavu
Black gram dal (split)	Urad dal	Ulutham paruppu
Chickpea	Kabuli Chana	Kondai kadalai
Green gram dal (split)	Moong dal	Payatham paruppu
Green gram, whole	Moong	Paasipayaru
Red lentil	Masoor dal	Mysoor paruppu
Red gram dal	Toovar (Toor) dal	Thuvaram paruppu
Sago (tapioca)	Sabudana	Javvarasi
Semolina	Sooji	Ravai
Vermicelli	Seviyan	Semiya
Wheat flour	Atta	Gothambai mavu

spices and other basics

The Indian Spice Box

In an Indian spice box there are seven small containers which usually contain the following spices for South Indian cooking. Under the cover of the spice box is another lid that holds the small containers in place.

Black mustard seeds   **Fenugreek seeds**

Urad dal   **Dried red chili pepper**

Cumin seeds   **Cinnamon sticks**

Fennel seeds

Storing Spices and Dals

Most spices keep best in covered glass bottles or containers. Spices will retain their quality for many months, tightly closed even for a year or two, provided they are stored in airtight containers. We highly recommend removing spices, powders, and dals from their plastic wraps and storing them in bottles with identifying labels. Spices kept in the kitchen cupboard in jars will retain flavor, aroma, and color. Dals can be stored in glass or metal containers. There are various size jars available in spice shops and in discount stores.

If you purchase spices, rice, and dals in bulk, you will have more than you will need for ready use in the kitchen. The remaining amount can be stored in dry, airtight containers on a cool pantry shelf.

spices and spice powders used in south indian cooking

With very few exceptions, the spices used in South Indian cooking can be found in most American supermarkets. Other spices can be bought economically from Indian and Oriental grocery stores or from stores specializing in spices. One may also mail-order spices from many Indian grocery stores or Web sites in the United States and in Canada. For suggestions visit Alamelu's Web site **www.curryonwheels.com.**

Once a basic pantry of Indian spices is assembled, you will be able to use them time and again in numerous recipes that often call for the same ingredients in similar order.

Asafoetida

A strongly scented resin used in small quantities in some vegetable and rice dishes, that imparts a flavor reminiscent of onion and garlic. Asafoetida is sold in lump or powdered form. The powdered form, available in Indian grocery stores, is recommended.

Bay Leaves

Long, dried green leaves that add a subtle flavor to dishes. Only one or two leaves are needed to flavor a recipe of vegetables or nonvegetarian foods.

Black Mustard Seeds

Small, round, black seeds which impart fundamental flavor and texture to dishes. Mustard seeds are often used in combination with urad dal in vegetable, rice, and sambhar dishes.

Black Pepper

Used whole or in powdered form. Powdered black pepper and cumin, mixed in equal portion, can be used in chicken recipes, over fried eggs, and in yogurt salads to enhance the flavor of the dish. The combination of black pepper and cumin powder in soups and rasams helps to relieve cold symptoms.

Black Pepper and Cumin Powder

Combine both spices in equal portion (for example, ¼ cup to ¼ cup) and grind to a fine powder. Delicious when used in nonvegetarian dishes and over fried eggs. It is also used in rasam preparation.

Cardamom

A highly aromatic spice with a delicate sweetness, used primarily to flavor tea, soup, and dessert dishes. The seeds may be used whole or in powdered form. Cardamom is also used as a breath freshener.

Cayenne Powder

Ground red chili pepper, readily available in regular and Indian grocery stores, often under the name "ground red pepper." Commonly used in both vegetarian and nonvegetarian dishes.

Chutney "Podi" Powder

This is a blend of various spices such as curry leaves, red chili peppers, toor dal, and urad dal. It is readily available in Indian grocery stores, sometimes labeled as "Chatney Powder." A recommended commercial preparation is the MTR brand. A unique Chettinad variation of chutney powder is known as "Podi." Podi is commonly served with such items as idlis and dosais, but the authors have found podi, or alternately chutney powder, to be a delicious ingredient in vegetable dishes as well.

The following is an easy-to-follow recipe for homemade Chutney "Podi" Powder:

> ½ cup whole dried red chili peppers (about 16)
>
> 2 tablespoons urad dal
>
> 1 tablespoon toor dal
>
> ¼ cup curry leaves
>
> 2 teaspoons canola oil
>
> ½ teaspoon asafoetida powder
>
> ½ teaspoon salt

1. Separately roast red chili peppers, urad dal, toor dal, and curry leaves, each in ½ teaspoon of oil over medium heat to a light golden color.

2. Combine the above roasted spices with asafoetida powder and salt.

3. In a spice or coffee grinder, grind the ingredients together to a fine powder.

Makes ½ cup.

Cinnamon

The aromatic reddish-brown bark of the cinnamon tree, it imparts a rich, sweet, pleasantly spicy flavor to foods. It is used, usually in stick form, in many vegetable and nonvegetarian dishes. Also available in powdered form.

Cloves

The aromatic unopened flower of the clove tree that imparts a rich and sweetly subtle flavor to rice and dessert dishes. Cloves are often chewed as mouth freshener after meals.

Coconut Powder

Available in Indian grocery stores and natural food stores as "unsweetened coconut powder." It is easier to use coconut powder than fresh coconut, which needs to be cracked and ground. Unsweetened coconut powder is used in various dishes. When coconut powder is ground with other seasonings to make kurma, it blends well with vegetables producing a smooth paste and allowing the flavors of the vegetables and meat to come through.

Coriander Seeds

Coriander seeds come from the same plant as coriander (cilantro) leaves. Coriander seeds can be used whole or ground. Usually a desired amount of coriander seeds is placed in an iron skillet, dry roasted over medium heat until dark brown, and then ground to a powder. Coriander seeds have a pleasant odor of sweetness with a bit of lemony taste. Coriander powder and cayenne powder are often combined together in equal portions in various dishes.

Cumin Powder

Powdered cumin is readily available in regular grocery stores. Cumin powder blends well with vegetables and has an aromatic flavor. Cumin powder blended with cayenne powder also lends distinctive flavor to any dish. Cumin powder, in combination with black pepper, is used over fried eggs and in soup and yogurt dishes. The combination of cumin powder and cayenne powder enhances the flavor of many dishes.

Cumin Seeds

An important spice, commonly used in whole or powdered form, that imparts a nutty, pleasantly bitter flavor to foods.

Curry Powder

A commercial blend of many spices such as coriander, fenugreek, turmeric, cumin, black pepper, bay leaves, cloves, onions, red chili peppers, and ginger. Readily available in regular grocery stores, domestic curry powder is used in some vegetable and meat dishes.

Fennel Seeds

Larger in size than cumin seeds, they have a delicate flavor similar to anise. Commonly used in nonvegetarian cooking and in soups. Roasted fennel seeds are also used as a breath freshener.

Fenugreek Seeds

Small brown seeds that are slightly bitter. Used sparingly in sambhar dishes and in nonvegetarian dishes such as seafood to enhance flavor. Also used with dosai batter to give a distinct and special flavor.

Garam Masala Powder

A mixture of several spices. It can be purchased in Indian grocery stores, but has a fresher taste if you personally roast and grind the spices, such as cardamom, black peppercorns, cumin seeds, coriander, cinnamon, and cloves. Garam masala powder is a spice mixture that is very aromatic. It is used in some nonvegetarian dishes.

Poppy Seeds (White)

The seeds from the poppy plant, used primarily as a thickening agent. White poppy seed is the only variety of poppy seed used in Indian cooking.

Rasam Powder

An aromatic blend of many spices including coriander seeds, red chili peppers, cumin seeds, curry leaves, and asafoetida. It comes prepackaged. We prefer to use the MTR brand of rasam powder that is available in Indian grocery stores.

Red Chili Pepper

Pungent dried pods of the pepper plant can be added whole or in powdered form. The use of one or two pods will increase the flavor level of dishes and enhance other seasonings. The perfect accompaniment for garnishing in hot oil with curry leaves and other seasonings, it enhances the flavor of chutneys and sambhar dishes.

Roasted Chickpeas

Known as *dhalia* in Hindi and *pottukadalai* in Tamil, roasted chickpeas give a pleasing texture and flavor particularly to chutneys and kurma dishes. If unavailable, dry roasted unsalted peanuts can be substituted with similar results.

Saffron

A rare and aromatic spice from the stigmas of the crocus plant that adds an exotic flavor and orange-red color to rice dishes. Known as "the queen of all spices," saffron is also used widely in desserts. Often saffron is soaked in water or milk to develop color and aroma.

Sambhar Powder

An aromatic blend of many spices including red chili peppers, cumin, curry leaves, fenugreek, asafoetida, chana dal, and toovar dal. Commonly used in sambhar and kulambu dishes.

Tamarind

A bean with a sweet and sour taste that adds a certain tartness to dishes. It is known as "Indian date." Bottled tamarind paste is available in Indian grocery stores. Lemon juice may be substituted for tamarind.

Tapioca

A beadlike starch obtained from the cassava root. It is used primarily in payasam (pudding) and served as dessert.

Turmeric Powder

One of the great Indian spices, turmeric powder is a yellow root-spice that has been dried and powdered. A natural food coloring that imparts a musty flavor and bright yellow color to any dish. Turmeric, which contains the compound curcumin, is an antioxidant and an anti-inflammatory substance. Growing research suggests that turmeric may help prevent arthritis and a host of other diseases including Alzheimer's.

Vindaloo Curry Paste

Pastes are convenient blends of ground spices preserved in oil for freshness. Vindaloo curry paste is spicy and sour and can be used to make chicken, shrimp, and lamb dishes. Ingredients in this paste are vegetable oil, coriander, cumin, turmeric, chili peppers, ginger, garlic, and tamarind. Available in small jars at Indian grocery stores.

NOTE: Many of the spices and spice powders can be obtained at major regular grocery stores. The Kohinoor or MTR brand are recommended. For additional suggestions visit Alamelu's Web site, www.curryonwheels.com.

Herbs and Fresh Ingredients

Coconut

The hard-shelled, edible nut of the coconut tree is widely used as a garnish for cooked vegetables and as a base for kurmas and chutneys. Fresh coconut is available in general grocery stores. Crack open the coconut with a hammer. Food processors or electric mini choppers may be used to shred the fresh coconut. Shredded unsweetened coconut powder is also available in natural food stores and in Indian grocery stores. The milk of the coconut is not used often in Indian cooking, but it is enjoyed as a cool, refreshing drink on a hot summer day.

Coriander

A distinctively aromatic herb of major importance, which may be purchased as leaves, seeds, or powder. Also called "cilantro" in Spanish and Mexican recipes, it is used both as a seasoning and as a garnish. Coriander chutney is a very popular accompaniment to vadais, idlis, and dosais.

Curry Leaves

The dark green leaves of the curry plant impart a savory taste and lingering aroma to South Indian dishes. They are one of the primary ingredients used in Madras sambhar powder and rasam powder. Curry leaves are dropped in hot oil before adding onions and other main ingredients or are used to flavor the oil that is poured over many dishes as a finishing step.

Garlic

A bulbous herb composed of individual cloves that is an essential ingredient in South Indian cooking. Used in most soups, vegetables, and meat dishes to enhance the flavor. Frequently sautéed in hot oil at the outset of a recipe, it infuses the entire dish with distinctively pleasing flavor. Garlic with ginger makes a delicious combination paste. Great curative powers are attributed to garlic.

Ginger Root

A root spice with a warm, fresh flavor that is used very often in Indian cooking both as a fundamental ingredient and as a garnish. Ginger in combination with garlic is very popular and adds wonderful flavor to any dish. Ginger also aids in digestion. Ginger is available in powdered form, but fresh ginger is highly recommended for its flavor and healthful qualities. It is valued as a medicinal and culinary spice.

Green Chili Peppers

Fresh unripe chili peppers are a common ingredient that imparts a spicy, hot flavor to many Indian dishes. There are a wide variety of chili peppers and you may use any of the many types available. Chili peppers are used in virtually every savory dish in India. Chili peppers may be used sparingly, however, or omitted altogether depending on your taste. In general, the smaller the chili pepper, the hotter it is.

Mint

Fragrant herb with a uniquely fresh flavor and aroma. Used primarily in cooling chutneys and relishes that balance the more spicy dishes.

Onion

Staple ingredient valued for its flavor and medicinal qualities. Onions sautéed in oil with various spices are the foundation of most dishes. Onions also appear raw in yogurt salad and as a garnish for other dishes.

Rice and oil used in south Indian cooking

Rice

Rice is a staple food of South India. Four types of rice, commonly used in our recipes for rice dishes, are outlined here.

Basmati rice is a fragrant, high-quality rice used in making both plain and flavored rice dishes. It has a nutlike flavor and comes packaged under several brand names. When purchasing basmati rice, look for a quality brand, such as Dehradun or Tilda. They are available in natural food stores and Indian grocery stores. The grains of basmati rice are finer than the grains of other types of rice, and they separate beautifully after they are cooked. Basmati rice is unexcelled in making pulaoo and flavored rice dishes.

Jasmine rice is a delicate and aromatic pure white rice. It is excellent for making plain or flavored rice dishes. It is available in Indian and Oriental grocery stores.

Extra long-grain rice is used in making plain and flavored rice dishes. It lacks the aromatic quality of the basmati and jasmine rice, but it is a good all-purpose rice. It is available in regular supermarkets.

Although white and basmati rice are commonly used in South Indian cooking, you may also prepare the recipes with **brown rice**. You may find that the nutty flavor and high fiber content of the brown rice compensates for its lack of lightness and delicacy.

To cook any type of rice, we highly recommend an automatic electric rice cooker. Rice cookers are readily available in department stores and in Indian and Oriental stores. Rice cookers come in various sizes, ranging from a small, four-cup size to larger sizes.

Cooking Oils

We prefer two types of light vegetable oils in preparing South Indian dishes. These are **canola oil** (for its mild flavor) and **corn oil** (for its rich corn taste). Both canola and corn oil provide a light cooking medium that will enhance the flavor of the dishes you are preparing. If you wish, you may also use olive oil as a cooking medium, although it is not an authentic South Indian cooking ingredient. The authors, therefore, recommend the more delicate canola and corn oils for South Indian cooking. Coconut oil is used in only one recipe in this book, Kerala Aviyal. While coconut oil lends a deliciously rich flavor to foods, it is rather high in saturated fat.

Ghee, clarified butter, is used in preparing delicious biriyani rice, chappatis, and desserts. Ghee is made by melting butter and seasoning the melted butter with curry leaves and cumin. Allow the melted butter to cool. Then pour off the clear butter into a bottle and discard the residue. The residue from the butter with all its seasonings is often used for making delicious ghee rice. Store ghee, covered, at room temperature or in the refrigerator. When you wish to use ghee, heat a small portion of ghee in a butter warmer and use as needed. Ghee adds a wonderful flavor to dishes, but should be used sparingly because of its high fat content.

Dals

Dals (lentils), legumes high in protein and fiber, are a staple ingredient in many South Indian dishes. There are numerous varieties of dals, but in most recipes no more than two dals are needed. The most common of these are toor dal (or moong dal) and urad dal. The following is a broad array of dals:

Toor Dal or Toovar Dal

A kind of yellow lentil that is split into two round halves. Sometimes toor dals are packaged in a slightly oiled form. Toor dal is cooked to a creamy consistency to make sambhars, kootus, and soups. It creates the rich base so characteristic of delicious sambhars. Toor dal is available in Indian grocery stores.

Yellow Split Peas

A familiar kind of legume, readily available in regular grocery stores. Yellow split peas appear often in the recipes in this book because of their distinctive texture and taste. Specifically yellow split peas are used to make dishes such as vadas, podimas, pachadis, and kootus.

Masoor Dal

An orange-red colored lentil, also known as red lentil, in split form, that is used in making sambhars. Masoor dal cooks faster than toor dal. Masoor dal can be substituted for toor dal in sambhars and other vegetable dishes. Masoor dal is available in natural food stores and Indian grocery stores.

Moong Dal

A golden yellow lentil used in split form. This most versatile of dals cooks quickly and is widely used in making vegetarian dishes. The whole moong bean, which is small, oval, and olive green in color, is called whole green gram dal. Available in Indian grocery stores.

Urad Dal

A creamy white split lentil. Fried urad dal gives a nutty, crunchy taste to dishes. Essential to South Indian cooking, urad dal is used both as a seasoning and as a base for vadas, idlis, and dosais. Urad dal, fried in oil with black mustard seeds and various seasonings, is an essential ingredient in many recipes. Available in Indian grocery stores. Urad dal, when whole, has a black skin and is known as black gram lentil. The recipes in this book use the split urad dal exclusively.

Chana Dal

A kind of yellow lentil, also called gram lentil, that resembles yellow split peas but is larger and coarser. When roasted, chana dal has a nutty taste and crunchy texture. Chana dal is used to make soondals, vadas, and kootus. Available in Indian grocery stores.

NOTE Dals are very easy to cook. In each recipe where dals are used, we have given easy-to-follow stovetop cooking instructions. Soaking toor dal and split peas in warm water for an hour prior to cooking will reduce the cooking time. The use of a pressure cooker can also reduce the cooking time considerably. Pressure cookers are often used in Indian households to cook all types of legumes. In case you prefer to use this method, the following instructions will be helpful.

Cooking dal in a pressure cooker (recommended size: 4 quarts)

Makes 1 cup cooked creamy dal

½ cup dal (toor dal, yellow split peas, masoor dal, or moong dal)

¼ teaspoon turmeric powder

1. Place 1 or 2 cups of water in a pressure cooker as specified by the manufacturer's instructions.

2. In a small stainless steel dish, place dal, turmeric powder, and 1 cup of water.

3. Place the stainless steel dish in the bottom of the pressure cooker in the water. Pressure cook for 5 to 7 minutes, according to manufacturer's instructions.

4. When the cooker is sufficiently cooled to open, remove dish with dal. Do not drain water.

Shopping List for Spices and Other Basics

Spices

- ❏ Asafoetida
- ❏ Bay leaves
- ❏ Black mustard seeds
- ❏ Black pepper (whole or powdered)
- ❏ Cayenne powder
- ❏ Cinnamon
- ❏ Cumin (seeds/powder)
- ❏ Fennel seeds
- ❏ Fenugreek seeds
- ❏ Poppy seeds (white)
- ❏ Red chili pepper (whole/powdered)
- ❏ Roasted chickpeas (known as chana dalia)
- ❏ Saffron
- ❏ Tamarind paste
- ❏ Turmeric powder
- ❏ Urad dal (split)

Spice Powders (MTR and Kohinoor brands recommended)

- ❏ Black pepper/cumin powder — combine in equal portion
- ❏ Cayenne powder
- ❏ Chutney powder
- ❏ Coconut powder (unsweetened)
- ❏ Cumin powder
- ❏ Curry powder
- ❏ Garam masala powder
- ❏ Rasam powder
- ❏ Sambhar powder

Rice and Lentils (Dals)

- ❏ Extra long-grain rice
- ❏ Basmati rice
- ❏ Jasmine rice
- ❏ Brown rice (if you prefer to make flavored rice with brown rice)
- ❏ Moong dal
- ❏ Toor dal
- ❏ Masoor dal
- ❏ Yellow split peas

GLOSSARY OF SOUTH INDIAN DISHES

Adai

A type of thick, fiber-rich pancake made from a variety of dals. Batter for adais does not require fermentation. Just soak dals, grind coarsely, and make adais immediately.

Aviyal

A delicious preparation of vegetables cooked with coconut, ginger, and green chili peppers. It has a consistency halfway between a thick kootu and a more liquid sambhar.

Bhaji

A vegetable fritter that can be made with potatoes, eggplants, or onions after dipping in a batter of besan flour and rice flour. Served as an appetizer or as a snack during teatime.

Bonda

Deep-fried dumplings coated with besan and rice flours and often filled with masala potatoes and peas. Served as an appetizer or as a snack during teatime.

Chappati

A flat, round, unleavened thin wheat bread, common in North and South India.

Chutney

A savory sauce used as an accompaniment to appetizers and breakfast items. There are a variety of delicious chutneys featured in this book. Unlike their North Indian counterparts, the South Indian chutneys are not sweet.

Dosai

A South Indian thin pancake or crepe made from rice and urad dal, ground and allowed to ferment. Dosai is a South Indian breakfast specialty and can be prepared in a variety of ways. One favorite variety is Masala Dosai, which is dosai stuffed with a delicious filling of potato masala and coconut chutney.

Idiyappam

A dish made with steam-cooked thin noodles made from rice flour called rice sticks. Packages of dry rice sticks are available in Indian and Oriental stores. Rice sticks are cooked in boiling water like pasta, and are drained and seasoned to make a delicious breakfast or a light supper.

Idli

Delicate steamed rice cake that is a South Indian specialty. Idli is made from a fermented batter similar to that used to make dosais. Idli or dosai is a popular breakfast food usually served with sambhar and chutney.

Kesari

A dessert made with cream of wheat, milk, sugar, cardamom, raisins, saffron, and cashews.

Kootu

A thick, creamy textured and mildly flavored vegetable dish prepared with dal, ginger, and cumin. Thicker than sambhar, kootus are often served as side dishes in a main meal.

Kulambu

A thick vegetable sauce usually made without dals. Kulambu features numerous individual vegetables, and occasionally meats, cooked with tamarind paste and a variety of spices.

Kurma

Exquisitely flavorful vegetable (or meat) sauce made from coconut and almonds ground with many spices to a creamy consistency. A uniquely aromatic and delicious preparation.

Pachadi

Vegetables cooked with a variety of spices in tamarind paste. Similar to kootu, but less creamy in texture, pachadi is a popular accompaniment to a meal.

Payasam

A sweet pudding-like dessert made with milk, cardamom, and saffron. Tapioca or vermicelli are the usual varieties. May be mixed with fruit cocktail or other fruit.

Podimas

A vegetable or meat dish with spices, split peas, and coconut.

Poori

A bread popular in both South and North India. Poori is made with unleavened wheat flour that puffs into airy rounds of bread when deep-fried.

Poriyal

A stir-fried vegetable without sauce that is served as a side dish in a main meal. Vegetables are cooked with seasonings and as a finishing touch combined with dals and coconut.

Pulaoo (Biriyani) Rice

A kind of aromatic fried rice infused with the flavors of cinnamon and clove. Two pulaoo rice recipes are included in this book: Vegetable Biriyani Rice and Chicken Biriyani Rice.

Rasam

A thin peppery soup made from garlic, onions, and tomatoes, rasam is usually served at mid-course in a meal with rice. It may also be enjoyed at the beginning of a meal. Rasams are believed to relieve the symptoms of colds and sore throats.

Sambhar

Vegetables and dals cooked with sambhar powder to make a hearty sauce of medium or thick consistency. There are a wide variety of sambhars to enjoy with idlis and dosais. Also served in main meals over plain rice.

Thuvaiyal

A kind of thick chutney made from coconut, chili peppers, and roasted dals. Sometimes made with vegetables such as eggplant.

Uppuma

A popular breakfast or snack item often made from cream of wheat, cream of rice, or cracked wheat seasoned with curry leaves, onions, and spices. Usually served with any sambhar or chutney.

Vadai

A fried doughnut-like patty made from urad dal or vegetables and yellow split peas ground with onions and chili peppers. Vadai is a popular breakfast and tea item. One particularly delicious variety is served marinated in seasoned yogurt and called *thayir vadai*.

General Cooking Tips

1. Relax and enjoy South Indian cooking. Preparing the dishes does not require a precise measurement of the ingredients. If you add a little more or less than the amount specified in the recipe, you are not going to spoil the preparation. Most cooks in India do not use measuring cups or spoons. If you like a certain spice, such as cumin, you may use more than the quantity indicated in the recipe. And if you dislike a particular spice, you may reduce the amount specified in the recipe or omit the ingredient altogether. There are very few absolutely essential spices or seasonings, given the wealth of spices and aromatic ingredients that make up almost every South Indian dish.

2. If you don't have a specific spice or other ingredient listed in the recipe, don't be disheartened. It is usually possible to substitute or omit ingredients and still produce a delicious dish, although with a different taste. Instead of mustard seeds and urad dal, for example, you may use whole cumin seeds. In a very short time, you will become familiar with the spices and the possible substitutions.

3. Indian food is not always hot and spicy. It is the chili peppers and cayenne powder that give the "kick" to a dish. We have indicated only minimal amounts of chili peppers and cayenne powder in our recipes. You may add more or less as you desire.

4. Use plump, ripened, round tomatoes. By adding more tomatoes, you can cut down on the tomato sauce if you prefer. In some recipes, however, tomato sauce enhances the flavor of the vegetable dish and should not be omitted.

5. Unsweetened coconut powder, available in Indian grocery stores, can be substituted for freshly ground coconut. The unsweetened coconut powder can be used as a garnish and also as a base for making chutneys and kurmas.

6. Most cities have Indian grocery stores. It is also possible to order spices on the Internet (an Internet search should provide you with retailers). For suggestions, visit **www.curryonwheels.com**.

7. Some recipes in our cookbook will yield more servings than you may wish to use in a single meal. That is no problem. The leftovers can be refrigerated or frozen with no detriment to flavor or nutritional value. Place leftovers in a plastic microwave dish or in a glass container. Just as wine tastes better with age, Indian food often tastes better after a day or two because of the rich blending of spices and seasonings. Most leftovers can be refrigerated for three to five days or kept frozen for weeks. Just reheat and enjoy.

8. Dals, such as toor dal and split peas, can be cooked in large quantities and can be kept frozen in one-cup portions for ready use any time. Freeze in a microwave container or any plastic container. Defrost, heat, and use as needed. Cooked dals can be frozen or refrigerated for many weeks with no loss of flavor or nutritional value.

9. Dal should be cooked on the stove or in a pressure cooker to achieve the creamy consistency so desirable for making delicious sambhars and kootus. For poriyals (stir-fry vegetables), however, dal should retain a firmer texture when cooked. Dals cooked in a microwave oven will take an excessive amount of time and will not attain a creamy consistency.

10. Our recipes are easy to follow. Once you have assembled all of your ingredients, it usually takes less than thirty minutes to prepare a dish. The more practiced you become in preparing a recipe, the easier it will become.

11. A word about vegetables: Even if you don't like a particular vegetable, you may be surprised at how much its taste is transformed and enhanced when prepared according to the recipes presented in this book. We have found that brussels sprouts, for example, won new fans by being prepared in the South Indian style. Allow this book to expand your taste and that of your family to include a variety of nutritious vegetables in your daily diet.

12. Here is a hint on using tamarind paste that comes in a bottle: Open the plastic seal and lightly microwave the thick tamarind paste for one minute. The paste will be converted to a thick liquid. Now, cover the bottle and store in the kitchen cupboard for any length of time. Tamarind paste, kept at room temperature in this way, is very easy to use.

13. If you are concerned about the amount of time you will need to prepare numerous Indian dishes for a big meal, you can always chop the vegetables ahead of time and keep them refrigerated in plastic wrap, ready for use.

14. You can also make the entire dinner early in the day and leave dishes at room temperature until dinnertime. Advance preparation actually enhances the flavor of the dishes. However, if a dish contains coconut or meat, it is important not to leave the cooked dish at room temperature for an extended period of time. The dish must be refrigerated. Before serving, heat and enjoy.

15. Regular stainless steel heavy bottomed saucepans, nonstick pots and pans, cast-iron skillets, and woks can be used in Indian cooking. Electric rice cookers and woks are useful but not necessary. Electric blenders, however, are necessary.

16. Combining Indian and western dishes makes for a very interesting and pleasing dining experience. Combining grilled chicken or fish with an Indian rice and vegetable dish can be a pleasant change of pace for your family and friends. Be certain to see the section on Fusion meals.

17. Spices are inexpensive, readily available and have a long shelf life. They do not have to be purchased frequently. They can be purchased as needed. When the spices are bought, you just have to take some time to empty the spices from plastic bags into bottles with lids, label the bottles for familiarity, and store them in the kitchen cabinet.

18. If you are a beginner and you do not know what spices and dals you need to buy in order to get started, here is a short, initial shopping list of essential ingredients:

❏ black mustard seeds	❏ turmeric powder	❏ moong or masoor dal
❏ split urad dal	❏ chutney or cayenne powder	❏ yellow split peas
❏ cumin powder	❏ cumin seeds	

With these spices and dals you can prepare many of the vegetable dishes in this book.

appetizers

Beet vadais

Makes 50 small vadas	1 cup yellow split peas	½ teaspoon fennel seeds	½ cup chopped fresh coriander	½ teaspoon salt
	1 or 2 whole dried red chili peppers	¼ cup finely shredded fresh beets	1 tablespoon minced ginger root	1 to 1½ cups plain dry bread crumbs
	¾ teaspoon whole cumin seeds	1½ cups chopped yellow onion	1 or 2 green chili peppers (optional)	canola oil for frying

Beet vadais are fried vegetable patties that can be served as appetizers or as an accompaniment to any meal.

Note   Any unused mixture may be refrigerated for further use, although it is advisable to use the refrigerated mix within a day or two.

variations   ONION VADAIS may be made by following the basic recipe for vadais without the beets.

CALORIES	64	CARBOHYDRATE	5g
FAT	5g	FIBER	1g
SATURATED FAT	1g	CHOLESTEROL	0mg
PROTEIN	1g	SODIUM	42mg

1. Soak yellow split peas in approximately 2 cups of warm water for 2 to 3 hours. Drain and grind split peas with red chili peppers, cumin seeds and fennel seeds in a blender to a coarse texture (similar to cornmeal). **Note:** *Grind about ½ cup of soaked split peas at a time with only enough water added each time to facilitate the grinding process. Do not grind the split peas too finely. It is desirable to have the split pea mixture coarsely ground to lend a crunchy texture to the finished vadais.*

2. Remove split pea mixture from blender and place in a large bowl. Use your hand to blend the mixture of split peas and spices thoroughly.

3. Add beets, onion, coriander, ginger, green chili peppers, and salt to the mixture. Blend thoroughly by hand.

4. Add bread crumbs to the mixture and blend by hand until mixture reaches a consistency sufficiently thick to form a ball. More bread crumbs may be added if the mixture is too watery.

5. Take a small portion of mixture (about 1 tablespoon) in the palm of your hand and form into a ball. With fingers, flatten ball into the shape of a patty, either in the palm of the hand or on a small plate. The patty should be about 1 inch in diameter. Repeat the procedure until the desired number of vadais has been made.

6. Heat enough oil in a skillet or wok for deep-frying. Drop a few patties at a time into the oil and fry until golden brown. Remove vadais from hot oil with a perforated spatula and drain them on paper towels.

spinach vadais

Makes about 30 small vadas

½ cup yellow split peas

½ cup moong dal

1 whole dried red chili pepper

¾ teaspoon whole cumin seeds

½ teaspoon fennel seeds

1 cup chopped fresh spinach

1 cup chopped onion

1 teaspoon salt

1 tablespoon minced ginger root

½ cup plain dry bread crumbs (more, if needed)

canola oil for frying

1. Soak yellow split peas and moong dal in 2 cups of water for 2 to 3 hours.

2. Drain split peas and moong dal and grind with red chili pepper, cumin seeds, and fennel seeds in a blender to a coarse texture (similar to cornmeal). **Note:** *Grind in two batches, add only enough water each time to facilitate the grinding process. It is desirable to have the dal mixture coarsely ground to lend a crunchy texture to the finished vadais. Do not grind the mixture too finely.*

3. Transfer the dal mixture from blender to a large bowl. Add chopped fresh spinach, onion, salt, and ginger. Blend thoroughly by hand.

4. Add bread crumbs to the mixture and mix well by hand until mixture reaches a consistency sufficiently thick to form a ball. More bread crumbs may be added if the mixture is too watery.

5. Take a small portion of mixture (about 1 tablespoon) in the palm of your hand and form into a ball. With fingers, flatten ball into the shape of a patty. Patty should be about 1 inch in diameter. Repeat until all of the spinach mixture is used.

6. Heat enough oil in a skillet for deep frying. Drop a few patties into hot oil and fry until golden brown. Do not crowd skillet—fry the vadais in several batches. Remove vadais from hot oil when golden brown and drain them on paper towels. Repeat the procedure until all the vadais have been fried. It is recommended that you use a perforated spatula in removing vadais from the hot oil.

7. Serve warm or at room temperature with any kind of chutney.

Fried vegetable patties may be served as appetizers or as an accompaniment to any meal.

CALORIES	40	CARBOHYDRATE	6g
FAT	1g	FIBER	2g
SATURATED FAT	trace	CHOLESTEROL	0mg
PROTEIN	2g	SODIUM	88mg

Bhajis

Makes about 30 bhajis	1 cup chickpea flour (gram or besan flour) ¼ cup rice flour 1 teaspoon salt	¼ teaspoon baking soda ½ teaspoon cayenne powder	½ teaspoon asafoetida powder ¼ teaspoon turmeric powder	30 thin potato slices with skin (about 3 inches in diameter), or eggplant slices, or onion slices canola oil for frying

Bhajis are flat vegetable fritters that can be served warm as a snack with any type of chutney.

1. Mix all of the dry ingredients together by hand in a medium bowl.

2. Add approximately 1 cup of water to dry ingredients to make a smooth, thick batter. Set aside for ½ hour.

3. Coat the potato or eggplant or onion slices by dipping them in the batter.

4. Heat enough oil in a deep skillet or wok for deep-frying. Fry a few slices at a time until golden brown on both sides, about 2 to 3 minutes. Drain the bhajis on paper towels. Repeat until all are fried.

HEALTHY SOUTH INDIAN COOKING

NOTE   Instant pakora mix may be purchased in some supermarkets and used in place of the dry ingredients.

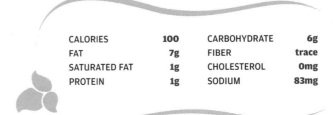

CALORIES	100	CARBOHYDRATE	6g
FAT	7g	FIBER	trace
SATURATED FAT	1g	CHOLESTEROL	0mg
PROTEIN	1g	SODIUM	83mg

bondas

Makes 25 small bondas	FOR POTATO FILLING	¼ teaspoon asafoetida powder	¼ cup chopped tomato	¼ cup chopped fresh coriander (cilantro) leaves	½ teaspoon turmeric powder
	2 medium Idaho potatoes	1 teaspoon black mustard seeds	1 green chili pepper, chopped	FOR BATTER	½ teaspoon cayenne powder
	¾ teaspoon turmeric powder	2 teaspoons urad dal	½ cup frozen green peas	1 cup chickpea flour (gram or besan flour)	½ teaspoon salt
	1 teaspoon salt	1 cup chopped onion	¼ cup roasted cashew halves	¼ cup rice flour	canola oil for frying
	2 tablespoons canola oil	1 teaspoon minced ginger root		¼ teaspoon baking soda	

1. **FOR POTATO FILLING** Scrub potatoes. Cut in half and place in a pressure cooker. Add enough water to cover potatoes, together with ½ teaspoon turmeric powder and ½ teaspoon salt. Cover and cook about 10 minutes until potatoes are tender. (You may also boil the potatoes in an uncovered saucepan.) Peel the potatoes, mash coarsely, and set aside.

2. Heat oil in skillet over medium heat. When oil is hot but not smoking, add asafoetida powder, mustard seeds, and urad dal. Cover and fry until mustard seeds pop and urad dal is golden brown, about 30 seconds.

3. Add the onion, ginger, tomato, and green chili pepper to skillet. Stir-fry for a few minutes. Add remaining ¼ teaspoon turmeric powder and ½ teaspoon salt.

4. Add mashed potatoes and stir well. Add green peas, cashews, and coriander and mix well. Set aside until batter is prepared.

5. **FOR BATTER** Mix chickpea flour, rice flour, baking soda, turmeric powder, cayenne powder, and salt. Add about 1 cup warm water to dry ingredients to form a thick and smooth paste. **Note:** *Batter must be thick, so be careful to add only a little water at a time.*

6. Shape the potato mixture into ¾ inch balls and coat balls with batter. Heat oil in a skillet over medium heat. Fry the coated balls in oil until golden brown. Drain on paper towels.

Bondas are deep-fried dumplings made with potatoes and mixed vegetables dipped in a batter of chickpea flour. They can be served warm as a snack with any type of chutney.

CALORIES	124	CARBOHYDRATE	6g
FAT	11g	FIBER	1g
SATURATED FAT	1g	CHOLESTEROL	0mg
PROTEIN	1g	SODIUM	147mg

Bell pepper pakoras

Makes 25 to 30 pakoras	1 cup chickpea flour (gram or besan flour)	½ teaspoon turmeric powder	1 cup chopped bell pepper	¼ cup chopped fresh coriander (cilantro) leaves
	½ cup rice flour	½ teaspoon cayenne powder	1 tablespoon minced ginger root	canola oil for frying
	¼ teaspoon baking soda	½ teaspoon salt	2 green chili peppers	½ cup roasted cashew halves (optional)
		1 cup chopped onion		

Pakoras are vegetable fritters that are served warm with any type of chutney.

1. In a medium bowl, mix together chickpea flour, rice flour, baking soda, turmeric powder, cayenne powder, and salt.

2. Add onion, bell pepper, ginger, green chili peppers, and coriander to the dry mixture.

3. Add ½ cup of water to the mixture. Use your hand to blend the ingredients into a smooth batter. Batter should be thick and should coat the vegetables thoroughly.

4. Add oil to a small wok over medium heat. When oil is hot, but not smoking, drop spoonfuls of thick batter into the oil and fry until golden yellow to brown. Drain on paper towels. Repeat until all of the batter is used.

NOTE   You may add ½ cup of cashew halves to the batter and mix well before frying. They will enhance the taste.

Instant pakora mix may be purchased in some grocery stores and used in place of the dry ingredients.

variation   Use fresh chopped spinach (1 cup) in above recipe instead of bell pepper to make SPINACH PAKORAS.

CALORIES	41	CARBOHYDRATE	8g
FAT	trace	FIBER	2g
SATURATED FAT	trace	CHOLESTEROL	0mg
PROTEIN	2g	SODIUM	52mg

appetizers

HEALTHY SOUTH INDIAN COOKING

pappadums

Makes 10 pappadums	10 pappadums	canola oil for deep-frying

1. Set a large platter, lined with paper towels, beside the stove to drain the pappadums.

2. Heat about 1 to 2 inches oil in a heavy skillet or wok over medium heat.

3. When oil is hot, but not smoking, put one pappadum in skillet. As the oil sizzles the pappadum will expand.

4. Turn pappadum over once and remove in a few seconds with slotted spoon. **Note:** *If pappadum becomes brown, then your cooking oil is too hot. Reduce the temperature to medium or low and then continue the frying.*

5. Prepare as many pappadums as you like, but fry only one at a time.

There are several varieties of the pappadum (called *appalam* in South India) which is essentially a wafer made from urad dal. Pappadums can be bought in grocery stores in spiced or unspiced forms. Madras pappadums are usually small and plain. When fried, they don't absorb much oil and are very crisp. Spiced pappadums vary from jeera- (cumin) to garlic- to black pepper-flavored pappadums. Pappadums can be deep-fried in hot oil and served as appetizers or as accompaniments to a meal. The frying takes just a few seconds. For convenience, pappadums can be broken in half before frying.

variations To make pappadums without deep-frying: place one pappadum in the microwave. Cook on high heat for 30 seconds to 1 minute depending on power of microwave.

CALORIES	131	CARBOHYDRATE	15g
FAT	8g	FIBER	4g
SATURATED FAT	trace	CHOLESTEROL	0mg
PROTEIN	5g	SODIUM	57mg

samosas

Makes about 40 samosas	1 package of 10 (6- to 7-inch) flour tortillas (or see recipe on following page)	1 recipe Potato Masala (page 206) or Tuna Masala (page 47)	canola oil for frying

Samosas are crispy savories stuffed with vegetables or meat that can be served warm as an appetizer or as a snack with any type of chutney.

variations Instead of deep-frying, brush each folded samosa on both sides with canola oil or use cooking oil spray and broil for about 5 minutes on each side.

Frying can be avoided completely by using frozen crescent dinner rolls or frozen puff-pastry sheets as a covering for the potato filling and baking them according to package directions.

1. Bring tortillas to room temperature before using so they will be softer and easy to fold.

2. Lightly moisten one side of each tortilla with warm water. Cut tortillas into quarters.

3. Take each quarter and fold it into a cone shape by bringing the two ends of tortilla together.

4. Stuff about a teaspoonful of masala into each cone, being careful not to overfill.

5. Moisten the edges of the tortilla cones and fold down to seal tightly into a triangular shape.

6. Heat enough oil in a small wok over medium heat. When the oil is hot, but not smoking, place a few filled samosas into the oil and deep-fry over medium heat to golden brown.

7. Set the fried samosas on paper towels to drain excess oil. Repeat until all are fried.

NUTRITIONAL ANALYSIS PER SAMOSA USING FLOUR TORTILLAS AND TUNA MASALA FILLING

CALORIES	175	CARBOHYDRATE	20g
FAT	8g	FIBER	1g
SATURATED FAT	2g	CHOLESTEROL	3mg
PROTEIN	5g	SODIUM	259mg

samosa dough

Makes 10 samosas

1 cup all-purpose flour

1 tablespoon butter

¼ teaspoon salt

1. Mix together all the ingredients with fingers, adding only enough water to form a soft dough. Knead it well to make a smooth dough. Allow the dough to settle for 1 hour at room temperature.

2. Divide the dough equally into about 10 smooth balls. Roll each ball evenly with a rolling pin into a circular shape as far as it can spread, about 4 inches in diameter.

3. Place a small spoonful of filling into the center of pastry. Lightly moisten the edge of the circle with water. Fold pastry in half and tightly seal the edges before frying.

The pastry for samosas can also be prepared from scratch according to this recipe.

stuffed mushrooms

Makes 12 stuffed mushrooms	12 large button mushroom caps	Spinach Poriyal (page 213) or Tuna Masala (page 47)	2 tablespoons butter

Mushrooms baked with spinach or tuna filling make a delicious appetizer.

NOTE Grated Parmesan cheese, if desired, may be sprinkled over tops of mushrooms.

1. Preheat oven to 350 degrees. Wash and dry mushrooms. Remove stems and hollow out mushroom pulp to form cups.

2. Fill mushroom caps with Spinach Poriyal or Tuna Masala.

3. Dot filled mushrooms with butter and bake, uncovered (or lightly tented), on a greased cooking sheet for 15 to 20 minutes.

NUTRITIONAL ANALYSIS OF ONE MUSHROOM STUFFED WITH TUNA MASALA

CALORIES	26	CARBOHYDRATE	2g
FAT	2g	FIBER	trace
SATURATED FAT	1g	CHOLESTEROL	5mg
PROTEIN	1g	SODIUM	21mg

tuna masala

Serves 6	2 tablespoons canola oil	1 cup chopped yellow onion	¼ teaspoon turmeric powder	¼ cup plain dry bread crumbs (optional)
	3 or 4 slivers cinnamon stick	¼ cup finely chopped tomato	2 teaspoons curry powder	½ teaspoon salt
	¼ teaspoon fennel seeds	¼ cup minced garlic cloves (less, if desired)	¼ cup tomato sauce	¼ cup minced fresh coriander (cilantro) leaves
	½ teaspoon cumin seeds	1 green chili pepper, chopped (more, if desired)	1 can (12 ounces) tuna in oil, drained	
	2 teaspoons urad dal			

1. Heat oil in an iron skillet over medium heat. When oil is hot, but not smoking, add cinnamon sticks, fennel seeds, cumin seeds, and urad dal.

2. When urad dal is golden, add the onion, tomato, garlic, and green chili pepper. Cook for 1 minute. Add turmeric, curry powder, and tomato sauce. Mix and cook for another minute.

3. Add tuna and mix thoroughly. Add bread crumbs, if desired, and salt and blend well with other ingredients. Cook for another 7 to 10 minutes over medium heat.

4. Add coriander and mix well.

Cooked with onions, tomatoes, and garlic with mild seasonings, Tuna Masala is an innovative and flavorful side dish which can be served over cocktail rye bread or with crackers as an appetizer or as a sandwich. It can also be used to make delicious Tuna Balls (page 48) or as a filler for Samosas (page 44).

CALORIES	145	CARBOHYDRATE	13g
FAT	7g	FIBER	3g
SATURATED FAT	1g	CHOLESTEROL	4mg
PROTEIN	9g	SODIUM	362mg

optional step   A slight amount of canola oil (1 to 2 teaspoons) may be added to skillet while cooking tuna masala over low heat for a few extra minutes to add crispiness.

note   You may use tuna packed in water instead of tuna in oil.

Tuna Balls

1 recipe Tuna Masala (page 47)

1 egg

¼ cup plain dry bread crumbs

canola oil for frying

Fried savories made with Tuna Masala, Tuna Balls are a delicious appetizer with beer or any beverage. Tuna Balls also make a unique side dish.

1. Mix the masala, egg, and bread crumbs with your hands to form a firm ball. You may need to add more bread crumbs if the tuna mixture is not firm enough.

2. Form the tuna mixture into small balls. Heat enough oil in a heavy skillet or wok over medium heat to fry tuna balls. Oil should be at least ½ inch deep. Fry 2 to 4 balls at a time until golden brown on all sides, about 2 minutes.

3. Drain on paper towels and serve either warm or cold. The tuna balls can be reheated in a toaster oven before serving.

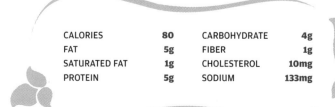

CALORIES	80	CARBOHYDRATE	4g
FAT	5g	FIBER	1g
SATURATED FAT	1g	CHOLESTEROL	10mg
PROTEIN	5g	SODIUM	133mg

vegetable cutlets

Makes about 16 vegetable cutlets	2 or 3 Idaho potatoes (enough for 2 cups mashed)	1 tablespoon minced ginger root	1½ teaspoons garam masala powder
	1 teaspoon turmeric powder	½ cup fresh green beans, finely diced	½ teaspoon salt
	2 tablespoons canola oil	½ cup shredded carrots	½ cup all-purpose flour
	½ cup chopped onion	¼ cup shredded beets	1 cup plain dry bread crumbs
	1 tablespoon minced garlic cloves	¼ cup chopped fresh coriander (cilantro) leaves	canola oil for frying

1. Cut potatoes in quarters and place potatoes in water with ½ teaspoon turmeric powder in a regular kettle to boil. (Or cut potatoes in half and cook in a pressure cooker with ½ teaspoon turmeric powder and enough water to cover potatoes.) When potatoes are tender, peel and mash them. Set aside.

2. Place oil in an iron skillet over medium heat. When oil is hot, but not smoking, add onion, garlic, and ginger. Stir-fry for a minute or two.

3. Add green beans, carrots, beets, and coriander. Stir and cook over medium heat for a minute or two.

4. Add remaining ½ teaspoon turmeric powder, garam masala powder, and salt. Stir the seasonings well with the vegetables.

5. When beans are tender, add the mashed potatoes to the mixture and cook over medium low heat, stirring well. Remove the vegetable mixture from heat and allow it to cool.

6. Form vegetable mixture into small patties using 2 tablespoons for each. Set aside.

CONTINUED

These cutlets are made from a variety of mildly seasoned vegetables that are pleasing to the palate. Serve as an appetizer or as a snack with any chutney.

49

appetizers

HEALTHY SOUTH INDIAN COOKING

7. In a small bowl, mix all-purpose flour with 1 cup of warm water to make a batter. Place bread crumbs on a separate plate.

8. Dip the vegetable patties into the batter. Then coat both sides of patties with the bread crumbs.

9. Set aside the coated vegetable patties on a platter. Place the platter with the patties in the refrigerator for ½ hour. (This helps the vegetables to bind well with the coating mixture.)

10. Place enough oil in a wok or skillet over medium heat. When oil is hot, but not smoking, fry the vegetable cutlets about a minute or two, until golden brown and crisp. Drain cutlets on paper towels.

CALORIES	130	CARBOHYDRATE	13g
FAT	8g	FIBER	1g
SATURATED FAT	1g	CHOLESTEROL	1mg
PROTEIN	2g	SODIUM	191mg

soups and rasam

Beet soup

Serves 6	¼ cup toor dal or moong dal	1 dry bay leaf	¼ cup sliced onion, cut lengthwise	½ cup tomato sauce
	½ teaspoon turmeric powder	4 to 6 curry leaves (optional)	½ cup chopped tomato	1 teaspoon salt
	2 tablespoons canola oil	¼ teaspoon fennel seeds	½ green chili pepper, finely chopped (more, if desired)	½ teaspoon cardamom powder
	2 or 3 slivers cinnamon stick	¼ teaspoon cumin seeds	¼ cup peeled and thinly sliced beets	½ teaspoon cumin powder

A thin dal-based soup with beets and delicate seasonings, Beet Soup is a great option as a first course or as part of a light lunch.

variation   To make **CARROT SOUP**, add ¼ cup peeled and thinly sliced carrots instead of beets.

NOTE   You may use vegetable broth instead of the dal-based broth. If using vegetable broth eliminate step 1, and start soup recipe from step 2. In step 5, add 2 cups of vegetable broth with 3 cups of warm water and follow the remaining directions.

1. Bring 3 cups of water to a boil in a deep saucepan. Add toor dal and ¼ teaspoon turmeric powder. Reduce heat to medium and cook, uncovered, for about 30 minutes until dal becomes creamy. Set aside.

2. Place the oil in a deep saucepan and heat over medium heat. When oil is hot, but not smoking, add cinnamon sticks, bay leaf, curry leaves, fennel seeds, and cumin seeds. Stir and heat until seeds are golden brown, about 30 seconds.

3. Add onion slices, tomato, and green chili pepper. Stir and cook for a few minutes. Add sliced beets and remaining ¼ teaspoon turmeric powder. Stir well to blend the seasonings with beets.

4. Add tomato sauce and cook over medium heat for another 1 to 2 minutes.

5. Add the dal mixture and an additional 5 cups of warm water to the saucepan.

6. Add salt, cardamom powder, and cumin powder to saucepan. Stir well. Cook, uncovered, over medium heat until mixture begins to boil. Let simmer for a few minutes until beets are tender.

7. Remove from heat. Serve immediately or cover and briefly reheat before serving.

CALORIES	99	CARBOHYDRATE	12g
FAT	5g	FIBER	4g
SATURATED FAT	1g	CHOLESTEROL	0mg
PROTEIN	3g	SODIUM	490mg

cauliflower soup

Serves 6

¼ cup toor dal or moong dal

½ teaspoon turmeric powder

2 tablespoons canola oil

2 or 3 slivers cinnamon stick

1 dry bay leaf

4 to 6 curry leaves (optional)

¼ teaspoon fennel seeds

¼ teaspoon cumin seeds

¼ cup sliced onion, cut lengthwise

½ cup chopped tomato

½ green chili pepper, finely chopped (more if desired)

½ cup tomato sauce

1 teaspoon salt

½ teaspoon cardamom powder

½ teaspoon cumin powder

1 cup 1-inch cauliflower florets

¼ cup finely chopped fresh coriander (cilantro) leaves

1. Bring 3 cups of water to a boil in a deep saucepan. Add toor dal and ¼ teaspoon turmeric powder. Reduce heat to medium and cook, uncovered, for about 30 minutes until dal becomes creamy. Set aside.

2. Place the oil in a deep saucepan and heat over medium heat. When oil is hot, but not smoking, add cinnamon sticks, bay leaf, curry leaves, fennel seeds, and cumin seeds. Stir quickly. Cover and heat until seeds are golden brown, about 30 seconds.

3. Add onion slices, tomato, and green chili pepper. Stir. Add remaining ¼ teaspoon turmeric powder. Stir well and cook, uncovered, until onions are tender.

4. Add tomato sauce and cook over medium heat for another 2 to 3 minutes. Stir until the ingredients in the saucepan reach a creamy consistency.

5. Add the dal mixture and an additional 5 cups of warm water to the saucepan.

6. Add salt, cardamom powder, and cumin powder to saucepan. Stir well. Cook, uncovered, over medium heat until mixture begins to boil.

7. Add cauliflower and cook, uncovered, until just tender, about 2 minutes. Be careful not to overcook the cauliflower.

8. Add coriander and let simmer for a few minutes. Remove from heat. Serve immediately or cover and briefly reheat before serving.

This is a thin dal-based soup with cauliflower and aromatic seasonings.

variation To make plain **TOMATO SOUP**, skip Step 7 in the recipe. In step 3, add 1 cup chopped tomato instead of ½ cup chopped tomato.

note You may use vegetable broth instead of the dal-based broth. If using vegetable broth eliminate step 1, and start the soup recipe from step 2 as directed. In step 5, add 2 cups of vegetable broth with 3 cups of warm water and follow the remaining directions.

CALORIES	100	CARBOHYDRATE	12g
FAT	5g	FIBER	3g
SATURATED FAT	1g	CHOLESTEROL	0mg
PROTEIN	3g	SODIUM	490mg

chettinad chicken soup

Serves 6

- ¼ cup toor dal
- ¾ teaspoon turmeric powder
- 4 garlic cloves
- 2 tablespoons canola oil
- 1 dry bay leaf
- 2 slivers cinnamon stick
- 2 to 4 curry leaves
- ½ teaspoon cumin seeds
- ¼ teaspoon fennel seeds
- ½ cup sliced onion, cut lengthwise
- ¼ cup chopped tomato
- 1 teaspoon minced ginger root
- ½ green chili pepper, chopped
- 1 cup chopped skinless chicken pieces
- ½ teaspoon curry powder
- ½ teaspoon salt (more, if desired)
- ¼ cup chopped fresh coriander (cilantro) leaves
- ½ teaspoon black pepper and cumin powder mixture

A flavorful chicken soup with ginger, garlic, and other herbs, this dish is a perfect starter at dinner or over rice as a main course. It's also a great remedy for colds!

NOTE You may use chicken broth instead of the dal-based broth. If using chicken broth eliminate step 1, and start the recipe from step 2 as directed. In step 5, add 2 cups of chicken broth with 3 cups of warm water and follow the remaining directions.

1. Bring 3 cups of water to a boil in a deep saucepan. Add toor dal and ¼ teaspoon turmeric powder. Reduce heat to medium and cook, uncovered, for about 30 minutes until dal becomes creamy. Set aside.

2. Peel the garlic cloves and cut 3 into halves or quarters.

3. Heat the canola oil in a deep saucepan over medium heat. When oil is hot, but not smoking, add bay leaf, cinnamon stick, curry leaves, cumin seeds, and fennel seeds. Immediately add garlic pieces, onions, tomato, ginger, and green chili pepper. Stir for a few seconds until onions are tender.

4. Add chicken and stir-fry with onions over medium heat. Add remaining ½ teaspoon turmeric powder and curry powder. Stir well and cook, uncovered, for 3 to 5 minutes. Add salt.

5. Add toor dal mixture and 4 cups of warm water to chicken. (See note at left.)

6. Add coriander and allow the soup to come to a boil. Crush the remaining 1 garlic clove and add along with the black pepper and cumin powder. Stir well.

7. After soup has come to a boil, reduce heat and allow to simmer until the chicken is tender. Stir frequently. If soup thickens, add a cup or two of water to thin it. When chicken is cooked, remove from heat.

CALORIES	140	CARBOHYDRATE	12g
FAT	6g	FIBER	3g
SATURATED FAT	1g	CHOLESTEROL	22mg
PROTEIN	12g	SODIUM	210mg

shrimp soup

Serves 4

½ cup coarsely chopped tomato

¼ cup tomato sauce

¼ teaspoon black pepper and cumin powder mixture

½ teaspoon rasam powder

¼ teaspoon salt (more, if desired)

3 tablespoons chopped green onion tops, plus additional for garnish

3 tablespoons chopped fresh coriander (cilantro) leaves, plus additional for garnish

½ teaspoon minced ginger root

1 garlic clove, peeled and crushed

½ pound fresh raw shrimp, shelled and cleaned, cut in half

1. Bring 6 cups of water to a boil. Add tomato and cook, uncovered, until tender.

2. Add tomato sauce, black pepper and cumin powder, rasam powder, and salt. Stir well and let it simmer over medium-low heat.

3. Add green onion, coriander, ginger, and garlic. Let it cook over medium heat for 2 to 3 minutes.

4. When the mixture begins to boil, add shrimp. Let shrimp cook over medium heat until they turn pink, 2 to 3 minutes.

5. Freshen the soup by garnishing with additional chopped green onion and chopped coriander.

This light, easy-to-make soup with shrimp and carefully blended seasonings will warm you up on cold winter nights!

CALORIES	38	CARBOHYDRATE	58g
FAT	trace	FIBER	trace
SATURATED FAT	trace	CHOLESTEROL	58mg
PROTEIN	7g	SODIUM	219mg

lemon rasam

Serves 6	¼ cup toor dal or moong dal	¼ cup chopped fresh coriander (cilantro) leaves	2 to 4 curry leaves
	½ teaspoon turmeric powder	1 teaspoon rasam powder	1 whole dried red chili pepper
	¼ cup chopped tomato	½ teaspoon salt (more, if desired)	1 teaspoon mustard seeds
	¼ teaspoon minced ginger root	1 teaspoon canola oil	2 tablespoons fresh lemon juice
	½ green chili pepper, finely chopped	¼ teaspoon asafoetida powder	

A thin peppery soup with lemon, Lemon Rasam is delightful when served over plain rice. Many claim it to be an effective cold remedy.

1. Bring 3 cups of water to a boil in a deep saucepan. Add toor dal and ¼ teaspoon turmeric powder. Reduce heat to medium and cook, uncovered, for about 30 minutes until dal becomes creamy.

2. Add 3 cups of warm water and the remaining ¼ teaspoon turmeric powder. Bring to a boil.

3. Add tomato and let cook for 2 to 4 minutes. (Cooked tomato will blend well with creamy dal.)

4. Add ginger, green chili pepper, and coriander to the dal mixture. Let simmer for about 2 minutes.

5. Add rasam powder and salt and let them blend with the seasonings for another minute or two.

6. Heat oil in a small butter warmer. When oil is hot, but not smoking, add asafoetida powder, curry leaves, red chili pepper, and mustard seeds. When mustard seeds burst add to the rasam mixture. Let rasam mixture come to a boil.

7. Immediately remove from heat. Add the lemon juice and stir well.

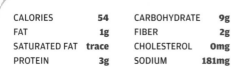

CALORIES	54	CARBOHYDRATE	9g
FAT	1g	FIBER	2g
SATURATED FAT	trace	CHOLESTEROL	0mg
PROTEIN	3g	SODIUM	181mg

moong dal rasam

Serves 4

- ¼ cup moong dal
- ½ cup chopped tomato
- 1 tablespoon minced ginger root
- ½ teaspoon asafoetida powder
- ¾ teaspoon cumin powder
- ½ teaspoon salt
- ½ teaspoon lemon juice
- 1 teaspoon canola oil
- 1 whole dried red chili pepper
- ½ teaspoon cumin seeds

1. Cook moong dal in 3 cups of water in a deep saucepan to a creamy consistency.

2. Add tomato, ginger, asafoetida powder, cumin powder, and salt to the creamy dal.

3. Add 3 cups of water and let simmer for 10 minutes. Add lemon juice.

4. In a small saucepan, heat oil. When oil is hot, but not smoking, add red chili pepper and cumin seeds. Stir-fry until cumin seeds turns brown. Add this seasoning to the dal mixture. Mix and serve warm.

This quick and easy dish of moong dals cooked with tomatoes and ginger and lightly garnished can be served as a soup.

CALORIES	49	CARBOHYDRATE	8g
FAT	trace	FIBER	4g
SATURATED FAT	trace	CHOLESTEROL	0mg
PROTEIN	4g	SODIUM	271mg

pineapple rasam

Serves 4	¼ cup chopped tomato	¼ cup tomato sauce	GARNISH (optional)	½ teaspoon cumin seeds
	¼ teaspoon minced ginger root	½ teaspoon salt (more, if desired)	½ teaspoon ghee (clarified butter)	
	½ teaspoon rasam powder	¼ cup chopped fresh coriander (cilantro) leaves	1 whole dried red chili pepper	
	¼ teaspoon black pepper and cumin powder mixture	1 cup freshly cut small pineapple chunks	2 to 4 curry leaves	
			½ teaspoon mustard seeds	

A thin peppery soup with the sweetness of pineapple, this rasam can be served hot as a first course or over rice at dinner.

1. Bring 4 cups of water to a boil. Add tomato and let simmer, uncovered, for 5 minutes.

2. Add ginger and simmer over medium heat for another 2 to 3 minutes.

3. Stir in rasam powder and black pepper and cumin powder.

4. Add tomato sauce, salt, and coriander. Stir well. Let all the ingredients simmer for 5 to 6 minutes.

5. *Optional:* Heat ghee in a butter warmer. When ghee is hot, but not smoking, add all of the garnish items. When mustard seeds pop, pour ingredients into rasam mixture.

6. Add pineapple chunks to the rasam mixture and let simmer for a few more minutes before serving.

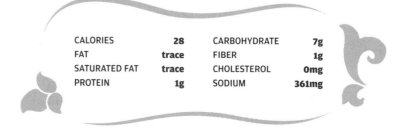

CALORIES	28	CARBOHYDRATE	7g
FAT	trace	FIBER	1g
SATURATED FAT	trace	CHOLESTEROL	0mg
PROTEIN	1g	SODIUM	361mg

tomato rasam

Serves 4

1 cup chopped tomato

½ teaspoon minced ginger root

¼ cup chopped fresh coriander (cilantro) leaves

1 teaspoon rasam powder

¼ teaspoon black pepper and cumin powder mixture

¼ cup tomato sauce

2 garlic cloves, peeled and crushed

½ teaspoon salt (more, if desired)

1. Bring 4 cups of water to a boil in a large saucepan. Add tomato and let simmer, uncovered, for 5 minutes.

2. Add ginger and coriander. Simmer over medium heat for another 2 to 3 minutes.

3. Stir in rasam powder and black pepper and cumin powder.

4. Add tomato sauce. When the mixture begins to boil, add the garlic and salt and stir well. Let all the ingredients simmer for 5 to 6 minutes.

A thin, delicious, traditional soup with garlic and cumin, Tomato Rasam is thought to be an excellent remedy for colds and sore throats. Serve hot as a first course or over plain rice as a main course.

variation   For enhanced flavor, heat 1 teaspoon oil in a small saucepan. When oil is hot, but not smoking, add 1 whole dried red chili pepper, ¼ teaspoon asafoetida powder, 2 to 4 curry leaves, 1 teaspoon mustard seeds, and 1 teaspoon urad dal. When mustard seeds pop and urad dal turns golden, add the seasonings to the above mixture. Let rasam simmer for a couple of minutes with the seasonings.

PER ½ CUP SERVING

CALORIES	16	CARBOHYDRATE	3g
FAT	trace	FIBER	1g
SATURATED FAT	trace	CHOLESTEROL	0mg
PROTEIN	1g	SODIUM	245mg

breads and grains

chappatis

Thin, flat wheat breads, chappatis are a staple of Indian cooking. They can be served with any kind of vegetable, kurma, or chutney.

1. Place the flour in a large mixing bowl. Add salt and oil. Mix well.

2. Gradually add approximately ¼ cup warm water to flour mixture, all the while working the dough with your hands. Knead with your hands or with a food processor to make dough elastic and pliable.

3. Moisten the palms of your hands with a small amount of canola oil and work with dough to make it soft. Shape the dough into 6 small balls.

4. Dust each of the balls of dough with flour and on a floured board roll out each ball evenly into a thin, flat, circular shape, 4 to 5 inches in diameter. At this point, the chappatis are ready for cooking.

   Note: *For more fluffy, flaky chappatis, brush half of each chappati circle lightly with canola oil. Fold dough over oiled half. Next, brush half of the folded dough lightly with oil. Again, fold over the oiled half. The dough should now be roughly triangular in shape. Dust well with additional wheat flour and roll out again evenly into a thin, flat, fanlike shape.*

5. For cooking, heat a nonstick skillet or iron skillet over medium heat. When the skillet is hot, add a chappati and cook both sides until slightly brown. Press the edge of the chappati lightly with a spatula until it puffs up. Remove the chappati from the skillet and brush lightly with butter or margarine, if desired. Repeat with remaining chappatis. Serve hot.

CALORIES	69	CARBOHYDRATE	15g
FAT	1g	FIBER	2g
SATURATED FAT	trace	CHOLESTEROL	0mg
PROTEIN	3g	SODIUM	90mg

pooris

Makes approximately 15 small pooris	1 cup graham (pastry) wheat flour	1 tablespoon cream of wheat (optional)	½ teaspoon salt
			Canola oil for frying

1. Place the first three ingredients in a large bowl and mix well with your hand.

2. Add approximately ⅓ cup warm water to flour mixture a little at a time. Work ingredients with your hands until they form a firm dough without sticking to the fingers.

3. Knead dough well with lightly oiled hands. Pound dough vigorously into bowl several times. (A food processor may also be used to form the dough.)

4. Roll the dough into a long, cord-like shape using the palms of both hands. Break off small pieces of dough and form small, smooth balls, approximately the size of a walnut. If large pooris are desired, the dough should be formed into larger equal-size balls.

5. Dab a very small amount of oil on a flat board or work surface. Place a ball of dough on oiled surface and roll evenly into a flat circular shape approximately 3 inches in diameter. After evenly rolling out balls of dough, keep pooris separate by placing them between grease-proof paper or on the top of wax paper.

6. Heat about 2 inches of canola oil in a small wok or electric fry pan until a poori dropped into the oil immediately sizzles and rises to the surface. Fry the pooris one at a time. The pooris will puff up only if the oil is hot enough but not smoking. Using a slotted spoon, turn the pooris over. Fry both sides evenly for 30 to 45 seconds. Lift pooris out from the pan, drain off the excess oil on paper towels, and serve hot.

Pooris are wheat breads that puff like a balloon when deep-fried in oil.

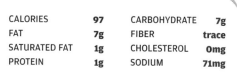

CALORIES	97	CARBOHYDRATE	7g
FAT	7g	FIBER	trace
SATURATED FAT	1g	CHOLESTEROL	0mg
PROTEIN	1g	SODIUM	71mg

dosais

Makes 16 dosais	2 cups raw extra long-grain rice	¼ cup urad dal 1 teaspoon fenugreek seeds	½ cup cooked plain rice 1 teaspoon salt

Dosais, thin, unsweetened pancakes made of rice and urad dal, are a delicious breakfast item that are also served for afternoon tea or for a light evening meal. Unique to South India, dosais can be made plain or as **onion dosais** or **masala dosais**. Serve any variety hot with chutney or sambhar.

The batter for dosais needs fermentation. Grind the batter for the dosais a day before you intend to prepare them in order for fermentation to take place. After you make the batter, you must wait 6 to 8 hours for fermentation to occur.

You may make a few dosais at a time. Save the remaining batter in the

1. Place raw rice, urad dal, and fenugreek seeds in enough warm water to cover generously. Soak at room temperature for about 6 hours.

2. Drain water and place rice and dal mixture in an electric blender. Add about 1½ cups of water to facilitate the grinding process.

3. Grind dal mixture on high power for several minutes. Add cooked rice a little at a time to the mixture, as it is being ground. (Cooked rice is added to improve the texture of the batter.) Grind to a fine paste.

4. Pour mixture into a bowl. Add the salt and mix well with your hand. **Note:** *It is essential to use your hand for mixing and not a spoon, because the warmth of the hand initiates the fermentation process.*

5. Cover bowl with a plate and place it in a warm place in the kitchen overnight. Do not use direct heat. The rice batter will begin to ferment and will double in quantity. Be certain that the bowl you are using will allow the batter to double its quantity.

Note: *Sometimes, because of cold weather, the batter will not ferment. You may place the bowl in a warmed oven. Just heat oven to 350 degrees for 10 minutes and then turn off the oven. Wait 10 to 15 minutes, then place the bowl with batter, still covered, in the oven.*

6. The next morning the fermented batter will be frothy.

Stir the batter with a large spoon for a few minutes and set aside. **Note:** *Depending upon the temperature and humidity, the batter might ferment in a shorter time and may overflow from the mixing bowl. This will still result in good dosais. Discard the overflow (it cleans up easily) and work with the batter in the bowl. Now you are ready to make dosais.*

TO MAKE PLAIN OR CRISPY DOSAIS:

1. Place about ½ cup of batter into the center of a hot, nonstick skillet. Spread the batter by moving the spoon in concentric circles, starting at the inside of the circle and working towards the outside, spreading the batter thinly and evenly.

2. Cover and cook over medium heat for 1 to 2 minutes. If added crispness is desired, when tiny bubbles appear on the dosai in the skillet place about ½ to 1 teaspoon canola oil around the dosai. Otherwise to make plain, soft dosais don't add oil and cook only on one side.

3. Lift the dosai with a spatula and turn over in skillet if both sides of dosai are to be cooked. After both sides are cooked evenly, transfer the dosai to a serving plate. Repeat with remaining batter.

Dosais are often served folded in a semicircular shape.

refrigerator for making dosais at a later time. The batter can be kept for several days in the refrigerator, but do not freeze.

There are 4 steps to making dosais:

1. Soak the ingredients for about 6 hours.

2. Grind for less than 15 minutes.

3. Ferment for 6 to 8 hours.

4. Cook dosais (only 3 minutes at most).

---

variation   **ONION DOSAIS** Following Step 1 for plain dosais, add about 1 teaspoon finely chopped onion over the batter spread in the skillet. Follow the remaining steps as for crispy dosai.

Makes 16 dosais

CALORIES	333	CARBOHYDRATE	63g
FAT	5g	FIBER	3g
SATURATED FAT	1g	CHOLESTEROL	0mg
PROTEIN	8g	SODIUM	361mg

NUTRITIONAL ANALYSIS OF DOSAI COOKED WITHOUT ADDITIONAL OIL

CALORIES	292	CARBOHYDRATE	62g
FAT	1g	FIBER	3g
SATURATED FAT	trace	CHOLESTEROL	0mg
PROTEIN	8g	SODIUM	361mg

NUTRITIONAL ANALYSIS OF CRISPY DOSAI

CALORIES	332	CARBOHYDRATE	62g
FAT	5g	FIBER	3g
SATURATED FAT	5g	CHOLESTEROL	0mg
PROTEIN	8g	SODIUM	361mg

masala dosais

1 batch dosai batter (page 66)

1 recipe Coconut Chutney (page 83)

1 recipe Potato Masala (page 206)

¼ to ½ teaspoon butter or margarine, melted

These dosais are stuffed with coconut chutney and potato masala.

1. Make the batter for plain dosais. Heat a nonstick skillet. Spread ½ cup batter in the skillet and spread as for plain dosais.

2. With a spoon, spread some coconut chutney evenly over top side of the dosai. Place 1 to 2 tablespoons of potato masala over the coconut chutney on one half of the dosai only. Fold the dosai up over the potato mixture and pat down with spatula. The dosai should now have a semicircular shape.

3. Lightly brush the dosai with melted butter and brown evenly one side at a time until desired crispness is reached.

4. Remove dosai to serving platter and repeat the same procedure with the rest of the batter. **Note:** *Be certain to wipe all butter from skillet with a paper towel before you start making the next dosai, otherwise the batter will not spread evenly in the skillet.*

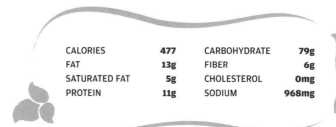

CALORIES	477	CARBOHYDRATE	79g
FAT	13g	FIBER	6g
SATURATED FAT	5g	CHOLESTEROL	0mg
PROTEIN	11g	SODIUM	968mg

uthappams (south Indian pancakes)

Makes 12	1 batch dosai batter (page 66)	6 to 12 teaspoons canola oil	Finely chopped onion

1. Heat nonstick skillet or iron skillet over medium heat. If you are using iron skillet, spray with nonstick cooking spray.

2. Pour ½ cup of the batter in the middle of the hot skillet and spread it to a small thick pancake of about 6 inches in diameter.

3. When tiny bubbles appear on the uthappam place ½ to 1 teaspoon oil around the uthappam.

4. Spread chopped onion over the uthappam as it cooks. After about 1 minute, turn the uthappam to the other side and cook until the uthappam becomes golden brown. Repeat with the remaining batter.

Uthappams are a thick variety of dosai.

variation   Uthappams can also be topped with other ingredients such as finely chopped tomatoes, chopped coriander, shredded carrots, or finely chopped chili peppers.

note   Uthappams go extremely well with any chutney, thuveyal, sambhar, or kulambu.

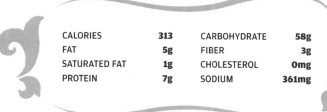

CALORIES	313	CARBOHYDRATE	58g
FAT	5g	FIBER	3g
SATURATED FAT	1g	CHOLESTEROL	0mg
PROTEIN	7g	SODIUM	361mg

adais

Makes about 10 adais	¼ cup urad dal	3 whole dried red chili peppers	¼ cup ground fresh coconut or unsweetened coconut powder	1 teaspoon salt
	¼ cup yellow split peas	1 teaspoon cumin seeds		1 cup chopped onion
	¼ cup toor dal	1 teaspoon fennel seeds	½ teaspoon asafoetida powder	¼ cup chopped fresh coriander (cilantro) leaves
	¼ cup moong dal		½ teaspoon turmeric powder	5 teaspoons canola oil
	1 cup extra long-grain rice			

Adais are pancakes made with lentils, rice, and spices that can be served with any type of chutney or kosamalli, usually for breakfast or for tea. Adai batter does not require fermentation.

1. Soak the urad dal, split peas, toor dal, moong dal, and rice with chili peppers and cumin seeds in water for 3 hours. Drain and put the soaked ingredients in a blender. Add the fennel seeds and about 2 cups of water and grind to a coarse and thick consistency.

2. Add fresh coconut powder, asafoetida powder, turmeric powder, salt, onion, and coriander to the ground mixture. Mix all the ingredients well. Now the batter is ready for making adais.

3. Spray an iron skillet with nonstick cooking oil spray.

4. Heat the iron skillet over medium heat. Spread about ⅓ cup of batter over the skillet in a circular pattern (like a thick pancake). Spread a small amount of oil (about ½ teaspoon) around the adai. Cook until the adai becomes golden brown and crunchy. With a stainless steel spatula turn it over and cook the other side. When the adai is crunchy and golden brown on both sides take it out of skillet and serve hot. Repeat with the rest of the batter.

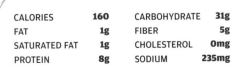

CALORIES	160	CARBOHYDRATE	31g
FAT	1g	FIBER	5g
SATURATED FAT	1g	CHOLESTEROL	0mg
PROTEIN	8g	SODIUM	235mg

idiyappam

Serves 4 to 6	1 pound thin rice sticks	3 teaspoons black mustard seeds	¼ cup low-fat buttermilk
	2 teaspoons salt	3 teaspoons urad dal	¼ cup chopped fresh coriander (cilantro) leaves
	4 tablespoons plus 1 teaspoon canola oil	2 onions, chopped	
	5 or 6 curry leaves	2 green chili peppers, chopped	

1. Remove rice sticks from package and break into small pieces. Set aside.

2. Bring 6 to 8 cups of water to a boil in a large saucepan.

3. When water is boiling vigorously, add salt, 1 teaspoon oil, and rice sticks. Boil, uncovered, for about 5 minutes. Do not overcook. (Oil is added to the boiling water to prevent rice sticks from sticking together.) When rice sticks are tender, drain thoroughly in a colander. Set aside.

4. Place remaining 4 tablespoons canola oil in a large skillet and heat over medium heat. When oil is hot, but not smoking, add curry leaves, mustard seeds, and urad dal. Cover and cook until mustard seeds pop and urad dal is golden brown, about 30 seconds.

5. Add onions and chili peppers to skillet. Stir-fry for a few minutes.

6. Add rice sticks from the colander to ingredients in the skillet and mix. Reduce heat to low while mixing well.

7. Add buttermilk to moisten rice sticks slightly. Stir carefully and add more salt, if desired.

8. Add coriander and stir. Serve.

This is a delicate dish made from rice sticks, onions, and chili peppers. Serve idiyappam with sambhar, chutney, or kosamalli as a breakfast item or for a light supper.

CALORIES	526	CARBOHYDRATE	104g
FAT	11g	FIBER	2g
SATURATED FAT	1g	CHOLESTEROL	trace
PROTEIN	2g	SODIUM	881mg

idlis (traditional)

Makes 60 idlis	4 cups idli rice	1 cup urad dal	1 teaspoon salt

Idlis are light, steamed rice-cakes. To make idlis you need an idli cooker, which is available in Indian stores. Plan to soak, grind, and ferment the batter a day in advance. The special rice for making them, called "idli rice," is available in Indian grocery stores. Some brands are Lakshmi or Swad, but you can use any idli rice in the following recipe.

1. **SOAKING** You will need 2 separate bowls for soaking the rice and urad dal. Soak the rice and urad dal in warm water to cover for six hours.

2. Drain the soaked rice and put the rice in a blender with enough water to facilitate grinding (about 1½ cups). Grind to a coarse cornmeal-like texture. Transfer ground rice to a deep bowl.

3. Drain water from soaked urad dal and place urad dal in blender. Add just enough water (about 1½ cups) to facilitate grinding. Grind to a fine smooth paste. Transfer ground dal to the deep bowl with the rice.

4. Add salt to the rice mixture in the deep bowl. With your hand mix the batters and the salt thoroughly. **Note:** *It is important to use your hand, and not a spoon, because the warmth from the hand will start the fermentation process of the batter.*

5. Cover the bowl and set aside in a warm place overnight—do not use direct heat.

Note: *Sometimes, because of cold weather, the batter may not readily ferment. To encourage the batter to ferment, place the bowl in a warmed oven. First heat oven to 350 degrees for 10 minutes and then turn off the oven. After a 10 to 15 minute wait, the bowl with batter can be placed, still covered, in the oven. You may also use the oven light to promote fermentation without turning on the oven. Place the bowl with batter for 4 to 6 hours inside the oven with oven light on.*

6. The following morning, or about 6 hours later depending upon the outside temperature and humidity, you will notice that the batter has risen in the bowl and has a foamy appearance. This is fermentation. Sometimes, depending upon the climate, the batter may over ferment and overflow the bowl. Discard spillage and just use the batter in the bowl to make idlis. (**Note:** *It is important not to stir the batter after fermentation.*) The batter is now ready for you to make idlis with an idli cooker.

use of an idli cooker   This is a special type of vessel (available in Indian grocery stores) that is used to make idlis. It has a bottom pan to hold water and a plate insert with 5 to 7 mold sections, similar in appearance to an egg poacher. A wet cloth is draped over the idli plate and the batter is poured into each mold over the steamed cloth. The steamed cloth is necessary to stop the batter from flowing into the water in the bottom vessel. The vessel has a tight cover to steam cook the idlis. Steam cook for 8 to 10 minutes.

note   A normal serving is about 2 idlis per person. Unused idlis from the above recipe can be refrigerated for up to 4 weeks and used later. Refrigerated idlis can be warmed in a microwave for 1 to 2 minutes before serving.

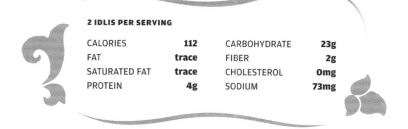

2 IDLIS PER SERVING

CALORIES	112	CARBOHYDRATE	23g
FAT	trace	FIBER	2g
SATURATED FAT	trace	CHOLESTEROL	0mg
PROTEIN	4g	SODIUM	73mg

rava idlis

1 package Rava idli mix

3 cups nonfat plain yogurt

1 cup low-fat cultured buttermilk

Rava idlis (MTR Brand) are made from instant mix. The ready-made package is available in most Indian grocery stores.

Serve Rava Idlis with coconut chutney and any sambhar.

1. Mix one package (about 3 cups) Rava idli mix with nonfat plain yogurt and cultured buttermilk.

2. Let the batter mixture sit for about 15 minutes.

3. Steam the batter in an idli cooker for about 10 to 12 minutes. (See page 73 for idli cooker information.)

rava kichadi

Serves 6				
	1 teaspoon canola oil	½ cup chopped onion	½ cup frozen mixed vegetables	¾ teaspoon garam masala powder
	2 teaspoons butter or ghee	½ cup chopped tomato	¼ teaspoon turmeric powder	½ teaspoon salt
	2 dry bay leaves	½ tablespoon minced ginger root	1 cup uncooked quick cream of wheat	¼ cup roasted cashew halves
	1 teaspoon cumin seeds			

1. Heat a nonstick skillet with oil and 1 teaspoon butter over medium heat. When oil is hot, but not smoking, add bay leaves and cumin seeds. Stir-fry for 1 minute.

2. Immediately add onion, tomato, ginger, and mixed vegetables. Stir well with the seasonings for a couple of minutes.

3. Add turmeric, cream of wheat, garam masala powder, and salt and mix well.

4. Add 3 cups of warm water to the mixture and stir well. Cook, covered over low medium heat for about 2 to 3 minutes.

5. Add 1 teaspoon butter and stir well. Garnish with cashew halves. Serve warm.

Rava Kichadi is a delicious dish of cream of wheat cooked with mixed vegetables, onions, tomatoes, and ginger.

CALORIES	174	CARBOHYDRATE	29g
FAT	5g	FIBER	2g
SATURATED FAT	1g	CHOLESTEROL	2mg
PROTEIN	5g	SODIUM	199mg

cream of wheat uppuma

Serves 4	1 tablespoon canola oil	¼ cup finely chopped onion	¼ cup minced fresh coriander (cilantro) leaves
	1 whole dried red chili pepper	1 cup uncooked quick or regular cream of wheat	1 teaspoon butter or margarine
	1 teaspoon black mustard seeds	½ teaspoon salt	2 tablespoons roasted cashew halves (optional)
	1 teaspoon urad dal	½ teaspoon finely minced ginger root	

This is cream of wheat cooked with onions and spices. Serve uppuma with sambhar or chutney.

variations **TOMATO UPPUMA** Follow the same recipe but after adding onion, add ¼ cup chopped tomato and ¼ teaspoon finely chopped green chili peppers. Stir well.

VEGETABLE UPPUMA Follow the same recipe but after adding water to cream of wheat, add 4 ounces frozen mixed vegetables and stir. Or add ¼ cup of shredded carrots together with ¼ cup of cooked green peas and stir. Cover and cook over low heat, stirring frequently.

1. Place oil in a skillet over medium heat. When oil is hot, but not smoking, add red chili pepper, mustard seeds, and urad dal.

2. When urad dal turns golden, add chopped onion and cook for 1 minute. Add cream of wheat and stir for 1 minute. Add salt and ginger.

3. Add 2 cups of warm water gradually to cream of wheat while stirring.

4. Cover and cook over low heat, stirring frequently for about 2 minutes. Add coriander and butter. Stir well. Add cashews, if desired, and mix well.

CALORIES	211	CARBOHYDRATE	35g
FAT	5g	FIBER	2g
SATURATED FAT	1g	CHOLESTEROL	0mg
PROTEIN	5g	SODIUM	280mg

soji uppuma

Serves 4	1 teaspoon canola oil	1 teaspoon urad dal	1 teaspoon minced green chili peppers
	2 teaspoons butter	1 cup soji	¼ cup shredded carrots
	4 to 6 curry leaves	¾ teaspoon salt	2 tablespoons roasted cashew halves (optional)
	1 teaspoon black mustard seeds	1 teaspoon minced ginger root (optional)	

1. Bring 2 cups of water to a boil in a saucepan. Set aside.

2. In a skillet or wok heat canola oil and 1 teaspoon butter together over medium heat. When oil is hot, but not smoking, add curry leaves, mustard seeds, and urad dal. Heat until mustard seeds pop and urad dal turns golden brown, about 30 seconds.

3. Add soji and salt to skillet and roast with spices over medium-low heat for 1 minute.

4. Add ginger, green chili peppers, and carrots to soji and mix well over low heat.

5. Slowly add the hot water to soji in skillet and keep stirring often, over low heat, for 2 to 4 minutes. Add 1 teaspoon butter and mix well.

6. Stir cashew halves into soji. Serve warm.

Soji is a special type of coarse cream of wheat that has a unique texture and taste when cooked. Soji is available in Indian grocery stores. This uppuma can be prepared in less than 15 minutes. This dish is wholesome, delicious, and satisfying. Soji can be served for breakfast, tea, or as a light evening meal with any chutney and sambhar.

HEALTHY SOUTH INDIAN COOKING

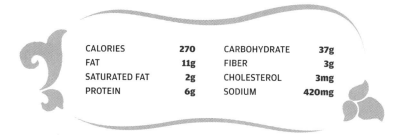

CALORIES	270	CARBOHYDRATE	37g
FAT	11g	FIBER	3g
SATURATED FAT	2g	CHOLESTEROL	3mg
PROTEIN	6g	SODIUM	420mg

cracked wheat uppuma

Serves 4	2 tablespoons canola oil	2 teaspoons urad dal	¼ cup shredded carrots
	4 to 6 curry leaves	1 cup cracked wheat	¼ cup ground fresh coconut or unsweetened coconut powder
	1 whole dried red chili pepper	1 teaspoon salt	
	1 teaspoon black mustard seeds	1 green chili pepper, chopped (optional)	

Cracked wheat cooked with shredded carrots and cashews, this uppuma can be served for breakfast or tea with any type of chutney or sambhar.

1. Place canola oil in a skillet over medium heat. When oil is hot, but not smoking, add curry leaves, red chili pepper, mustard seeds, and urad dal. Cook until mustard seeds pop and urad dal turns golden brown, about 30 seconds.

2. Add cracked wheat and roast, uncovered, over medium heat for a few minutes.

3. Add salt and 4 cups of warm water. Blend carefully with ingredients in the skillet.

4. Add green chili pepper and carrots. Stir and cook briefly over low heat, covered, until water evaporates.

5. Stir in coconut powder and mix well. Serve warm.

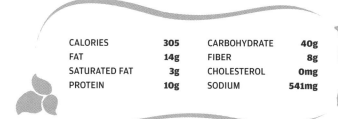

CALORIES	305	CARBOHYDRATE	40g
FAT	14g	FIBER	8g
SATURATED FAT	3g	CHOLESTEROL	0mg
PROTEIN	10g	SODIUM	541mg

urad dal vadais

Makes 12 vadais

½ cup urad dal

2 tablespoons urad flour (optional)

¼ cup finely chopped onion

1 green chili pepper, finely chopped

½ teaspoon salt

¼ cup chopped fresh coriander (cilantro) leaves

canola oil for frying

1. In a bowl, soak urad dal in water to cover for 2 hours.

2. Drain water from urad dal. Transfer soaked urad dal to blender and grind with ¼ cup of water to facilitate the grinding process. Add urad flour to thicken batter if desired. **Caution:** *Do not make the batter too watery, otherwise the vadais will become oily when fried.*

3. In a bowl mix batter with onion and green chili pepper. (The quantity of onion and chili pepper may be adjusted to taste.)

4. Add salt and coriander to batter and mix well.

5. Heat oil in a wok. Oil must be hot, but not smoking. Take about 1½ tablespoons of batter in hand. Form into a doughnut shape over a wet cloth (to prevent sticking to hands) and transfer directly to the hot oil. Deep-fry until one side is cooked, turn with a slotted spoon to the other side and cook until vadai becomes golden brown. Repeat with remaining batter.

Note: *If the above method seems complicated, you may also drop batter by the spoonfuls directly into the oil, as though making dumplings. Fry until golden brown and drain on paper towels.*

Urad Dal Vadais, donut-shaped snacks made of lentils, are a unique South Indian food. They are also known as Medhu Vadais. Urad Dal Vadais are commonly served in South India for breakfast and tea. They are delicious served with Coconut Chutney (page 83).

variation **THAYIR VADAIS** (*vadais soaked in yogurt*): Soak the cooked vadais in hot water for 3 to 5 minutes in a wide-bottomed bowl. Scoop vadais without water to a deep platter. Blend 2 cups of fat-free plain yogurt with 1 tablespoon minced ginger root, ½ green chili pepper, and ½ teaspoon cumin seeds in a blender. Pour the ground mixture over the vadais and let them soak in the yogurt mixture for an hour before serving. Garnishing: Fry ½ teaspoon mustard seeds, ½ teaspoon urad dal, and 2 to 4 curry leaves in a teaspoon of oil in a small saucepan and pour it over the thayir vadais. Leftover thayir vadais can be refrigerated and served at a later time.

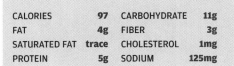

CALORIES	71	CARBOHYDRATE	7g
FAT	4g	FIBER	3g
SATURATED FAT	trace	CHOLESTEROL	0mg
PROTEIN	3g	SODIUM	94mg

CALORIES	97	CARBOHYDRATE	11g
FAT	4g	FIBER	3g
SATURATED FAT	trace	CHOLESTEROL	1mg
PROTEIN	5g	SODIUM	125mg

chutneys and salads

chettinad onion kose

Serves 6	FOR GRINDING	2 garlic cloves, peeled and cut in half	1 teaspoon urad dal	¼ teaspoon turmeric powder
	2 dried red chili peppers	———————	1½ cups coarsely chopped onion (¼-inch pieces)	½ teaspoon salt (more, if desired)
	1 teaspoon fennel seeds	2 tablespoons canola oil	1½ cups chopped tomato	¼ cup tomato sauce
	10 to 12 almonds	2 dry bay leaves	1 cup chopped Idaho potato, (about ½-inch pieces)	
	2 tablespoons unsweetened coconut powder	1 teaspoon black mustard seeds		

This kose is an authentic Chettinad speciality sauce. It is an excellent accompaniment to any bread.

1. In a blender mix all of the grinding ingredients with 1 cup of warm water and grind to a smooth paste. Set aside.

2. Heat saucepan over medium heat. Add oil and when oil is hot, but not smoking, stir in bay leaves, mustard seeds, and urad dal. Cover and heat till mustard seeds pop and urad dal turns golden brown, about 30 seconds.

3. Add onion, tomato, potato, and turmeric powder. Stir-fry for 2 to 3 minutes.

4. Add the ground mixture with 2 cups of warm water, salt, and tomato sauce. Cover and cook over low medium heat until the potatoes are cooked.

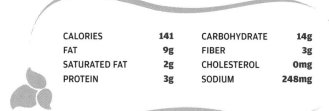

CALORIES	141	CARBOHYDRATE	14g
FAT	9g	FIBER	3g
SATURATED FAT	2g	CHOLESTEROL	0mg
PROTEIN	3g	SODIUM	248mg

coconut chutney

Makes 2 ½ cups	1 heaping cup fresh coconut, cut in small chunks or 1 heaping cup unsweetened coconut powder	3 green chili peppers or 3 dried red chili peppers (more if desired) 2 small slices ginger root	1 tablespoon roasted chickpeas or dry roasted peanuts ½ teaspoon salt (more, if desired)

Grind all of the ingredients in a blender with 1½ cups of hot water to create a smooth paste. Transfer chutney paste from blender to a bowl before serving. **Note:** *Always keep coconut chutney refrigerated.*

A delicious optional enhancement:

>   1 tablespoon canola oil
>   ¼ teaspoon asafoetida powder
>   4 curry leaves (optional)
>   1 whole dried red chili pepper (more, if desired)
>   1 teaspoon black mustard seeds
>   1 teaspoon urad dal

Heat oil over medium heat in a butter warmer or a small saucepan. When oil is hot, but not smoking, add asafoetida powder, curry leaves, and chili pepper. Add mustard seeds and urad dal. Cover and fry until mustard seeds burst and urad dal is golden brown, about 30 seconds. Pour over chutney and mix well.

A condiment-like sauce with fresh coconut, Coconut Chutney is a delicious accompaniment to a number of dishes, including many listed as appetizers and breads in this book. Coconut chutney is one of the outstanding specialties of South Indian cuisine.

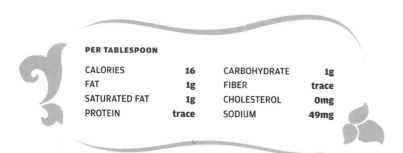

PER TABLESPOON

CALORIES	16	CARBOHYDRATE	1g
FAT	1g	FIBER	trace
SATURATED FAT	1g	CHOLESTEROL	0mg
PROTEIN	trace	SODIUM	49mg

coconut thuvaiyal

Makes 2 cups	1 tablespoon canola oil	1 teaspoon black mustard seeds	2 tablespoons roasted chickpeas or dry roasted peanuts	¼ teaspoon tamarind paste
	½ teaspoon asafoetida powder	1 teaspoon urad dal	4 dried red chili peppers (more, if desired)	½ teaspoon salt (more, if desired)
	4 to 6 curry leaves (optional)	1 heaping cup fresh coconut, cut in small pieces, or 1 heaping cup unsweetened coconut powder	¼ cup chopped onion	

Thuvaiyal is a thick variation of chutney. It is a finely ground paste-like accompaniment for various appetizers, breads, and rice dishes. Thuvaiyal goes particularly well with idlis, dosais, Yogurt Rice (page 123), Lemon Rice (page 114), and Tamarind Rice (page 118).

1. Heat oil in a skillet over medium heat. When oil is hot, but not smoking, add asafoetida powder, curry leaves, mustard seeds, and urad dal. Cover and cook over medium heat until mustard seeds burst and urad dal is golden brown, about 30 seconds.

2. Add coconut and the remaining ingredients (except salt) to the skillet. Stir-fry for 2 minutes.

3. Grind ingredients in a blender with 1½ to 2 cups of hot water and salt for 2 to 3 minutes to create a smooth thick paste.

PER TABLESPOON

CALORIES	27	CARBOHYDRATE	2g
FAT	2g	FIBER	trace
SATURATED FAT	1g	CHOLESTEROL	0mg
PROTEIN	1g	SODIUM	44mg

coriander chutney 1

Makes 2 cups	1 teaspoon canola oil	3 cups chopped fresh coriander (cilantro) leaves	⅓ cup roasted chickpeas or roasted peanuts
	1 teaspoon asafoetida powder	2 green chili peppers (more, if desired)	¼ teaspoon tamarind paste
	½ teaspoon black mustard seeds	2 or 3 small slices ginger root	½ teaspoon salt (more, if desired)
	½ teaspoon urad dal		

1. Place oil in a wok or skillet over medium heat. When oil is hot, but not smoking, add asafoetida powder, mustard seeds, and urad dal. Cover and fry until mustard seeds pop and urad dal is golden brown, about 30 seconds.

2. Add coriander, chili peppers, ginger, and chickpeas. Stir-fry for a few minutes.

3. Transfer all ingredients to a blender. Add tamarind paste and about 1½ cups hot water (enough water to grind ingredients smoothly). Grind all the ingredients to a smooth consistency. Add salt to taste.

A chutney with sautéed spices, fresh coriander, and ginger.

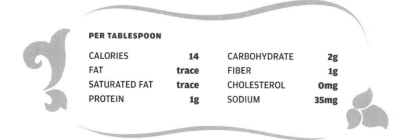

PER TABLESPOON

CALORIES	14	CARBOHYDRATE	2g
FAT	trace	FIBER	1g
SATURATED FAT	trace	CHOLESTEROL	0mg
PROTEIN	1g	SODIUM	35mg

coriander chutney II

Makes 2 cups	2 cups chopped fresh coriander (cilantro) leaves	1 tablespoon minced ginger root	1/3 cup roasted chickpeas or dry roasted peanuts
	1 or 2 green chili peppers (more, if desired)	1/4 cup ground fresh coconut or 1 tablespoon unsweetened coconut powder	1/4 teaspoon tamarind paste
			1 teaspoon salt

An easy-to-prepare chutney with fresh coriander and coconut.

1. Place all the ingredients, except salt, in a blender.

2. Add 1½ cups of hot water and grind ingredients to a smooth paste.

3. Add salt to taste and mix well.

PER TABLESPOON

CALORIES	10	CARBOHYDRATE	2g
FAT	trace	FIBER	trace
SATURATED FAT	trace	CHOLESTEROL	0mg
PROTEIN	1g	SODIUM	47mg

eggplant chutney 1

Makes 3 cups	3 tablespoons canola oil	2 cups unpeeled chopped eggplant	1 tablespoon minced ginger root	¼ teaspoon tamarind paste
	¼ teaspoon asafoetida powder	½ cup coarsely chopped tomato	2 or 3 dried red chili peppers (more, if desired)	2 tablespoons tomato sauce
	1 teaspoon black mustard seeds	1 cup coarsely chopped onion	¼ cup ground fresh coconut or unsweetened coconut powder	1 teaspoon salt
	1 teaspoon urad dal	4 garlic cloves, chopped		

1. Heat the oil in a skillet over medium heat. When the oil is hot, but not smoking, add asafoetida powder, mustard seeds, and urad dal. Cover and fry until mustard seeds pop and urad dal is golden brown, about 30 seconds.

2. Add eggplant, tomato, onion, garlic, and ginger to skillet. Stir-fry for 5 to 7 minutes. Add red chili peppers, coconut powder, tamarind paste, tomato sauce, and 1½ cups of hot water. Add salt and mix well. Cover and cook over medium heat until eggplant becomes somewhat soft, about 3 minutes.

3. Transfer ingredients from skillet to a blender and grind coarsely. Transfer eggplant chutney to a bowl and serve.

A condiment-like sauce made from eggplant, tomatoes, and garlic, Eggplant Chutney is served as an accompaniment to many Indian breads and appetizers.

PER TABLESPOON

CALORIES	13	CARBOHYDRATE	1g
FAT	1g	FIBER	trace
SATURATED FAT	trace	CHOLESTEROL	0mg
PROTEIN	trace	SODIUM	49mg

eggplant chutney II

Makes 2 cups	2 tablespoons canola oil	1 cup unpeeled chopped eggplant	2 garlic cloves, peeled and cut in half	2 thick slices ginger root
	1 dried red chili pepper (more, if desired)	½ cup coarsely chopped onion	½ teaspoon turmeric powder	½ teaspoon salt (more, if desired)
		½ cup coarsely chopped tomato	¼ cup dry roasted peanuts	½ teaspoon fresh lemon juice

A simpler version of Eggplant Chutney I (page 87).

1. Place oil in a warmed skillet. When oil is hot, add red chili pepper, eggplant, onion, tomato, and garlic. Stir-fry for about 2 minutes.

2. Add turmeric powder and stir well. Cover and cook over medium heat until eggplant becomes soft, about 7 to 10 minutes.

3. Transfer ingredients from skillet to a blender and grind together with peanuts, ginger, and salt. Add ½ cup of warm water and grind to a thick paste. Add 1 to 2 tablespoons more water, if needed, to facilitate the grinding process.

4. Transfer eggplant mixture to a serving bowl and stir in fresh lemon juice. Mix well. Serve.

chutneys and salads

HEALTHY SOUTH INDIAN COOKING

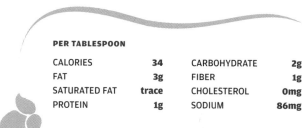

PER TABLESPOON

CALORIES	34	CARBOHYDRATE	2g
FAT	3g	FIBER	1g
SATURATED FAT	trace	CHOLESTEROL	0mg
PROTEIN	1g	SODIUM	86mg

kosamalli

Serves 6	3 cups chopped eggplant with skin	2 tablespoons canola oil	¼ teaspoon turmeric powder	½ teaspoon tamarind paste
	1 cup chopped onion	4 to 6 curry leaves	½ teaspoon cayenne powder	½ cup tomato sauce
	¼ cup chopped tomato	¼ teaspoon asafoetida powder	½ teaspoon cumin powder	¼ cup chopped fresh coriander (cilantro) leaves
	1 green chili pepper, chopped (more, if desired)	1 teaspoon black mustard seeds	1 teaspoon salt	
		1 teaspoon urad dal		

1. Put the eggplant in a saucepan and add enough water to cover. Cook, uncovered, for a few minutes until it is soft. Use a masher to mash the eggplant with the water. Set aside.

2. In a small bowl, combine onion, tomato, and green chili pepper and set aside.

3. Heat oil in a saucepan over medium heat. When oil is hot, but not smoking, add curry leaves, asafoetida powder, mustard seeds, and urad dal. Fry until mustard seeds pop and urad dal turns golden brown, about 30 seconds.

4. Immediately add onion mixture and cook until onions are tender. Add turmeric powder and mix well.

5. Add the mashed eggplant and stir into the mixture. Add cayenne powder, cumin powder, salt, tamarind paste, and tomato sauce.

6. Add 2 cups of water and stir. When the mixture begins to boil, add coriander and let it simmer over low heat for 7 to 10 minutes.

This Chettinad specialty is an eggplant dish with onions and tomatoes cooked in tamarind paste. Serve with adais, idlis, dosais, or idiyappam.

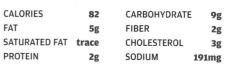

PER TABLESPOON

CALORIES	82	CARBOHYDRATE	9g
FAT	5g	FIBER	2g
SATURATED FAT	trace	CHOLESTEROL	3g
PROTEIN	2g	SODIUM	191mg

mango and ginger chutney

Makes 1 cup	½ cup chopped unripe mango	¼ cup unsweetened coconut powder	1 green chili pepper (more if desired)
	¼ cup minced ginger root	¼ cup roasted peanuts	¼ teaspoon salt (more, if desired)

Another variety of chutney made from a delicious combination of mango and ginger.

1. Place all the ingredients in a blender with approximately ½ cup of warm water.

2. Blend for a few minutes until ingredients become smooth. If more water is needed to facilitate the grinding process, add ¼ cup of warm water at a time, as needed.

PER TABLESPOON

CALORIES	54	CARBOHYDRATE	4g
FAT	4g	FIBER	1g
SATURATED FAT	2g	CHOLESTEROL	0mg
PROTEIN	1g	SODIUM	106mg

masoor dal supreme

Makes 4 cups	¼ cup masoor dal	1 teaspoon black mustard seeds	1 teaspoon minced ginger root
	½ teaspoon turmeric powder	1 teaspoon urad dal	½ teaspoon cumin powder
	2 tablespoons canola oil	1 cup chopped onion	½ teaspoon salt (more, if desired)
	4 to 6 curry leaves	1 cup chopped tomato	½ cup chopped fresh coriander (cilantro) leaves
	1 whole dried red chili pepper	1 green chili pepper, minced	

1. Bring 2 cups of water to a boil. Add masoor dal and ¼ teaspoon turmeric powder. Cook, uncovered, over medium heat for about 15 minutes until dal becomes soft and well cooked. Mash cooked masoor dal. Set aside.

2. Place canola oil in a saucepan over medium heat. When oil is hot, but not smoking, add curry leaves, red chili pepper, mustard seeds, and urad dal. Fry until mustard seeds pop and urad dal turns golden brown, about 30 seconds.

3. Add onion, tomato, green chili pepper, and ginger. Cook until onion is tender.

4. Add remaining ¼ teaspoon turmeric powder and mashed masoor dal and stir well. Add about ¾ cup of warm water and mix well.

5. Add cumin powder and salt. When the mixture begins to boil, add coriander and let it simmer for about 3 minutes.

A hearty sauce made from tomatoes and masoor dal (also known as red lentils) that can be served with pooris, chappatis, or any Indian breads. It can also be served over any plain or basmati rice. Masoor dal cooks quickly and has a delicate texture.

Note   Instead of 2 tablespoons of canola oil, the dish can be enhanced in flavor by adding 1 tablespoon of ghee (clarified butter) and 1 tablespoon of oil in Step 2, if you desire.

variation   For a delicious variation in flavor, you may substitute moong dal for the masoor dal to create MOONG DAL SUPREME.

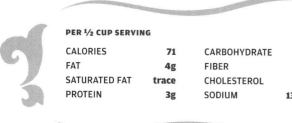

PER ½ CUP SERVING

CALORIES	71	CARBOHYDRATE	8g
FAT	4g	FIBER	3g
SATURATED FAT	trace	CHOLESTEROL	0mg
PROTEIN	3g	SODIUM	138mg

mint chutney

Makes 1 cup

1 tablespoon canola oil

¼ teaspoon asafoetida powder

1 teaspoon black mustard seeds

1 teaspoon urad dal

½ cup chopped onion

1 green chili pepper (more, if desired)

1 cup fresh mint leaves

1 tablespoon ground fresh coconut or unsweetened coconut powder

1 tablespoon roasted chickpeas or roasted peanuts

¼ teaspoon tamarind paste

½ teaspoon salt (more, if desired)

A refreshing condiment-like sauce with fresh mint, Mint Chutney is an accompaniment to any appetizer and goes well with yogurt rice.

1. Heat oil in a heavy skillet until hot, but not smoking. Add asafoetida powder, mustard seeds, and urad dal. Cover and fry until mustard seeds pop and urad dal is golden brown, about 30 seconds.

2. Add onion and green chili pepper to skillet and stir-fry for a few minutes.

3. Add mint, coconut powder, and roasted chickpeas to skillet and stir-fry for at least 2 minutes. Mix well.

4. Transfer ingredients to a blender and finely grind. Add 1½ cups of hot water to facilitate the grinding.

5. Add tamarind paste and salt and continue grinding until ingredients reach a fine medium-thick consistency.

PER TABLESPOON			
CALORIES	11	CARBOHYDRATE	1g
FAT	1g	FIBER	trace
SATURATED FAT	trace	CHOLESTEROL	0mg
PROTEIN	trace	SODIUM	35mg

mint and yogurt chutney

Makes 1 cup	1 cup fresh mint leaves	4 raw almonds	½ teaspoon salt
	½ teaspoon cumin seeds	½ green chili pepper (more, if desired)	¾ cup nonfat plain yogurt
	1 tablespoon unsweetened coconut powder	¼ teaspoon lemon juice	

Blend all of the above ingredients to a smooth paste in a blender. Serve at room temperature or slightly chilled.

An easy to make chutney that can be used as a spread to make chutney sandwiches. Delicious served as a dip or as an accompaniment with Indian breads.

PER TABLESPOON

CALORIES	15	CARBOHYDRATE	2g
FAT	1g	FIBER	trace
SATURATED FAT	trace	CHOLESTEROL	trace
PROTEIN	1g	SODIUM	77mg

onion and potato kose

Serves 6	2 tablespoons canola oil	1 teaspoon urad dal	1 cup small oblong pieces Idaho potato with skin	1½ teaspoons cumin powder
	2 to 4 slivers cinnamon stick	½ cup chopped onion	¼ teaspoon turmeric powder	½ cup tomato sauce
	1 dry bay leaf	½ cup chopped tomato	½ teaspoon cayenne powder	½ teaspoon salt
	1 teaspoon black mustard seeds			¼ cup chopped fresh coriander (cilantro) leaves

A thick tomato-based sauce with onions and potatoes, Onion and Potato Kose is an excellent accompaniment to chappatis, pooris, idlis, dosais, or tortillas.

variations In a spice grinder or coffee grinder, grind together 1 teaspoon unsweetened coconut powder, 1 dried red chili pepper, ½ teaspoon fennel seeds, and ½ teaspoon cumin seeds. Stir into cooked kose. Simmer over low heat for an additional 2 to 3 minutes.

For a lighter version, omit potatoes and increase both onion and tomato to 1 cup each to create a delicious ONION AND TOMATO KOSE.

1. Heat oil in a medium saucepan over medium heat. When oil is hot, but not smoking, add cinnamon sticks and bay leaf. Immediately add mustard seeds and urad dal. Cover and fry until mustard seeds pop and urad dal is golden brown, about 30 seconds.

2. Immediately add onion, tomato, and potatoes to saucepan. Add turmeric powder and stir well. Cook, uncovered, over medium-low heat for 1 to 2 minutes.

3. Add cayenne powder, cumin powder, tomato sauce, and salt. Blend well. Add 2 cups of water and blend well. When the ingredients start to boil, add coriander. Cook, covered, over medium-low heat until potatoes are tender, 8 to 10 minutes, stirring frequently.

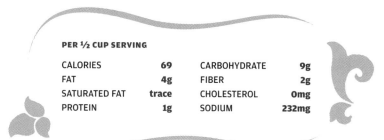

PER ½ CUP SERVING

CALORIES	69	CARBOHYDRATE	9g
FAT	4g	FIBER	2g
SATURATED FAT	trace	CHOLESTEROL	0mg
PROTEIN	1g	SODIUM	232mg

onion and tomato chutney

Makes 2 ½ cups	2 tablespoons canola oil ¼ teaspoon asafoetida powder 4 or 5 curry leaves	2 to 4 whole dried red chili peppers (more, if desired) 1 teaspoon black mustard seeds	1 teaspoon urad dal 1 cup coarsely chopped onion 1 cup chopped tomato	3 garlic cloves, peeled ¼ teaspoon tamarind paste ½ teaspoon salt

1. Heat canola oil in a small skillet or wok over medium heat. When oil is hot, but not smoking, add asafoetida powder, curry leaves, red chili peppers, mustard seeds, and urad dal. Cover and heat until mustard seeds pop and urad dal turns golden brown, about 30 seconds.

2. Add onion, tomato, and garlic cloves to skillet and stir-fry until tender.

3. Add tamarind paste and salt. Stir and cook for a few minutes until mixture is well blended. Remove from heat.

4. Transfer ingredients from skillet to a blender. Add 1 cup of warm water. Grind on high speed for a few minutes until the ingredients are ground thoroughly and have reached a thick consistency.

Onion and Tomato Chutney can be served with any bread and is an excellent accompaniment to dosais, adais, and idlis. This chutney is also delicious with pakora and bhaji.

PER TABLESPOON

CALORIES	11	CARBOHYDRATE	1g
FAT	1g	FIBER	trace
SATURATED FAT	trace	CHOLESTEROL	0mg
PROTEIN	trace	SODIUM	27mg

paruppu thuvaiyal

Makes 1 cup	½ cup moong dal	2 garlic cloves, peeled	¼ teaspoon salt (more, if desired)
	¼ cup unsweetened coconut powder	2 whole dried red chili peppers	

A thick condiment-like sauce made from lentils, coconut, and garlic, this thuvaiyal can be served with buttered plain rice, yogurt rice, or as a spread over any bread.

1. In a nonstick skillet, dry roast moong dal for about 2 minutes over medium heat.

2. In a blender, mix roasted moong dal with coconut powder, garlic, red chili pepper, salt, and 1 cup of warm water and grind.

PER TABLESPOON

CALORIES	35	CARBOHYDRATE	5g
FAT	1g	FIBER	2g
SATURATED FAT	trace	CHOLESTEROL	0mg
PROTEIN	2g	SODIUM	38mg

peanut chutney

Makes about 1½ cups	1 cup dry roasted peanuts (lightly salted)	3 garlic cloves, peeled and quartered	¼ teaspoon salt (more, if desired)
	¼ cup unsweetened coconut powder or ground fresh coconut	1 whole dried red chili pepper (more, if desired)	

1. Place peanuts, coconut powder, garlic cloves, red chili pepper, and salt in a blender with approximately 1¾ cups warm water.

2. Blend for a few minutes until ingredients become smooth.

A wonderful combination of peanuts and coconut. Can be used as a spread to make chutney sandwiches or served as a dip.

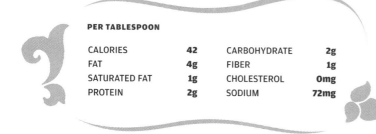

PER TABLESPOON

CALORIES	42	CARBOHYDRATE	2g
FAT	4g	FIBER	1g
SATURATED FAT	1g	CHOLESTEROL	0mg
PROTEIN	2g	SODIUM	72mg

tomato chutney

Makes 2 cups	2 tablespoons canola oil	3 or 4 curry leaves (optional)	¼ teaspoon turmeric powder	¼ cup minced fresh coriander (cilantro) leaves
	¼ teaspoon asafoetida powder	1 cup finely chopped tomato	¼ teaspoon cayenne powder	¾ teaspoon salt (more, if desired)
	1 teaspoon black mustard seeds	1 cup finely chopped onion	1 teaspoon cumin powder	
	2 teaspoons urad dal		1 cup tomato sauce	

A salsa-like South Indian chutney! This easy-to-prepare chutney may be served with many appetizers or Indian breads.

1. Place oil in a small saucepan or small skillet over medium heat. When oil is hot, but not smoking, add asafoetida powder, mustard seeds, urad dal, and curry leaves. Fry, covered, until mustard seeds pop and urad dal is golden brown, about 30 seconds.

2. Add tomato and onion. Sauté for a few minutes.

3. Add turmeric powder, cayenne powder, and cumin powder and stir well.

4. Add tomato sauce, coriander, and salt. Cook, covered, over low heat for approximately 10 minutes. The tomato will blend with other ingredients over low heat to become somewhat smooth and thickened.

PER TABLESPOON

CALORIES	10	CARBOHYDRATE	1g
FAT	1g	FIBER	trace
SATURATED FAT	trace	CHOLESTEROL	0mg
PROTEIN	trace	SODIUM	65mg

sweet mango pachadi

Serves 4	2 cups chopped ripe mango	1 teaspoon canola oil	½ teaspoon black mustard seeds
	½ cup light brown sugar (more, if desired)	1 whole dried red chili pepper	1 teaspoon urad dal
	1 teaspoon minced ginger root		

1. In a medium saucepan, cook mango in 2 cups of water until it becomes creamy.

2. Add brown sugar and minced ginger to mango and mix well.

3. Heat a small skillet. Add oil. When oil is hot, but not smoking, add red chili pepper, black mustard seeds, and urad dal. Cover and fry until mustard seeds burst and urad dal is golden brown, about 30 seconds.

4. Add the seasoning to the cooked mango mixture and mix well.

A Chettinad speciality—ripe mango cooked with light brown sugar! It can be served as a chutney, as a side dish to a meal, or as a dessert.

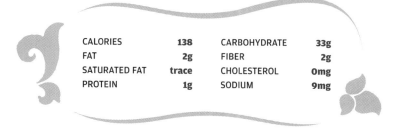

CALORIES	138	CARBOHYDRATE	33g
FAT	2g	FIBER	2g
SATURATED FAT	trace	CHOLESTEROL	0mg
PROTEIN	1g	SODIUM	9mg

cauliflower and pasta salad

Serves 6	1 cup small pasta shells	1 teaspoon urad dal	1 teaspoon salt	½ cup roasted cashew halves (optional)
	2 tablespoons canola oil	½ onion, chopped	½ teaspoon chutney powder (more, if desired)	
	1 teaspoon black mustard seeds	1 or 2 green chili peppers, chopped	¼ cup chopped fresh coriander (cilantro) leaves	
		3 cups cauliflower florets		

An innovative and refreshing dish, Cauliflower and Pasta Salad can be served as a light snack or as an accompaniment to any grilled or baked meat dish.

1. Bring 3 cups of water to a boil. When water is at boiling point, add pasta. Cook pasta until tender. Drain and set cooked pasta aside.

2. In a skillet or wok, heat oil over medium heat. When oil is hot, but not smoking, add mustard seeds and urad dal. Cover and fry over medium heat until mustard seeds pop and urad dal is golden brown, about 30 seconds.

3. Add onion and green chili peppers. Stir-fry for 1 minute. (Onion should remain crisp.) Then add cauliflower and cook for about 2 minutes.

4. Add cooked pasta shells and stir. Add salt and chutney powder and mix well. Cook, covered, for an additional minute or two.

5. Garnish with coriander and cashew halves.

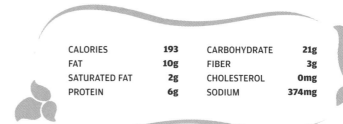

CALORIES	193	CARBOHYDRATE	21g
FAT	10g	FIBER	3g
SATURATED FAT	2g	CHOLESTEROL	0mg
PROTEIN	6g	SODIUM	374mg

yogurt salad

Serves 2 to 4	1 cup red onion slices (cut lengthwise)	½ cup chopped tomato	½ teaspoon salt (or to taste)
	1 green chili pepper, chopped	1½ cups low-fat or fat-free plain yogurt	1 teaspoon chopped fresh coriander (cilantro) leaves

1. Combine onion slices, chili pepper, and tomato with yogurt. Add salt to taste. Chill at least 1 hour before serving.

2. Garnish with coriander.

A creamy salad featuring red onions and tomatoes, yogurt salad is particularly delicious served with Vegetable Biriyani Rice (page 121) or Chicken Biriyani Rice (page 224).

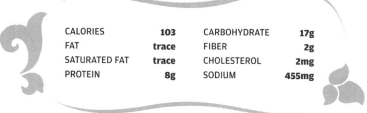

CALORIES	103	CARBOHYDRATE	17g
FAT	trace	FIBER	2g
SATURATED FAT	trace	CHOLESTEROL	2mg
PROTEIN	8g	SODIUM	455mg

cucumber and tomato yogurt salad

Serves 4	1½ cups peeled and diced fresh pickling cucumbers	1 green chili pepper, finely diced (optional)	1½ cups fat-free plain yogurt
	¾ cup diced tomato	1 teaspoon black pepper and cumin powder mixture	¼ cup chopped fresh coriander (cilantro) leaves
	¾ cup diced red onion	½ teaspoon salt	

Refreshing and easy-to-make, this salad is very colorful and pleasing to the palate. It is an excellent accompaniment to any meal.

1. Place all the vegetables in a serving bowl.

2. Blend black pepper and cumin powder and salt into yogurt.

3. Pour yogurt mixture over diced vegetables and stir to coat vegetables. Taste and add additional seasonings if desired.

4. Refrigerate at least 1 hour. Garnish with coriander before serving.

NOTE You may use regular cucumbers instead of fresh pickling cucumbers if you desire. Fresh pickling cucumbers are used in this recipe for extra crunchiness.

chutneys and salads

HEALTHY SOUTH INDIAN COOKING

CALORIES	101	CARBOHYDRATE	18g
FAT	1g	FIBER	6g
SATURATED FAT	trace	CHOLESTEROL	2mg
PROTEIN	8g	SODIUM	346mg

tomato pachadi

Serves 4

1 teaspoon canola oil

1 whole dried red chili pepper

¼ teaspoon asafoetida powder

1 teaspoon black mustard seeds

1 teaspoon urad dal

1 cup chopped onion

1 cup chopped tomato

¼ teaspoon turmeric powder

½ teaspoon cayenne powder

2 cups plain fat-free yogurt

1 teaspoon salt

2 tablespoons chopped fresh coriander (cilantro) leaves

1. Place oil in saucepan over medium heat. When oil is hot, but not smoking, add red chili pepper, asafoetida powder, mustard seeds, and urad dal. Cook, covered, until mustard seeds pop and urad dal is golden brown, about 30 seconds.

2. Add chopped onion and tomato and stir-fry for a few minutes.

3. Add turmeric and cayenne powders and cook for a few more minutes. Transfer ingredients from saucepan to a bowl and allow to cool.

4. Stir yogurt into cooled spice mixture. Add salt and stir. Garnish with coriander leaves.

Seasoned yogurt salad with onions and tomatoes, this pachadi is a refreshing accompaniment to any other dish.

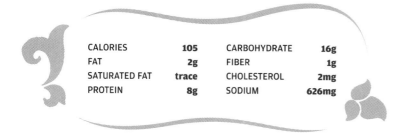

CALORIES	105	CARBOHYDRATE	16g
FAT	2g	FIBER	1g
SATURATED FAT	trace	CHOLESTEROL	2mg
PROTEIN	8g	SODIUM	626mg

onion and tomato salad

Serves 2	1 cup sliced onion (cut lengthwise)	½ green chili pepper, chopped	¼ teaspoon salt
	1 cup chopped tomato	1 cup plain fat-free yogurt	

This yogurt salad is a delightful accompaniment to any meal, eastern or western.

1. Mix onion slices, tomato, and green chili pepper.

2. Add enough yogurt to blend well with the vegetables.

3. Add salt and mix well.

NOTE It is not necessary to have precise measurements for the onions and tomatoes. Quantities of each can be blended to one's taste with the yogurt.

CALORIES	107	CARBOHYDRATE	18g
FAT	1g	FIBER	2g
SATURATED FAT	trace	CHOLESTEROL	2mg
PROTEIN	8g	SODIUM	368mg

seasoned pomegranate yogurt salad

Serves 4

1 teaspoon canola oil

1 or 2 curry leaves (optional)

¼ cup chopped onion

½ teaspoon cumin powder

1 cup pomegranate seeds

1 cup nonfat plain yogurt (more, if desired)

1. Heat a small skillet over medium heat. When oil is hot, but not smoking, add curry leaves and onion. Cook until onion is translucent.

2. Add cumin powder and mix well. Set aside to cool.

3. In a bowl, add pomegranate seeds and the onion mixture to yogurt and mix well.

4. Refrigerate until serving.

Ruby red pomegranate juice is very popular in India. The seeds with the flesh are separated by hand and are eaten as fruit and made into delicious juice. Pomegranate Yogurt Salad can be a complement to any meal.

CALORIES	69	CARBOHYDRATE	11g
FAT	1g	FIBER	trace
SATURATED FAT	trace	CHOLESTEROL	1mg
PROTEIN	4g	SODIUM	45mg

rice

basmati rice with green peas

Serves 6	2 cups basmati rice	1 tablespoon cashew halves (more, if desired)	2 whole cloves (optional)	¼ teaspoon ground cardamom or 2 whole cardamoms
	2 tablespoons butter		¼ teaspoon turmeric powder	
	4 or 5 slivers cinnamon stick	¼ teaspoon saffron (optional)		½ teaspoon salt (more, if desired)
	2 dry bay leaves			½ cup frozen peas

An aromatic rice dish flavored with saffron and cardamom.

1. Wash basmati rice well and rinse thoroughly.

2. Bring 4 cups of water to a boil in a microwave oven or on stovetop and set aside.

3. Heat butter over medium heat in a saucepan. When butter is hot, but not smoking, add cinnamon sticks, bay leaves, and cashews. Fry over medium heat until cashew pieces become golden brown.

4. Add rice to saucepan and stir well to mix all ingredients.

5. Add saffron, cloves, turmeric powder, cardamom, and salt. Mix well. Fry for a minute or two.

6. Pour 4 cups hot water over rice. Stir and wait until mixture begins to boil. Reduce heat to low. Cover and cook for 20 minutes or until rice is fluffy and water has evaporated.

7. Cook green peas for 2 minutes in microwave oven until just tender. Drain peas and set aside. Add the peas to cooked rice just before serving.

CALORIES	271	CARBOHYDRATE	48g
FAT	6g	FIBER	3g
SATURATED FAT	3g	CHOLESTEROL	10mg
PROTEIN	6g	SODIUM	277mg

bell pepper and tomato rice with cashews

Serves 12	2 cups basmati rice	4 or 5 slivers cinnamon stick	1 cup sliced onion, cut lengthwise	1 cup tomato sauce
	1 box (10 ounces) frozen baby lima beans	1 dry bay leaf	1 cup diced tomato	1 tablespoon curry powder
	¾ teaspoon turmeric powder	½ teaspoon cumin seeds	1 green chili pepper, finely chopped	2 teaspoons salt
	4 tablespoons canola oil	½ teaspoon fennel seeds	2 cups coarsely chopped green bell peppers	½ cup cashew halves

1. Cook rice in a rice cooker or saucepan in 4 cups of water. Transfer cooked rice to a bowl and let it cool for about 15 minutes so grains do not stick together.

2. Cook lima beans in a saucepan in 1 cup of water with ¼ teaspoon turmeric powder. When beans are tender, drain and set aside to cool.

3. Heat oil in a wok or large fry-pan over medium heat. When oil is hot, but not smoking, add cinnamon, bay leaf, cumin seeds, and fennel seeds. Brown for a few seconds.

4. Add ¾ cup of the onion slices, tomato, and chili pepper. Stir-fry for 1 minute.

5. Add bell peppers, cooked lima beans, and remaining ½ teaspoon turmeric powder. Mix well.

6. Add tomato sauce. Blend ingredients well. Cook, covered, over medium heat, until bell pepper becomes slightly tender, approximately 1 minute, stirring occasionally. Do not overcook bell pepper.

7. Stir in curry powder and salt.

8. Add cooked rice to wok and blend well with sauce. Immediately reduce heat to low and stir in cashew halves.

9. Sprinkle remaining ¼ cup onion slices over rice. Fluff and mix the rice gently. Turn off heat.

This hearty, flavorful, and nutritious rice dish is filling and delicious by itself. It also can be served with chicken or turkey. This recipe uses a large quantity of rice and keeps well in the refrigerator for many days. If a smaller quantity is desired, you may prepare the dish with half the stated amount of ingredients.

HEALTHY SOUTH INDIAN COOKING

CALORIES	443	CARBOHYDRATE	74g
FAT	13g	FIBER	6g
SATURATED FAT	2g	CHOLESTEROL	0mg
PROTEIN	12g	SODIUM	618mg

black pepper rice with cashews

| Serves 8 | 2 cups extra long-grain white rice or basmati rice

2 tablespoons canola oil | 4 to 6 curry leaves (optional)

1 whole dried red chili pepper

2 teaspoons black mustard seeds | 3 teaspoons urad dal

1 cup chopped yellow onion

2 teaspoons black pepper and cumin powder mixture | 1 teaspoon salt (more, if desired)

¼ cup dry roasted cashews |

A distinctly savory rice dish, Black Pepper Rice goes well with both vegetable and meat dishes and also with yogurt salad.

1. Cook rice in rice cooker or in a saucepan in 4 cups of water following directions for fluffy rice on the box but omitting salt and oil if included in the directions. Cool rice about 1 hour so grains do not stick together.

2. Heat oil in a wok or in a large skillet over medium-high heat. When oil is hot, but not smoking, add curry leaves and red chili pepper. Stir briefly. Add mustard seeds and urad dal. Cover and heat until mustard seeds pop and urad dal is golden brown, about 30 seconds.

3. Add onion and cook for 1 minute. Add cooked rice and stir well. Add black pepper and cumin powder to rice, and salt and mix well.

4. Add cashews and stir well.

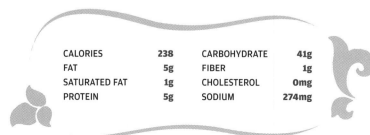

CALORIES	238	CARBOHYDRATE	41g
FAT	5g	FIBER	1g
SATURATED FAT	1g	CHOLESTEROL	0mg
PROTEIN	5g	SODIUM	274mg

carrot rice with cashews

Serves 6			
	2 cups basmati rice	½ cup sliced onion (cut lengthwise)	½ cup roasted cashew halves
	3 tablespoons butter	2 cups shredded carrots	
	3 dry bay leaves	½ teaspoon garam masala powder	
	4 or 5 slivers cinnamon stick	1 teaspoon salt	
	1 teaspoon cumin seeds		

1. Rinse and drain basmati rice. Cook basmati rice in 4 cups of warm water in a rice cooker or on stovetop. Transfer cooked rice to a bowl. Set aside to cool.

2. Heat butter over medium heat in a wide saucepan. When butter is hot, but not smoking, add bay leaves and cinnamon stick. Stir-fry for 1 minute. Add cumin seeds and stir-fry for another minute.

3. Add onions and 1 cup of shredded carrots and stir-fry for about two minutes.

4. Add garam masala powder and salt. Stir well. Add the cooked rice and stir well.

5. Add the remaining 1 cup of shredded carrots and ½ cup of cashews to the rice and fluff the rice gently.

An innovative and aromatic rice dish, that will prove a sure winner on the dinner table.

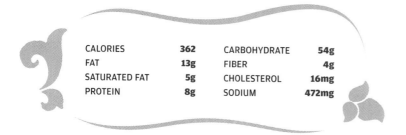

CALORIES	362	CARBOHYDRATE	54g
FAT	13g	FIBER	4g
SATURATED FAT	5g	CHOLESTEROL	16mg
PROTEIN	8g	SODIUM	472mg

cauliflower rice

Serves 4

1 cup basmati rice

1 tablespoon butter (plus 1 teaspoon, optional)

1 tablespoon canola oil

4 to 6 curry leaves

1 dry bay leaf

2 to 4 slivers cinnamon stick

1 teaspoon cumin seeds

1 teaspoon urad dal

1 cup sliced onion (cut lengthwise)

2 cups cauliflower florets

½ teaspoon black pepper and cumin powder mixture

1 teaspoon salt

¼ cup peanuts or cashews

½ cup chopped fresh coriander (cilantro) leaves

A unique cauliflower-based adaptation of South Indian flavored rice dishes.

1. Rinse basmati rice and cook in 2 cups of water. Set aside.

2. Melt 1 tablespoon butter in a wok or wide-bottomed skillet. Add oil and heat over medium heat. When oil is hot, but not smoking, add curry leaves, bay leaf, and cinnamon sticks.

3. Add cumin seeds and urad dal and cover and fry over medium heat until cumin seeds and urad dal are golden brown, about 30 seconds.

4. Add onion and cauliflower florets and stir-fry for a few minutes.

5. Add black pepper and cumin powder and salt. Add 1 tablespoon of water and continue cooking, covered, over medium heat until cauliflower is tender.

6. Add cooked basmati rice. Stir well into cauliflower mixture. Cover and allow to steam over low heat until rice becomes softer and absorbs the flavor of the cauliflower.

7. Add peanuts and coriander and fluff the rice gently.

8. **Optional step:** 1 teaspoon of melted butter or ghee may be added to rice to enhance flavor. Mix well.

NUTRITIONAL ANALYSIS WITHOUT OPTIONAL BUTTER OR GHEE

CALORIES	314	CARBOHYDRATE	43g
FAT	13g	FIBER	5g
SATURATED FAT	3g	CHOLESTEROL	10mg
PROTEIN	8g	SODIUM	622mg

NUTRITIONAL ANALYSIS WITH OPTIONAL BUTTER OR GHEE

CALORIES	342	CARBOHYDRATE	43g
FAT	16g	FIBER	5g
SATURATED FAT	5g	CHOLESTEROL	19mg
PROTEIN	8g	SODIUM	622mg

coconut rice

Serves 8	2 cups long-grain rice or basmati rice	2 whole dried red chili peppers (more, if desired)	¼ cup cashew halves (raw or roasted)
	3 cups shredded fresh coconut	6 to 8 curry leaves (optional)	1 teaspoon salt (more if desired)
	¼ cup canola oil	1½ teaspoons black mustard seeds	¼ cup chopped fresh coriander (cilantro) leaves
	½ teaspoon asafoetida powder	1½ teaspoons urad dal	

1. Cook rice in 4 cups of water. Cool and set aside.

2. Heat a wok and dry roast the shredded coconut, stirring constantly, until golden, approximately 3 minutes. Remove coconut from wok and set aside.

3. Heat oil in the wok over medium heat. When oil is hot, but not smoking, add asafoetida powder, red chili peppers, and curry leaves. Add mustard seeds and urad dal. Cover and fry until mustard seeds pop and urad dal turns golden brown, about 30 seconds.

4. Add cashews (if using raw) to the wok and roast for 2 to 3 minutes.

5. Add cooked rice to the wok and mix well.

6. Stir in the roasted coconut and mix well.

7. Add cashews (if using roasted), salt, and coriander. Mix well.

This exquisite dish is served on auspicious occasions and even in temples in South India. It goes well with light vegetable dishes, such as Cauliflower Masala Poriyal (page 178) and Green Bean Podimas (page 165 var). Be careful not to overpower this delicate dish with heavy sauces.

CALORIES	365	CARBOHYDRATE	44g
FAT	19g	FIBER	4g
SATURATED FAT	10g	CHOLESTEROL	0mg
PROTEIN	5g	SODIUM	278mg

lemon rice

Serves 8	2 cups jasmine rice or extra long-grain rice or basmati rice	1½ teaspoons turmeric powder	4 to 6 curry leaves (optional)	2 tablespoons dry roasted unsalted peanuts (more, if desired)
	¼ cup dry yellow split peas	3 tablespoons canola oil	2 teaspoons black mustard seeds	2 tablespoons minced fresh coriander (cilantro) leaves
	½ cup lemon juice	1 whole dried red chili pepper	2 teaspoons urad dal	
	2 teaspoons salt	½ teaspoon asafoetida powder	1 teaspoon chutney powder	1 teaspoon minced ginger

This popular rice dish is served on special social and religious occasions. Indeed, lemon is considered a very auspicious fruit. Lemon rice goes particularly well with Potatoes Roasted with Garlic and Tomatoes (page 207). It keeps well at room temperature and can be packed for lunch.

1. Cook rice in 4 cups of water, following directions for fluffy rice but omitting salt and oil if included in directions. Cool rice about 1 hour, so grains do not stick together. If time is limited, a little of the lemon juice mixture (see Step 3) can be stirred into the cooling rice to help separate the grains.

2. Soak split peas in 1 cup hot water for about 20 minutes. (Or microwave split peas with enough water to cover, uncovered at high heat for 5 to 6 minutes until peas becomes soft.) Drain and set peas aside.

3. Combine lemon juice, salt, and turmeric powder; set aside.

4. Heat oil in a large skillet or wok over medium heat. When oil is hot, but not smoking, add red chili pepper, asafoetida powder, and curry leaves. Immediately stir in mustard seeds and urad dal. Cover and heat until mustard seeds pop and urad dal is golden brown, about 30 seconds.

5. Immediately stir in soaked split peas. Reduce heat and cook, uncovered, for 2 to 3 minutes.

6. Immediately stir in lemon juice mixture and chutney powder. Simmer 2 to 4 minutes, reducing heat if mixture starts to boil.

7. Reduce heat to low. Add cooked rice and stir gently with minced ginger.

8. Taste and add additional seasonings, if desired. Serve garnished with peanuts and coriander.

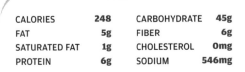

CALORIES	248	CARBOHYDRATE	45g
FAT	5g	FIBER	6g
SATURATED FAT	1g	CHOLESTEROL	0mg
PROTEIN	6g	SODIUM	546mg

savory mushroom rice

Serves 6	1 tablespoon butter	3 cups chopped mushrooms (portobello, cremini, etc.)	½ teaspoon salt
	1 tablespoon canola oil	1 cup basmati rice, rinsed and drained	
	1 dry bay leaf		
	1 teaspoon cumin seeds	1 teaspoon black pepper and cumin powder mixture	
	½ cup chopped onion		

1. Heat 1 tablespoon butter with oil. When oil is hot, but not smoking, add bay leaf.

2. Add cumin seeds and heat until golden brown.

3. Add onion and sauté for a few minutes.

4. Add mushrooms and sauté for a few additional minutes over medium-high heat until mushrooms become brown and aromatic.

5. Add basmati rice and blend well.

6. Add black pepper and cumin powder mixture and salt.

7. Add 2 cups of hot water to the rice mixture in the pan. Bring to a boil and then reduce to low heat. Cook, covered, for 20 to 30 minutes until rice becomes fluffy.

8. **Optional step:** When rice is cooked, you may add an additional 1 tablespoon butter, an additional ½ cup chopped onion, and ¼ cup of roasted cashews and mix well to enhance the flavor.

This rice dish with mushrooms is a variation of Basmati Rice with Green Peas (page 108). It can be served with turkey, chicken, fish, or any meat during the holidays. It also makes a good accompaniment to any potato, vegetable, or chicken kurma sauce.

CALORIES	156	CARBOHYDRATE	24g
FAT	5g	FIBER	1g
SATURATED FAT	2g	CHOLESTEROL	5mg
PROTEIN	4g	SODIUM	220mg

spinach rice

Serves 8	1 recipe Basmati Rice with Green Peas, omitting peas (page 108)	1 teaspoon salt	¼ cup unsalted roasted cashews
		1 teaspoon cumin powder	
	1 recipe Spinach Poriyal (page 213)	1 green chili pepper, minced (optional)	

Spinach rice with split peas or moong dal is another variety of flavored rice. It is delicious by itself and is also an excellent accompaniment to any chicken or fish recipe, vegetable side dish, or yogurt salad.

1. In a large heavy-bottomed saucepan or skillet over medium heat, mix Basmati Rice with 1½ cups of Spinach Poriyal.

2. Add salt and cumin powder to the spinach-rice mixture and fluff rice gently. Add green chili pepper, if desired.

3. Garnish rice with cashews.

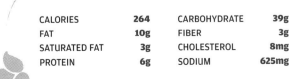

CALORIES	264	CARBOHYDRATE	39g
FAT	10g	FIBER	3g
SATURATED FAT	3g	CHOLESTEROL	8mg
PROTEIN	6g	SODIUM	625mg

sweet pongal rice

Serves 8	1 cup extra long-grain rice or jasmine rice	½ teaspoon powdered cardamom	¼ cup raw cashews
	3 cups 2% milk	2 very small pieces crystalline camphor (optional)	½ tablespoon butter (plus 2 tablespoons, optional)
	2 cups packed dark brown sugar		
	¼ teaspoon saffron threads	2 tablespoons raisins (more, if desired)	

1. Cook rice to a creamy consistency in either a saucepan or rice cooker. One cup of rice to 4 cups water will result in a creamy consistency.

2. As soon as rice is cooked, use a masher to mash the rice. Transfer the mashed rice to a saucepan if rice has been cooked in a rice cooker.

3. Add milk to rice. Stir for about 2 minutes over medium-low heat.

4. Add the dark brown sugar, saffron, cardamom, camphor, and raisins. Stir all ingredients and let simmer, covered, over low heat for about fifteen minutes, stirring frequently.

5. Fry raw cashews to a golden brown in ½ tablespoon butter and add to rice mixture when it is cooked.

6. You may add 2 additional tablespoons of butter to the rice while simmering to enhance the flavor.

Cooked in milk with brown sugar, cardamom and saffron, Sweet Pongal Rice is often served during religious holidays or on special social occasions as a dessert.

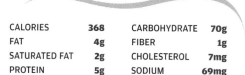

CALORIES	368	CARBOHYDRATE	70g
FAT	4g	FIBER	1g
SATURATED FAT	2g	CHOLESTEROL	7mg
PROTEIN	5g	SODIUM	69mg

tamarind rice

Serves 8 to 10

2 cups extra long-grain white rice or jasmine rice

¼ cup yellow split peas

3 teaspoons tamarind paste

2 teaspoons salt

¼ cup canola oil

6 to 8 curry leaves

1 or 2 whole dried red chili peppers

½ teaspoon asafoetida powder

1½ teaspoons black mustard seeds

1½ teaspoons urad dal

¾ teaspoon turmeric powder

1 pinch brown sugar (optional)

1 teaspoon chutney powder

¼ cup unsalted roasted peanuts

Tamarind paste is made from the fruit of the tamarind tree, which is indigenous to tropical countries. This rice is served on auspicious occasions and even in temples in South India. Tamarind Rice is often taken for lunch during trips. It keeps well for several days in the refrigerator.

1. Cook rice with 4 cups of water in a rice cooker or in an open saucepan over medium heat. Transfer cooked rice into a bowl and cool for about 15 minutes.

2. Soak yellow split peas in 1 cup of hot water for about 20 minutes. (Or microwave split peas with enough water to cover, uncovered at high heat for 5 to 7 minutes until peas become soft.) Set aside.

3. In a small bowl, mix tamarind paste, salt, and ¼ cup of warm water. Stir to achieve a smooth consistency.

4. Place oil in wok over medium heat. When oil is hot but not smoking, add curry leaves, red chili peppers, asafoetida powder, mustard seeds, and urad dal. Cover and fry over medium heat until mustard seeds pop and urad dal is golden brown, about 30 seconds.

5. Drain water from split peas and stir peas into spice mixture in wok. Stir-fry for 30 seconds. Add tamarind mixture and turmeric powder and mix well.

6. Add brown sugar, if desired. Add chutney powder.

7. When the mixture begins to boil, add rice and blend thoroughly. Add peanuts and stir into rice.

CALORIES	258	CARBOHYDRATE	41g
FAT	8g	FIBER	3g
SATURATED FAT	1g	CHOLESTEROL	0mg
PROTEIN	6g	SODIUM	481mg

tomato rice with cashews

Serves 8	¼ cup diced fresh coconut (or unsweetened coconut powder)	4 small slices ginger root	1 dry bay leaf	½ cup chopped fresh coriander (cilantro) leaves
		2 cups basmati rice	1 cup onion slices (cut lengthwise; plus additional for garnish)	1 tablespoon lemon juice
	4 green chili peppers (more, if desired)	3 tablespoons ghee or butter		
	5 garlic cloves, peeled	3 or 4 slivers cinnamon stick	1 cup chopped tomato	2 teaspoons salt
				1 cup cashews

1. Grind coconut, chili peppers, garlic, and ginger in a blender with about ¼ cup warm water (only enough to facilitate the grinding process).

2. Wash rice thoroughly and drain.

3. Put 2 tablespoons ghee in a large wide-bottomed saucepan and melt over medium heat. Add cinnamon and bay leaf.

4. Add rice to saucepan and fry until golden brown. Transfer rice mixture to a bowl and set aside.

5. Add remaining 1 tablespoon of ghee to the saucepan. When ghee is hot, but not smoking, add onion slices, tomato, and ¼ cup of coriander and cook until tender.

6. Add the contents from the blender and the lemon juice. Simmer for a few minutes. Add 2 cups of water and the salt and continue to simmer.

7. When the mixture is ready to boil, add the browned rice. Cover and cook over low heat until rice is cooked, approximately 10 minutes.

8. As soon as rice is cooked, turn off heat. Gently stir well and add cashews and remaining ¼ cup of coriander. You may add some additional chopped raw onion as a garnish.

Basmati rice cooked with tomatoes in an aromatic mixture of coconut, garlic, and ginger, this dish is particularly delicious served with Potato Kurma (page 204) or Chettinad Chicken Kurma (page 228).

CALORIES	316	CARBOHYDRATE	42g
FAT	14g	FIBER	2g
SATURATED FAT	5g	CHOLESTEROL	12mg
PROTEIN	8g	SODIUM	617mg

tomato rice with green onions

Serves 4			
	1 cup basmati rice or extra long-grain rice or jasmine rice	½ teaspoon cumin seeds	¼ cup chopped fresh coriander (cilantro) leaves	½ teaspoon garam masala powder
	2 tablespoons canola oil	½ cup chopped onion	¼ teaspoon turmeric powder	½ teaspoon salt
	1 dry bay leaf	½ cup chopped tomato	½ cup tomato sauce	½ cup chopped green onion tops
	3 or 4 slivers cinnamon stick		¼ teaspoon ground cloves (optional)	½ cup roasted cashews

This easy-to-prepare rice dish in a seasoned tomato base may be served with any vegetable dish, cucumber yogurt salad, Potato Kurma (page 204), or any grilled or baked meat.

1. Cook rice in 2 cups of water in a rice cooker or covered saucepan over low heat. Set aside to cool for about 10 minutes.

2. Place oil in a wok or wide-bottomed skillet and heat over medium heat. When oil is hot, but not smoking, add bay leaf, cinnamon sticks, and cumin seeds. Fry until cumin seeds are golden.

3. Add onion, tomato, and coriander to wok and sauté for a few minutes.

4. Add turmeric powder, tomato sauce, ground cloves, and garam masala powder. Stir well and reduce heat to low. Continue cooking uncovered for a few minutes.

5. Add salt and mix well with ingredients in wok. Add rice and stir carefully into the mixture.

6. Add green onion to rice and stir gently. Add cashew nuts and stir well.

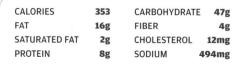

CALORIES	353	CARBOHYDRATE	47g
FAT	16g	FIBER	4g
SATURATED FAT	2g	CHOLESTEROL	12mg
PROTEIN	8g	SODIUM	494mg

vegetable biriyani rice

Serves 8	2 cups basmati rice	½ cup chopped tomato	½ cup frozen lima beans	¼ cup shredded beets
	1 tablespoon butter	2 tablespoons minced garlic cloves	½ cup peeled and sliced carrots	1 cup frozen peas, defrosted
	1 tablespoon canola oil	2 tablespoons minced ginger root	½ cup diced green beans	½ cup cashew halves
	3 whole dry bay leaves	¾ teaspoon turmeric powder	1 cup 1-inch cauliflower florets	½ cup chopped red onion
	2 or 3 slivers cinnamon stick	1 cup peeled and cubed Idaho potato	2 teaspoons garam masala powder	
	1 cup chopped onion			

1. Rinse rice thoroughly in cold water and drain. Bring 4 cups of water to a boil and cook rice over medium heat on stovetop or in a rice cooker. Place the cooked rice in a bowl and gently fluff the rice. Set aside.

2. Heat a saucepan over medium heat. Add butter and oil. When butter is melted, but not smoking, add bay leaves and cinnamon sticks and sauté until bay leaves become brown and aromatic.

3. Immediately add onion, tomato, garlic, ginger, and turmeric powder. Mix well.

4. Add the potatoes, lima beans, carrots, green beans, and cauliflower. Coat the vegetables well with the seasonings.

5. Add garam masala powder. Stir well. Add 1 to 2 tablespoons of water and cook the vegetables covered over low-medium heat, until potatoes and lima beans are tender.

CONTINUED

An easy-to-prepare aromatic basmati rice cooked with a variety of vegetables—potatoes, lima beans, carrots, beans, cauliflower, beets and peas—and garnished with cashews. (This dish is also known as Vegetable Pulaoo Rice.)

6. Add cooked rice to the vegetable mixture and gently fold the rice in.

7. Add shredded beets and peas and gently stir into the rice mixture.

8. Garnish the rice with cashews and chopped red onion. Stir well and serve the biriyani rice warm.

CALORIES	302	CARBOHYDRATE	50g
FAT	8g	FIBER	4g
SATURATED FAT	2g	CHOLESTEROL	4mg
PROTEIN	9g	SODIUM	83mg

yogurt rice

Serves 4

1 cup long-grain rice or jasmine rice

2 cups fat-free plain yogurt

1 cup buttermilk (optional)

¼ teaspoon salt

1 teaspoon minced ginger root

1. Cook rice in 3 cups of water to achieve a creamy consistency. You might use a masher to soften the rice to ensure the creamy consistency.

2. Add yogurt and buttermilk and mix very well. More yogurt may be added, if desired.

3. Add salt and ginger and mix well.

variations **YOGURT RICE WITH CUCUMBERS AND CARROTS** To enhance the Yogurt Rice as prepared above, add 1 tablespoon minced cucumbers, 1 tablespoon shredded carrots, and 1 tablespoon minced coriander. Mix well.

SEASONED YOGURT RICE Place 1 teaspoon oil in a small saucepan or butter warmer over medium heat. When oil is hot, but not smoking, add 4 to 6 curry leaves, 1 teaspoon mustard seeds, and 1 teaspoon urad dal. When mustard seeds pop and urad dal is golden brown, pour mixture over yogurt rice. Mix well. Add ¼ cup chopped coriander. Add ¼ cup of 2% milk to prevent the yogurt rice from turning sour. Leave rice at room temperature until you are ready to serve.

Cooling and satisfying, Yogurt Rice, also known as Curd Rice, is traditionally served as a final course in a South Indian meal. It can accompany any vegetable dish or Indian pickles (lime or mango, for example), which are available in Indian grocery stores. Nutritious and tasty, Yogurt Rice can be packed for lunch at work or for an outing and is very soothing to the stomach.

STANDARD YOGURT RICE

CALORIES	171	CARBOHYDRATE	32g
FAT	1g	FIBER	trace
SATURATED FAT	trace	CHOLESTEROL	3mg
PROTEIN	8g	SODIUM	191mg

SEASONED YOGURT RICE

CALORIES	180	CARBOHYDRATE	34g
FAT	3g	FIBER	1g
SATURATED FAT	trace	CHOLESTEROL	4mg
PROTEIN	9g	SODIUM	196mg

sambhar, kulambu and dals

acorn squash pulikulambu

Serves 4	1 acorn squash	½ teaspoon fenugreek seeds	¼ cup chopped tomato	¼ teaspoon tamarind paste
	1 tablespoon canola oil	1 teaspoon black mustard seeds	¼ teaspoon turmeric powder	1 teaspoon salt
	¼ teaspoon asafoetida powder	1 teaspoon urad dal	2 teaspoons sambhar powder	¼ cup chopped fresh coriander (cilantro) leaves
	4 to 6 curry leaves	½ cup chopped onion	1 cup tomato sauce	

A unique dish of assorted vegetables cooked with spices in tamarind sauce.

1. Acorn squash has a tough skin. Cut squash in half and cook one half in microwave for 2 to 3 minutes so that it is easy to cut the squash. Remove the seeds and skin. Cut squash into small cubes (you should have about 2 cups). Save the other half in the refrigerator for later use.

2. In a small saucepan heat oil over medium heat. When oil is hot, but not smoking, add asafoetida powder, curry leaves, fenugreek seeds, mustard seeds, and urad dal. Cover and fry until mustard seeds pop and urad dal turns golden brown, about 30 seconds.

3. Add onion and tomato and cook for a minute or two.

4. Add squash and stir. Add turmeric powder and mix well over medium heat.

5. Stir in sambhar powder, tomato sauce, tamarind paste, and salt. Add 1 cup of water to the mixture.

6. Add coriander. Cook, covered, over low heat, stirring often until squash becomes tender.

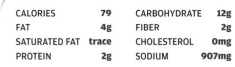

CALORIES	79	CARBOHYDRATE	12g
FAT	4g	FIBER	2g
SATURATED FAT	trace	CHOLESTEROL	0mg
PROTEIN	2g	SODIUM	907mg

asparagus sambhar

Serves 6

- ½ cup toor dal or moong dal
- ½ teaspoon turmeric powder
- 2 tablespoons canola oil
- ¼ teaspoon asafoetida powder
- 4 to 6 curry leaves
- 1 whole dried red chili pepper
- 1 teaspoon black mustard seeds
- 1 teaspoon urad dal
- ½ cup chopped onion
- ½ cup chopped tomato
- 1 teaspoon sambhar powder
- ½ cup tomato sauce
- ½ teaspoon salt (more, if desired)
- 1 pound green asparagus, ends trimmed and cut in half horizontally
- ½ cup chopped coriander (cilantro) leaves

1. Bring 4 cups of water to a boil in a deep saucepan. Add toor dal and ¼ teaspoon turmeric powder. Reduce heat to medium and cook, uncovered, for about 30 minutes until dal becomes creamy. If water evaporates during the cooking process, add another cup of water and cook until dal becomes creamy in texture. Set aside. (You may also cook the dal more quickly in a pressure cooker.)

2. In a saucepan add oil over medium heat. When oil is hot, but not smoking add asafoetida, curry leaves, red chili pepper, mustard seeds, and urad dal. Cover and fry until mustard seeds pop and urad dal turns golden, about 30 seconds.

3. Add onion and tomato and cook for 1 minute. Add remaining ¼ teaspoon turmeric powder, sambhar powder, tomato sauce, and salt. Blend the seasonings well with tomato and onion mixture.

4. Add cut asparagus and stir for a minute. Add creamy dal with 1½ cups of warm water. Stir and let mixture come to a boil. Cover and simmer over reduced heat approximately 5 to 7 minutes until asparagus is tender.

5. Add coriander and let simmer for a few minutes.

Asparagus cooked with mild spices in a creamy dal base is an innovative dish that is best served over plain rice or with any bread.

CALORIES	136	CARBOHYDRATES	18g
FAT	5g	FIBER	7g
SATURATED FAT	trace	CHOLESTEROL	0mg
PROTEIN	7g	SODIUM	312mg

bangalore sambhar

Serves 6	½ cup toor dal	¼ cup unsweetened powdered coconut	1 teaspoon salt (more, if desired)	¼ teaspoon asafoetida powder
	¼ teaspoon turmeric powder	5 whole dried red chili peppers	¼ cup tomato sauce	4 to 6 curry leaves (optional)
	1 cup peeled and cubed Idaho potato	2 garlic cloves, peeled	¼ cup chopped fresh coriander (cilantro) leaves	1 teaspoon black mustard seeds
	1 cup frozen Fordhook (large size) lima beans	1 teaspoon cumin seeds	1 tablespoon canola oil	1 teaspoon urad dal

A mixture of vegetables and spices cooked in a base of creamy dal, this sambhar should be served over plain rice as an accompaniment to a meal.

1. Bring 4 cups of water to a boil in a deep saucepan over medium heat. Add toor dal and turmeric powder. Reduce heat to medium and cook, uncovered, for about 30 minutes, until dal becomes creamy. If water evaporates during the cooking process, add another cup of water and cook until dal becomes creamy.

2. When dal is cooked, add potatoes and lima beans with 2 cups of water to cover the vegetables. Cook over medium heat until vegetables are tender, about 10 minutes.

3. Place coconut, 4 red chili peppers, garlic, and cumin in blender. Add about ½ cup of warm water to facilitate the grinding. Grind until smooth.

4. Add contents of blender to the vegetable mixture. Add salt and tomato sauce. Stir well.

5. Add coriander and continue to simmer, covered, until potatoes are tender.

6. Place oil in a small skillet over medium heat. When oil is hot, but not smoking, add remaining 1 red chili pepper, asafoetida powder, curry leaves, mustard seeds, and urad dal. Cover and fry until mustard seeds pop and urad dal is golden brown, about 30 seconds. Add spice mixture to sambhar. Stir and let it simmer for a few minutes. If sambhar seems too thick, add ½ to 1 cup of warm water as desired and stir. Let it simmer for another minute or two.

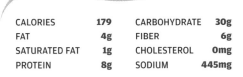

CALORIES	179	CARBOHYDRATE	30g
FAT	4g	FIBER	6g
SATURATED FAT	1g	CHOLESTEROL	0mg
PROTEIN	8g	SODIUM	445mg

Green Beans Kulambu

Serves 4

- ¼ cup toor dal
- ½ teaspoon turmeric powder
- 1 cup green beans
- 2 tablespoons canola oil
- ¼ teaspoon asafoetida powder
- 4 to 6 curry leaves
- 1 whole dried red chili pepper
- 1 teaspoon black mustard seeds
- 1 teaspoon urad dal
- ½ cup chopped tomato
- 1 teaspoon sambhar powder
- ½ teaspoon salt (more, if desired)
- ¼ teaspoon tamarind paste
- ¼ cup tomato sauce
- ¼ cup chopped fresh coriander (cilantro) leaves

1. Bring 3 cups of water to a boil in a deep saucepan. Add toor dal and ¼ teaspoon turmeric powder. Reduce heat to medium and cook, uncovered, for about 30 minutes, until dal becomes creamy. If water evaporates during the cooking process, add another cup of water and cook until dal becomes creamy. Set aside.

2. Wash the green beans and cut off the ends. Cut each bean in half. Place in a bowl and set aside.

3. In a saucepan heat oil over medium heat. When oil is hot, but not smoking, add asafoetida powder, curry leaves, red chili pepper, mustard seeds, and urad dal. Cover and fry until mustard seeds pop and urad dal turns golden brown, about 30 seconds.

4. Add tomato and green beans and cook for 1 minute.

5. Add remaining ¼ teaspoon turmeric powder, sambhar powder, and salt. Blend the seasonings well with vegetables in the saucepan.

6. Add cooked creamy dal, tamarind paste, and tomato sauce to the mixture in the saucepan. Add 1 cup of warm water. Stir and let mixture come to a boil.

7. Add coriander and let mixture simmer for a few more minutes.

Green beans cooked with tomatoes and spices in a creamy dal base, Green Beans Kulambu is delicious served over plain rice, with idlis and dosais, or with toasted bread.

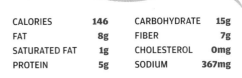

CALORIES	146	CARBOHYDRATE	15g
FAT	8g	FIBER	7g
SATURATED FAT	1g	CHOLESTEROL	0mg
PROTEIN	5g	SODIUM	367mg

bell pepper and radish sambhar

Serves 6

½ cup toor dal

¾ teaspoon turmeric powder

3 tablespoons canola oil

¼ teaspoon asafoetida powder

1 whole dried red chili pepper

½ teaspoon fenugreek seeds

1 teaspoon black mustard seeds

1 teaspoon urad dal

½ cup chopped onion

½ cup coarsely chopped tomato

1 cup thinly sliced white or red radish

½ teaspoon tamarind paste

2 teaspoons sambhar powder

1½ teaspoons salt

1 cup tomato sauce

¼ cup chopped fresh coriander (cilantro) leaves

2 cups coarsely cut green bell peppers

Bell peppers and radishes cooked with spices in a creamy dal base, this sambhar is best served over plain rice.

NOTE   If the finished sambhar is very thick, add an additional cup of warm water.

CALORIES	194	CARBOHYDRATE	27g
FAT	9g	FIBER	9g
SATURATED FAT	1g	CHOLESTEROL	0mg
PROTEIN	8g	SODIUM	527mg

1. Bring 4 cups of water to a boil in a deep saucepan. Add toor dal and ¼ teaspoon turmeric powder. Reduce heat to medium and cook, uncovered, for about 30 minutes until dal becomes creamy. If water evaporates during the cooking process, add another cup of water and cook until dal becomes creamy. Set aside.

2. Warm oil in a saucepan over medium heat. When the oil is hot, but not smoking, add asafoetida powder, red chili pepper, fenugreek seeds, mustard seeds, and urad dal. Fry, covered, until mustard seeds pop and other ingredients are golden brown, about 30 seconds.

3. Add the onion and tomato. Cook for 1 minute. Add the remaining ½ teaspoon turmeric powder and radish. Cook over medium heat, stirring constantly, for a few minutes.

4. Add the creamy toor dal mixture plus 2 cups of water to the ingredients in the saucepan.

5. Add the tamarind paste, sambhar powder, and salt. Cook, covered, over low heat for 10 minutes.

6. Add tomato sauce and coriander. When the mixture begins to boil add green bell peppers. Cover and cook over low heat for 5 to 7 minutes. Do not overcook the green peppers.

blackeye peas kulambu

Serves 4	2 tablespoons canola oil	1 teaspoon black mustard seeds	2 cups frozen blackeye peas or canned blackeye peas, rinsed and drained	2 garlic cloves, peeled and crushed
	¼ teaspoon asafoetida powder	1 teaspoon urad dal		¼ cup chopped fresh coriander (cilantro) leaves
	1 whole dried red chili pepper	1 onion, chopped	1 teaspoon sambhar powder	
	½ teaspoon fenugreek seeds	1 tomato, chopped	½ teaspoon salt	
		¼ teaspoon turmeric powder	1 cup tomato sauce	

1. Place oil in a warmed saucepan. When oil is hot, add asafoetida powder, red chili pepper, fenugreek seeds, mustard seeds, and urad dal. Cover and cook over medium heat until mustard seeds pop and urad dal is golden brown, about 30 seconds.

2. Add onion and tomato to saucepan and stir well. Add turmeric powder and cook until onions are translucent. Add blackeye peas, sambhar powder, and salt and stir.

3. Add tomato sauce and 3 cups of warm water to the mixture. When mixture begins to boil, add the crushed garlic and let simmer over low heat until blackeye peas are tender. Add chopped coriander and serve warm.

A quick blend of blackeye peas cooked with tomatoes, garlic, and spices without a creamy dal base. This kulambu is best served over plain rice. It can also be served as a soup with any bread.

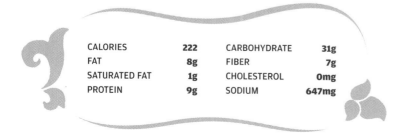

CALORIES	222	CARBOHYDRATE	31g
FAT	8g	FIBER	7g
SATURATED FAT	1g	CHOLESTEROL	0mg
PROTEIN	9g	SODIUM	647mg

blackeye peas sambhar

Serves 6	¼ cup toor dal	1 whole dried red chili pepper	2 teaspoons sambhar powder
	¾ teaspoon turmeric powder	½ teaspoon fenugreek seeds	1½ teaspoons salt
	1 cup dried or frozen blackeye peas	1 teaspoon black mustard seeds	½ cup tomato sauce
	2 tablespoons canola oil	1 teaspoon urad dal	2 garlic cloves, peeled and crushed
	¼ teaspoon asafoetida powder	1 onion, chopped	¼ cup chopped fresh coriander (cilantro) leaves
		1 tomato, chopped	

A blend of blackeye peas cooked with tomatoes, garlic, and spices in a creamy dal base, this sambhar is best served over plain rice or with idlis and dosais.

1. Bring 3 cups of water to a boil in a deep saucepan. Add toor dal and ¼ teaspoon turmeric powder. Reduce heat to medium and cook, uncovered, for about 30 minutes, until dal becomes creamy. If water evaporates during the cooking process, add another cup of water and cook until dal becomes creamy. Set aside.

2. If using dried blackeye peas: In another saucepan bring 4 cups of water to a boil, add dried blackeye peas and ¼ teaspoon turmeric powder. Cook blackeye peas, uncovered, until they are tender. When peas are tender, rinse well in a colander and set aside. (If using frozen blackeye peas, set out to defrost.)

3. In a saucepan, heat oil over medium heat. When oil is hot, but not smoking, add asafoetida powder, red chili pepper, fenugreek seeds, mustard seeds, and urad dal. Cover and cook over medium heat until mustard seeds pop and urad dal is golden brown, about 30 seconds.

4. Add onion and tomato to saucepan and stir well. Add remaining ½ teaspoon turmeric powder.

5. Add sambhar powder and salt. Stir well. Add tomato sauce.

6. Add cooked creamy dal and 2 additional cups of warm water. Stir and heat to boiling point.

7. When mixture is ready to boil, add cooked (dried) blackeye peas or thawed (frozen) blackeye peas. Let the sambhar simmer for about 5 minutes.

8. Add garlic and coriander and allow to simmer for another 5 to 7 minutes. If sambhar seems too thick, add additional (up to 1 cup) warm water and let simmer.

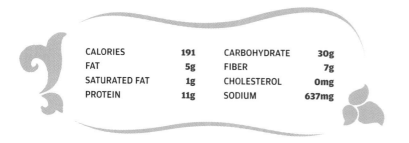

CALORIES	191	CARBOHYDRATE	30g
FAT	5g	FIBER	7g
SATURATED FAT	1g	CHOLESTEROL	0mg
PROTEIN	11g	SODIUM	637mg

brussels sprouts kulambu

Serves 4	2 tablespoons canola oil	½ teaspoon fenugreek seeds	½ cup chopped tomato	1 teaspoon salt
	¼ teaspoon asafoetida powder	1 teaspoon black mustard seeds	¼ teaspoon turmeric powder	¼ teaspoon tamarind paste
	4 to 6 curry leaves (optional)	1 teaspoon urad dal	2 teaspoons sambhar powder	1½ cups fresh brussels sprouts, cut in half (if large, cut in quarters)
		½ cup chopped onion	1 cup tomato sauce	

These brussels sprouts are cooked with onions and tomatoes and simmered in tamarind sauce with spices. This kulambu is best served over plain rice or with idlis and dosais.

1. Place oil in a saucepan over medium heat. When the oil is hot, but not smoking, add asafoetida powder, curry leaves, fenugreek seeds, mustard seeds, and urad dal. Cover and fry over medium heat until the mustard seeds pop and urad dal is golden brown, about 30 seconds.

2. Add onion, tomato, and turmeric powder, stirring constantly.

3. Add sambhar powder, tomato sauce, and salt. Stir well. Add 2 cups of warm water to saucepan. Stir and cook for a few minutes.

4. Add tamarind paste and mix thoroughly.

5. When the mixture in saucepan begins to boil, add brussels sprouts. Cover and cook over low heat until brussels sprouts are just tender, about 10 minutes. Be careful not to overcook.

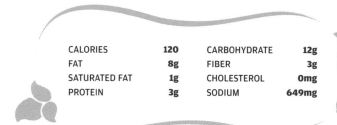

CALORIES	120	CARBOHYDRATE	12g
FAT	8g	FIBER	3g
SATURATED FAT	1g	CHOLESTEROL	0mg
PROTEIN	3g	SODIUM	649mg

sambhar, kulambu and dals

HEALTHY SOUTH INDIAN COOKING

carrot sambhar

Serves 6	½ cup toor dal	4 to 6 curry leaves (optional)	¼ cup chopped tomato	½ cup tomato sauce
	¾ teaspoon turmeric powder	¼ teaspoon fenugreek seeds	1 cup peeled and sliced fresh carrots (thin rounds)	1 teaspoon salt (more, if desired)
	2 tablespoons canola oil	1 teaspoon black mustard seeds	2 teaspoons sambhar powder	¼ cup chopped fresh coriander (cilantro) leaves
	1 whole dried red chili pepper	1 teaspoon urad dal	¼ teaspoon tamarind paste	
	¼ teaspoon asafoetida powder	½ cup chopped onion		

1. Bring 4 cups of water to a boil in a deep saucepan. Add toor dal and ¼ teaspoon turmeric powder. Reduce heat to medium and cook, uncovered, for about 30 minutes until dal becomes creamy. If water evaporates during the cooking process, add another cup of water and cook until dal becomes creamy. Set aside.

2. Place oil in a large saucepan over medium heat. When oil is hot, but not smoking, add whole red chili pepper, asafoetida powder, curry leaves, fenugreek seeds, mustard seeds, and urad dal. Fry, covered, until mustard seeds pop and other ingredients are a golden brown, about 30 seconds.

3. Add onion, tomato, and remaining ½ teaspoon turmeric powder and stir-fry for 1 to 2 minutes.

4. Add carrots and stir-fry for 1 minute.

5. Add sambhar powder, tamarind paste, tomato sauce, and salt. Cook, covered, over medium-low heat for 3 minutes, stirring occasionally.

6. Add the toor dal mixture plus 2 cups of warm water, and stir into carrot mixture. Add coriander. Cook, covered, over medium-low heat for another 5 to 7 minutes, until carrots are tender.

Carrots cooked with spices in a creamy dal base, this sambhar is delicious served over plain rice and with idlis, dosais, and chappatis.

NOTE   You may substitute masoor dal (also known as red lentil) for toor dal. Cooking instructions for masoor dal are the same as for toor dal but cooking time is usually less.

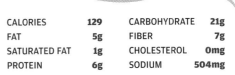

CALORIES	129	CARBOHYDRATE	21g
FAT	5g	FIBER	7g
SATURATED FAT	1g	CHOLESTEROL	0mg
PROTEIN	6g	SODIUM	504mg

carrot and zucchini sambhar

Serves 6			
½ cup toor dal or moong dal	¼ teaspoon asafoetida powder	½ cup chopped onion	1 teaspoon sambhar powder
¾ teaspoon turmeric powder	4 to 6 curry leaves	¼ cup chopped tomato	¼ teaspoon tamarind paste
2 tablespoons canola oil	¼ teaspoon fenugreek seeds	1 cup peeled and sliced fresh carrots (thin rounds)	¼ cup tomato sauce
1 whole dried red chili pepper	1 teaspoon black mustard seeds	1 cup sliced zucchini	1 teaspoon salt
	1 teaspoon urad dal		¼ cup chopped coriander (cilantro) leaves

A delicious combination of vegetables cooked in a creamy dal base, this sambhar is best served over plain rice or with any meal.

NOTE You may substitute masoor dal (also known as red lentil) for toor dal. Cooking instructions for masoor dal are the same as for toor dal, but cooking time is usually less.

1. Bring 4 cups of water to a boil in a saucepan. Add toor dal and ¼ teaspoon turmeric powder. Reduce heat to medium and cook, uncovered, for about 30 minutes until dal becomes creamy. If water evaporates during the cooking process, add another cup of water and cook until dal becomes creamy. Set aside.

2. Add oil to a saucepan over medium heat. When oil is hot, but not smoking, add whole chili pepper, asafoetida powder, curry leaves, fenugreek seeds, mustard seeds, and urad dal. Fry, uncovered, until mustard seeds burst and other ingredients are golden brown.

3. Add onion, tomato, and remaining ½ teaspoon turmeric powder and stir-fry for 1 to 2 minutes. Add sliced carrots and zucchini and stir-fry for 1 minute.

4. Add sambhar powder, tamarind paste, tomato sauce, and salt.

5. Add the toor dal mixture plus 2 cups of warm water. Add coriander. Cook, covered, over medium heat for approximately 7 to 10 minutes or until carrots and zucchini are tender.

CALORIES	142	CARBOHYDRATE	19g
FAT	5g	FIBER	8g
SATURATED FAT	1g	CHOLESTEROL	0mg
PROTEIN	7g	SODIUM	456mg

eggplant pulikulambu

Serves 4			
3 tablespoons canola oil	½ teaspoon fenugreek seeds	1 small tomato, chopped	½ teaspoon sambhar powder (more, if desired)
1 whole dried red chili pepper	1 teaspoon black mustard seeds	2 cups diced unpeeled eggplant	1 teaspoon salt
3 or 4 curry leaves (optional)	1 teaspoon urad dal	¼ teaspoon turmeric powder	1 cup tomato sauce
¼ teaspoon asafoetida powder	1 small onion, chopped		½ teaspoon tamarind paste

1. Add canola oil to a saucepan or a pressure cooker over medium heat. When oil is hot, but not smoking, add red chili pepper, curry leaves, asafoetida powder, fenugreek seeds, mustard seeds, and urad dal. Fry, covered, for a few minutes until mustard seeds pop and urad dal becomes golden.

2. Add onion and tomato and sauté for a few minutes.

3. Add eggplant and stir-fry for a few minutes over low heat.

4. Add turmeric powder, sambhar powder, and salt. Stir the seasonings into the mixture over medium heat.

5. Add tomato sauce and 1½ cups of warm water. Add tamarind paste. Blend the ingredients well in saucepan.

6. Cook, covered, over low heat until eggplant becomes soft and blends well with other ingredients in the saucepan to become a delicious thickened kulambu.

Eggplant is cooked with onions, tomatoes, and tamarind paste to make a delicious sauce.

NOTES You may follow the recipe up to Step 5, cover and then pressure cook, if you prefer.

Thai eggplant or baby eggplant is particularly delicious in this recipe. You need to remove the stem and cut the eggplants in halves or in quarters, all the same size!

CALORIES	125	CARBOHYDRATE	14g
FAT	7g	FIBER	3g
SATURATED FAT	1g	CHOLESTEROL	0mg
PROTEIN	3g	SODIUM	910mg

eggplant and potato pulikulambu

Serves 6

2 tablespoons canola oil

1/8 teaspoon asafoetida powder

4 to 6 curry leaves (optional)

1 whole dried red chili pepper

1/4 teaspoon fenugreek seeds

1 teaspoon black mustard seeds

1 teaspoon urad dal

2 cups chopped unpeeled eggplant

1 cup peeled, chopped potato, cut slightly bigger than eggplant

1/2 cup sliced onion (cut lengthwise)

1/2 cup chopped tomato

1/2 teaspoon turmeric powder

2 teaspoons sambhar powder

1 cup tomato sauce

1/4 teaspoon tamarind paste

1 teaspoon salt (more, if desired)

1/4 cup chopped fresh coriander (cilantro) leaves

Simmered in a rich tamarind-based sauce, Eggplant and Potato Pulikulambu takes only 15 minutes to prepare using a pressure cooker. At least a 2.5-quart-size pressure cooker is necessary. This pulikulambu can be served over plain rice, Yogurt Rice (page 123), idlis, dosais, uthappams, or with Indian breads.

1. Place oil in a pressure cooker or saucepan over medium heat. When oil is hot, but not smoking, add asafoetida powder, curry leaves, red chili pepper, fenugreek seeds, mustard seeds, and urad dal. Cover and fry until mustard seeds pop and urad dal is golden brown, about 30 seconds.

2. Add eggplant, potatoes, onion slices, tomato, and turmeric powder and stir-fry for a few minutes over medium heat.

3. Add sambhar powder, tomato sauce, tamarind paste, salt, and coriander. Blend the seasonings well into the vegetables.

4. Add about 2 cups of water to the mixture. Be sure that there is enough liquid to cover the vegetables.

5. If cooking in a saucepan, cover and cook over medium heat, stirring often, until potatoes and eggplant are tender. (Or cook in a pressure cooker covered over medium heat for 10 minutes. Check for doneness. If the potatoes are not tender, cook the kulambu for a few additional minutes, uncovered, in the pressure cooker over low heat or transfer the kulambu to a saucepan and cook over low heat until the potatoes are tender.)

CALORIES	105	CARBOHYDRATE	14g
FAT	5g	FIBER	3g
SATURATED FAT	1g	CHOLESTEROL	0mg
PROTEIN	2g	SODIUM	608mg

garlic kulambu

Serves 4

3 tablespoons canola oil

¼ teaspoon asafoetida powder

4 to 6 curry leaves (optional)

½ teaspoon fenugreek seeds

1 teaspoon black mustard seeds

1 teaspoon urad dal

½ cup chopped onion

½ cup chopped tomato

½ cup whole peeled garlic cloves

½ teaspoon turmeric powder

2 teaspoons sambhar powder

¼ teaspoon tamarind paste

½ teaspoon salt (more, if desired)

1 cup tomato sauce

½ cup minced fresh coriander (cilantro) leaves

1. Place oil in a saucepan over medium heat. When oil is hot, but not smoking, add asafoetida powder, curry leaves, fenugreek seeds, mustard seeds, and urad dal. Stir quickly and cover. Fry until mustard seeds pop and urad dal is golden, about 30 seconds.

2. Add onion, tomato, and garlic. Stir-fry for 1 minute. Add turmeric powder and mix well. Cook, covered, over medium-low heat, for about 3 minutes, until onion and garlic are tender.

3. Add sambhar powder, tamarind paste, and salt. Mix all the ingredients thoroughly while cooking over medium heat.

4. Add tomato sauce, 1 cup of warm water, and coriander. Continue to cook, covered, until garlic is tender. The cooking time will vary with the size of the garlic cloves, about 4 to 6 minutes.

Garlic is delicious when slow-cooked with onions, tomatoes, and spices in tamarind sauce. Garlic Kulambu is wonderful served over plain rice. It also goes well with any Indian breads.

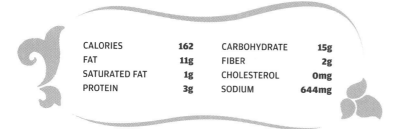

CALORIES	162	CARBOHYDRATE	15g
FAT	11g	FIBER	2g
SATURATED FAT	1g	CHOLESTEROL	0mg
PROTEIN	3g	SODIUM	644mg

kohlrabi sambhar

Serves 6

- ½ cup toor dal
- ½ teaspoon turmeric powder
- 2 tablespoons canola oil
- ¼ teaspoon asafoetida powder
- 1 whole dried red chili pepper
- ½ teaspoon fenugreek seeds
- 1 teaspoon black mustard seeds
- 1 teaspoon urad dal
- ¼ cup chopped onion
- ½ cup chopped tomato
- 1 cup peeled and thinly sliced kohlrabi
- 1 teaspoon sambhar powder
- ¼ cup tomato sauce
- ¼ teaspoon tamarind paste
- 1 teaspoon salt
- 2 tablespoons chopped fresh coriander (cilantro) leaves

Kohlrabi Sambhar is cooked with kohlrabi, tomatoes, and toor dal. It is light, flavorful, and easy to prepare. This sambhar is delicious served over plain rice, with uppuma, idlis, dosais, or any Indian breads.

1. Bring 4 cups of water to a boil in a deep saucepan. Add toor dal and ¼ teaspoon turmeric powder. Reduce heat to medium and cook, uncovered, for about 30 minutes, until dal becomes creamy. If water evaporates during the cooking process, add another cup of water and cook until dal becomes creamy. Set aside.

2. In another saucepan, heat oil over medium heat. When oil is hot, but not smoking, add asafoetida powder, whole red chili pepper, fenugreek seeds, mustard seeds, and urad dal. Cook, covered, until mustard seeds pop and urad dal is golden brown, about 30 seconds.

3. Add chopped onion and tomato. Cook 2 to 3 minutes, until onion is tender. Add kohlrabi and the remaining ¼ teaspoon turmeric powder. Stir well.

4. Stir in sambhar powder and tomato sauce. Add toor dal mixture plus 2 cups of warm water. Stir well.

5. Add tamarind paste and salt. When mixture begins to bubble, reduce heat and cook kohlrabi until tender, 4 to 6 minutes. Add coriander and simmer for an additional few minutes.

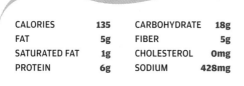

CALORIES	135	CARBOHYDRATE	18g
FAT	5g	FIBER	5g
SATURATED FAT	1g	CHOLESTEROL	0mg
PROTEIN	6g	SODIUM	428mg

masoor dal vegetable sambhar

Serves 4

¼ cup masoor dal

½ teaspoon turmeric powder

1 cup peeled and sliced Idaho potato

¼ cup chopped tomato

1 teaspoon sambhar powder

1 teaspoon salt

¼ cup chopped fresh coriander (cilantro) leaves

½ cup chopped bell pepper

½ cup tomato sauce

1. In a medium saucepan, bring 2 cups of water to a boil and add masoor dal and ¼ teaspoon turmeric powder. Cook, uncovered, over medium-low heat until dal becomes soft, about 15 minutes. If water evaporates during the cooking process, add another ½ cup water and cook until dal becomes creamy.

2. After dal is cooked, add potato, tomato, and the remaining ¼ teaspoon turmeric powder to dal mixture in saucepan.

3. Add sambhar powder, salt, coriander, and an additional 2 cups of warm water to the vegetables. Cook over medium-low heat, covered, until potatoes are tender.

4. When potatoes are almost cooked, add bell pepper and tomato sauce. Let sambhar simmer for a few more minutes until bell pepper is cooked to desired degree of doneness.

This sambhar takes only a few minutes to cook, as masoor dal cooks quickly. Potatoes, bell peppers, and tomatoes are cooked with the masoor dal to make a delicious sambhar, which is very satisfying served over plain rice.

variation To enhance the flavor of this sambhar, heat 1 tablespoon oil in a butter warmer. When oil is hot, but not smoking, add 2 to 4 curry leaves, ¼ teaspoon asafoetida powder, 1 red chili pepper, 1 teaspoon mustard seeds, and 1 teaspoon urad dal. Cover and heat until mustard seeds pop and urad dal turns golden brown, about 30 seconds. Add this garnish to above sambhar in the saucepan and let it simmer over low heat for about 2 minutes before serving.

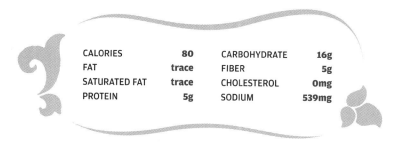

CALORIES	80	CARBOHYDRATE	16g
FAT	trace	FIBER	5g
SATURATED FAT	trace	CHOLESTEROL	0mg
PROTEIN	5g	SODIUM	539mg

mixed vegetable sambhar

Serves 6				
	½ cup toor dal	½ teaspoon cumin seeds	1 teaspoon urad dal	½ teaspoon sambhar powder (more, if desired)
	¾ teaspoon turmeric powder	¾ teaspoon yellow split peas	½ cup sliced onion (cut lengthwise)	2 green bell peppers, cut into small pieces
	2½ tablespoons canola oil	1 tablespoon unsweetened coconut powder	1 cup chopped tomato	¼ cup chopped fresh coriander (cilantro) leaves
	3 dried red chili peppers	¼ teaspoon asafoetida powder	2 small Idaho potatoes, washed, peeled, and cut into cubes	
	1 teaspoon coriander seeds	1 teaspoon black mustard seeds	1 teaspoon salt	

Potatoes, bell peppers, and tomatoes are cooked in a creamy dal base. In this preparation, roasted and ground aromatic spices are added to the sambhar. Serve with plain rice, idlis, or dosais.

1. Bring 4 cups of water to a boil in a deep saucepan. Add toor dal and ¼ teaspoon turmeric powder. Reduce heat to medium and cook, uncovered, for about 30 minutes, until dal becomes creamy. If water evaporates during the cooking process, add another cup of water and cook until dal becomes creamy. Set aside.

2. Place ½ tablespoon oil in a cast-iron skillet and heat over medium heat. When oil is hot, but not smoking, add 2 red chili peppers, coriander seeds, cumin seeds, and yellow split peas. Fry over low heat until golden brown. Add coconut powder and stir 1 minute.

3. Put all the above fried ingredients in a spice or coffee grinder and grind (without water) to a powdery consistency. Set aside.

4. Heat remaining 2 tablespoons oil in a saucepan over medium heat. When oil is hot, but not smoking, add the remaining red chili pepper, asafoetida powder, mustard seeds, and urad dal. Cover and fry until mustard seeds pop and urad dal is golden brown, about 30 seconds.

5. When urad dal turns golden, add onion slices and tomato. Stir-fry briefly. Add potatoes together with remaining ½ teaspoon turmeric powder. Stir well, uncovered, over medium heat.

6. Add creamy dal, 3 additional cups of warm water, salt, and sambhar powder. Cook potatoes, covered, over medium heat about 5 minutes, until partially cooked.

7. Add ground spices to the mixture in the saucepan. Stir and cook, covered, over medium heat. When potatoes are tender, add bell peppers and fresh coriander. Cook over low heat until peppers are tender.

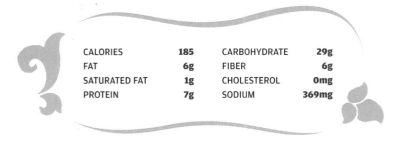

CALORIES	185	CARBOHYDRATE	29g
FAT	6g	FIBER	6g
SATURATED FAT	1g	CHOLESTEROL	0mg
PROTEIN	7g	SODIUM	369mg

moore kulambu

Serves 6
(Makes about
3 cups)

2 teaspoons canola oil

1 tablespoon cumin seeds

1 tablespoon chana dal or
yellow split peas

1 tablespoon white rice

¼ cup unsweetened coconut
powder

1 tablespoon sliced ginger
root

1 green chili pepper (more,
if desired)

1½ cups buttermilk

¼ teaspoon asafoetida
powder

1 dried red chili pepper

4 to 6 curry leaves

1 teaspoon mustard seeds

1 teaspoon urad dal

¼ cup sliced onion (cut
lengthwise)

¼ cup chopped tomato

¼ cucumber, unpeeled and
cut lengthwise into thin
slices

½ teaspoon salt

¼ cup chopped fresh
coriander (cilantro) leaves

This buttermilk sauce, similar to a sambhar, is blended with coconut, cumin seeds, ginger, and chili pepper. Vegetables of your choice can be added to this dish. Moore Kulambu is delicious served over plain rice.

variation Skip the first 2 steps in the above recipe. In a grinder blend 1 cup of buttermilk with 1 tablespoon sliced ginger, ¼ cup unsweetened coconut powder, 1 green chili pepper, and 2 teaspoons cumin seeds. Grind the ingredients to create a smooth paste. Then follow the recipe from Step 3 through Step 6.

1. Place 1 teaspoon oil in a small skillet over medium heat. When oil is hot, but not smoking, add cumin seeds, chana dal, and rice. Fry to a golden brown. Turn off heat. Add coconut powder, ginger, and green chili pepper to the seasonings in skillet.

2. Transfer all the ingredients from the skillet to a blender. Add buttermilk to cover the ingredients and 1 cup of warm water. Grind the ingredients to create a smooth mixture.

3. Heat remaining 1 teaspoon oil in a saucepan over medium heat. When oil is hot, but not smoking, add asafoetida powder, red chili pepper, curry leaves, mustard seeds, and urad dal. Cover and fry until mustard seeds pop and urad dal is golden brown, about 30 seconds.

4. Add onion slices and tomato and stir-fry for 1 minute. Add cucumber, salt, and coriander.

5. Add buttermilk mixture to the saucepan and stir well.

6. When the mixture begins to boil remove from heat. Do not let buttermilk simmer as it will begin to curdle.

PER ½ CUP SERVING

CALORIES	79	CARBOHYDRATE	9g
FAT	4g	FIBER	2g
SATURATED FAT	1g	CHOLESTEROL	1mg
PROTEIN	3g	SODIUM	228mg

okra sambhar

Serves 6	¼ cup toor dal	1 whole dried red chili pepper	1 teaspoon black mustard seeds	2 cups frozen cut okra
	½ teaspoon turmeric powder	4 to 6 curry leaves (optional)	1 teaspoon urad dal	2 teaspoons sambhar powder
	2 tablespoons canola oil	¼ teaspoon fenugreek seeds	⅓ cup chopped onion	½ cup tomato sauce
	½ teaspoon asafoetida powder		¼ cup chopped tomato	1 teaspoon salt

1. Bring 3 cups of water to a boil in a deep saucepan over medium heat. Add toor dal and ¼ teaspoon turmeric powder. Reduce heat to medium and cook, uncovered, for about 30 minutes, until dal becomes creamy. If water evaporates during the cooking process, you may add another cup of water and cook until dal becomes creamy. Set aside.

2. In a saucepan, place oil over medium heat. When oil is hot, but not smoking, add asafoetida powder, red chili pepper, curry leaves, fenugreek seeds, mustard seeds, and urad dal. Cover and cook over medium heat until mustard seeds pop and urad dal is golden brown, about 30 seconds.

3. Add onion and tomato to saucepan and stir well.

4. Add okra and the remaining ¼ teaspoon turmeric powder to saucepan and sauté for 2 to 3 minutes over medium heat.

5. Add sambhar powder, tomato sauce, and salt. Stir well.

6. Add cooked creamy dal with about 2 cups of water to the okra mixture. Stir the mixture well. Let okra continue to cook over medium-low heat for 3 to 5 minutes.

Okra cooked with tomatoes in a creamy dal, this nutritious and satisfying sambhar is best served over plain rice.

NOTE You may also use fresh cut okra for making Okra Sambhar. Cut the ends off fresh okra and slice in ½-inch to ¾-inch slices. The authors prefer to use frozen cut okra because it is cut evenly and cooks faster than fresh okra.

CALORIES	107	CARBOHYDRATE	13g
FAT	5g	FIBER	3g
SATURATED FAT	1g	CHOLESTEROL	0mg
PROTEIN	4g	SODIUM	483mg

pearl onion and tomato sambhar

Serves 6	¼ cup toor dal	4 to 6 curry leaves	1 teaspoon urad dal	1 teaspoon salt
	½ teaspoon turmeric powder	1 whole dried red chili pepper	½ cup (about 12) fresh pearl onions, peeled	¼ cup tomato sauce
	3 tablespoons canola oil	¼ teaspoon fenugreek seeds	1 cup chopped tomato	¼ teaspoon tamarind paste
	¼ teaspoon asafoetida powder	1 teaspoon black mustard seeds	2 teaspoons sambhar powder	¼ cup chopped fresh coriander (cilantro) leaves

This aromatic sambhar is a popular and traditional dish. Pearl Onion and Tomato Sambhar is served over plain rice with any vegetable kootu, poriyal, and pappadums. It can also be served with idlis and dosais during breakfast.

1. Bring 3 cups of water to a boil in a deep saucepan. Add toor dal and ¼ teaspoon turmeric powder. Reduce heat to medium and cook, uncovered, for about 30 minutes, until dal becomes creamy. If water evaporates during the cooking process, add another cup of water and cook until dal becomes creamy. Set aside.

2. Place oil in a saucepan and heat over medium heat. When the oil is hot, but not smoking, add asafoetida powder, curry leaves, red chili pepper, fenugreek seeds, mustard seeds, and urad dal. Cover and fry until mustard seeds pop and urad dal turns golden brown, about 30 seconds.

3. Add onions and tomato to saucepan. Cook, covered, for about 2 minutes, until onions are tender.

4. Add remaining ¼ teaspoon turmeric powder and blend well. Add sambhar powder and salt. Blend the seasonings well with onions and tomato. Cook for 1 minute.

5. Add cooked creamy dal to the onion mixture with about 2½ cups of warm water. Stir well.

6. Add tomato sauce, tamarind paste, and coriander to the sambhar mixture. Let onions cook with sauce over low heat, covered, for about 3 minutes.

CALORIES	118	CARBOHYDRATE	11g
FAT	7g	FIBER	3g
SATURATED FAT	1g	CHOLESTEROL	8mg
PROTEIN	3g	SODIUM	442mg

potato sambhar

½ cup toor dal

2 whole dried red chili peppers

¼ teaspoon turmeric powder

2 cups unpeeled, chopped potato

1 cup chopped tomato

1 green chili pepper, chopped

1 teaspoon salt

1 teaspoon sambhar powder

½ teaspoon asafoetida powder

3 or 4 curry leaves or ¼ cup chopped fresh coriander (cilantro) leaves (optional)

2 tablespoons canola oil

1 teaspoon mustard seeds

1½ teaspoons urad dal

1. Place toor dal, 1 red chili pepper, turmeric powder, and 3 cups of water in a medium stainless steel mixing bowl that will fit into a pressure cooker.

2. Add potato, tomato, and green chili pepper to the bowl.

3. Add salt, sambhar powder, and ¼ teaspoon asafoetida powder with several curry leaves or chopped coriander, if desired, to the mixing bowl.

4. Place 1 or 2 cups of water in bottom of pressure cooker according to manufacturer's direction and size of pressure cooker. Place the bowl containing all the above ingredients in the pressure cooker. Cook in pressure cooker for 10 to 15 minutes.

5. Place oil in a medium saucepan over medium heat. When oil is hot, but not smoking, add remaining 1 red chili pepper, remaining ¼ teaspoon asafoetida powder, mustard seeds, and urad dal. Cover and fry until mustard seeds pop and urad dal is golden brown, about 30 seconds.

6. Stir the ingredients from pressure cooker plus 2 cups warm water into the spice mixture. Heat for a few minutes over low heat to blend all the ingredients thoroughly.

This quick and easy-to-prepare recipe for Potato Sambhar uses a pressure cooker (at least a 2.5-quart-size pressure cooker is necessary for this recipe). This sambhar may be served with idlis, dosais, uppuma, or idiyappam.

CALORIES	170	CARBOHYDRATE	26g
FAT	5g	FIBER	5g
SATURATED FAT	1g	CHOLESTEROL	0mg
PROTEIN	7g	SODIUM	365mg

thannir kulambu

Serves 4

2 tablespoons canola oil

¼ teaspoon asafoetida powder

4 or 5 curry leaves

1 whole dried red chili pepper

¼ teaspoon fenugreek seeds

1 teaspoon black mustard seeds

1 teaspoon urad dal

½ cup chopped onion

½ cup chopped tomato

¼ teaspoon turmeric powder

½ teaspoon sambhar powder (more, if desired)

¼ cup tomato sauce

2 garlic cloves, peeled and crushed

½ teaspoon salt

2 tablespoons minced fresh coriander (cilantro) leaves

A Chettinad favorite featuring onions and tomatoes in a mildly flavored tomato base, this light kulambu is best served over plain rice or uppuma.

1. Heat oil in a saucepan over medium heat. When oil is hot, but not smoking, add asafoetida powder, curry leaves, red chili pepper, fenugreek seeds, mustard seeds, and urad dal. Cover and fry until mustard seeds pop and urad dal is golden brown, about 30 seconds.

2. Add onion and tomato. Sauté for a few minutes. Add turmeric powder.

3. When onion and tomato are tender, add sambhar powder. Blend well.

4. Add tomato sauce and 2 cups of warm water. Simmer over medium heat. When kulambu begins to boil, add crushed garlic, salt, and coriander. Simmer for a few more minutes.

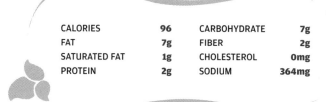

CALORIES	96	CARBOHYDRATE	7g
FAT	7g	FIBER	2g
SATURATED FAT	1g	CHOLESTEROL	0mg
PROTEIN	2g	SODIUM	364mg

zucchini sambhar

Serves 6

- ½ cup toor dal
- ½ teaspoon turmeric powder
- 2 tablespoons canola oil
- ½ teaspoon asafoetida powder
- 1 whole dried red chili pepper
- ½ teaspoon fenugreek seeds

- 1 teaspoon black mustard seeds
- 1 teaspoon urad dal
- ½ medium onion, sliced lengthwise
- 1 small tomato, chopped
- 2 teaspoons sambhar powder
- ¼ cup tomato sauce

- ¼ teaspoon tamarind paste
- 1 teaspoon salt (more, if desired)
- 2 cups peeled and cubed zucchini
- 2 to 3 tablespoons chopped fresh coriander (cilantro) leaves

1. Bring 4 cups of water to a boil in a deep saucepan. Add toor dal and ¼ teaspoon turmeric powder. Reduce heat to medium and cook, uncovered, for about 30 minutes, until dal becomes creamy. If water evaporates during the cooking process, add another cup of water and cook until dal becomes creamy. Set aside.

2. In another saucepan, heat oil over medium heat. When oil is hot, but not smoking, add asafoetida powder, whole red chili pepper, fenugreek seeds, mustard seeds, and urad dal. Cook, covered, until mustard seeds pop and urad dal is golden brown, about 30 seconds.

3. Add onion and tomato. Cook 2 to 3 minutes, until onion is tender. Add remaining ¼ teaspoon turmeric powder and sambhar powder and stir well.

4. Add tomato sauce, toor dal mixture, and 3 cups of warm water to the mixture in the saucepan. Stir well.

5. Add tamarind paste and salt. When mixture begins to bubble, add zucchini and cook, covered, over low heat, until zucchini is tender.

6. Add coriander and simmer for a few more minutes.

This sambhar is made from zucchini, onions, and tomatoes in a creamy dal base. It is delicious served over plain rice, with uppuma, idlis, dosais, or any Indian breads.

HEALTHY SOUTH INDIAN COOKING

CALORIES	130	CARBOHYDRATE	17g
FAT	5g	FIBER	4g
SATURATED FAT	1g	CHOLESTEROL	0mg
PROTEIN	6g	SODIUM	425mg

paruppu masiyal

Serves 4	¼ cup toor dal	2 garlic cloves, peeled and crushed	¾ teaspoon cumin powder
	¼ teaspoon turmeric powder	¼ teaspoon salt	2 to 4 curry leaves, chopped

A Chettinad favorite, Paruppu Masiyal is often served with ghee (clarified butter) over plain rice as a first course in a meal. Even when served over just plain rice without ghee, this creamy base dal is a delightful dish.

1. Bring 3 cups of water to a boil in a deep saucepan. Add toor dal and turmeric powder. Reduce heat to medium and cook, uncovered, for about 30 minutes until dal becomes creamy. If water evaporates during the cooking process, you may add another ½ cup of water and cook until dal becomes creamy. If needed you may use a masher to achieve the correct consistency of the dal.

2. Transfer dal to a bowl, add ½ cup water and mix well.

3. Add garlic, salt, cumin powder, and curry leaves to creamy dal. Mix well.

CALORIES	54	CARBOHYDRATE	10g
FAT	trace	FIBER	2g
SATURATED FAT	trace	CHOLESTEROL	0mg
PROTEIN	3g	SODIUM	136mg

vegetables

acorn squash masala poriyal

Serves 6	2 cups peeled, cubed acorn squash (see Step 1)	1 whole dried red chili pepper
	2 tablespoons canola oil	1 teaspoon black mustard seeds
	¼ teaspoon asafoetida powder	1 teaspoon urad dal
	4 to 6 curry leaves (optional)	1 medium onion, sliced lengthwise
		1 small tomato, chopped

½ teaspoon turmeric powder	
½ teaspoon cayenne powder (more, if desired)	
¾ cup tomato sauce	
1 teaspoon salt	
¼ cup unsweetened coconut powder	

A seasoned stir-fry vegetable dish that can be served with Lemon Rice (page 114), Yogurt Rice (page 123), or as a side dish with any meal.

1. Acorn squash has a tough skin. To peel and cube, cut the squash in half and cook the halves in a microwave for 1 to 2 minutes so that it is easy to cut the squash. Remove the pulp from the skin. Cut squash into small chunks.

2. Place oil in skillet over medium heat. When oil is hot, but not smoking, add asafoetida powder, curry leaves, red chili pepper, mustard seeds, and urad dal. Cover and fry until mustard seeds pop and urad dal is golden brown, about 30 seconds.

3. Add onion and tomato and stir-fry for 1 minute. Add turmeric powder and cayenne powder. Stir well.

4. Add tomato sauce and salt. Mix well. When the mixture begins to bubble, add the acorn squash and stir well.

5. Cover and cook over medium heat until the squash becomes somewhat soft. Add a small amount of water (about 1 tablespoon) periodically to facilitate the cooking process.

6. Add coconut powder and stir well.

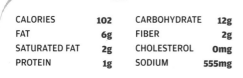

CALORIES	102	CARBOHYDRATE	12g	
FAT	6g	FIBER	2g	
SATURATED FAT	2g	CHOLESTEROL	0mg	
PROTEIN	1g	SODIUM	555mg	

asparagus poriyal

Serves 4

- 1 teaspoon canola oil
- 1 whole dried red chili pepper
- 1 teaspoon cumin seeds
- ¼ cup chopped onion
- 1 pound green asparagus, ends removed and diced
- 1 teaspoon cumin powder
- ½ teaspoon salt
- 1 tablespoon unsweetened coconut powder

1. Heat canola oil in a skillet over medium heat. When oil is hot, but not smoking, stir in red chili pepper and cumin seeds. Stir-fry 1 minute.

2. Add onion and asparagus. Stir-fry for another minute.

3. Add cumin powder and salt. Mix asparagus with seasonings, cover and let it cook in its own steam over low heat until tender.

4. Add coconut powder at end of cooking.

This great asparagus stir-fry with light seasonings can be served as a side dish with any meal.

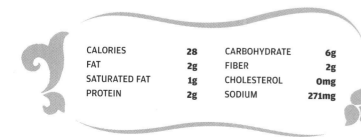

CALORIES	28	CARBOHYDRATE	6g
FAT	2g	FIBER	2g
SATURATED FAT	1g	CHOLESTEROL	0mg
PROTEIN	2g	SODIUM	271mg

avocado in yogurt

Makes 1 cup

1 avocado, peeled and mashed

1 teaspoon chopped red onion

1 teaspoon lemon juice

½ green chili pepper, minced

½ teaspoon cumin powder

¼ teaspoon salt

Nonfat plain yogurt (just enough to moisten avocado)

Avocado in yogurt can be served as a dip with any cocktail bread, chips, crackers or as an accompaniment to any meal.

Mix all the above ingredients in a bowl and refrigerate until serving.

CALORIES	47	CARBOHYDRATE	3g
FAT	4g	FIBER	1g
SATURATED FAT	1g	CHOLESTEROL	trace
PROTEIN	1g	SODIUM	75mg

green beans kootu

Serves 4

½ cup yellow split peas or moong dal

½ teaspoon turmeric powder

2 tablespoons canola oil

2 to 4 curry leaves

1 teaspoon black mustard seeds

1 teaspoon urad dal

⅓ cup chopped onion

1 tablespoon minced ginger root

1 green chili pepper, chopped

2 cups chopped green beans

1 teaspoon cumin powder

1 teaspoon salt

1. Bring 3 cups of water to a boil in a saucepan over medium heat. Add split peas or moong dal and ¼ teaspoon turmeric powder. Cook, uncovered, for about 30 minutes, until split peas or dal become creamy. If water evaporates during cooking process, add ½ cup more water to the saucepan. Mash the cooked split peas with masher while they are hot. Set aside.

2. Heat oil in a saucepan over medium heat. When oil is hot, but not smoking, add curry leaves, mustard seeds, and urad dal. Cover and fry until mustard seeds pop and urad dal turns golden brown, about 30 seconds.

3. Immediately add onion, ginger, and green chili pepper. Stir well and add remaining ¼ teaspoon turmeric powder.

4. Add green beans to the saucepan. Stir and add cumin powder and salt. Blend the ingredients well.

5. Add creamy split pea mixture together with just enough water to cover the beans and cook, covered, over medium-low heat about 10 minutes, until beans are tender but not overcooked.

Green beans cooked with creamy yellow split peas, cumin, and ginger, Beans Kootu is delicious served with plain rice, Yogurt Rice (page 123), or as a side dish with any meal.

157

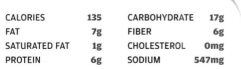

CALORIES	135	CARBOHYDRATE	17g
FAT	7g	FIBER	6g
SATURATED FAT	1g	CHOLESTEROL	0mg
PROTEIN	6g	SODIUM	547mg

green beans poriyal 1

Serves 6	¼ cup yellow split peas or moong dal	1 teaspoon black mustard seeds	1 teaspoon minced ginger root	¼ cup ground fresh coconut or unsweetened coconut powder
	¾ teaspoon turmeric powder	2 teaspoons urad dal	1 green chili pepper, finely chopped (optional)	
	2 tablespoons canola oil	1 pound green beans, diced (stems removed), about 3 cups	1 teaspoon salt	
	4 to 6 curry leaves (optional)		½ teaspoon chutney powder	

Green beans with split peas, ginger, and coconut, Beans Poriyal makes a tasty side dish for any meal.

variation   To make **GREEN BEANS AND CABBAGE PORIYAL**, use 1½ cups diced green beans and 1½ cups coarsely shredded cabbage. Follow the recipe through Step 4. In Step 5, when beans are tender but still crisp, add shredded cabbage. Stir-fry for about 3 minutes until cabbage is slightly cooked, then add cooked split peas and coconut powder. Stir well.

1. Bring 2 cups of water to a boil in a saucepan. Add split peas or moong dal and ¼ teaspoon turmeric powder. Cook over medium heat, uncovered, for about 20 minutes. Drain and set aside.

2. Heat oil in a large skillet over medium heat. When oil is hot, but not smoking, stir in curry leaves, mustard seeds, and urad dal. Cover and heat until mustard seeds pop and urad dal is golden brown, about 30 seconds.

3. Add green beans and stir well. Add ginger and green chili pepper. Cook over medium heat for about 1 minute. Add salt, remaining ½ teaspoon of turmeric powder, and chutney powder. Mix well.

4. Cover beans and cook over low heat without water for 5 to 7 minutes. **Note:** *a sprinkle or two of water may, however, be added on top of the green beans to facilitate the cooking process.*

5. When beans are tender but still crisp, add cooked split peas and coconut powder. Stir well. Serve immediately or remove from heat and keep covered until serving time. Be careful not to overcook beans.

CALORIES	125	CARBOHYDRATE	15g
FAT	7g	FIBER	7g
SATURATED FAT	2g	CHOLESTEROL	0mg
PROTEIN	5g	SODIUM	440mg

green beans poriyal II

Serves 4	2 teaspoons canola oil	2 teaspoons urad dal	½ teaspoon salt (more, if desired)
	1 whole dried red chili pepper	3 cups diced green beans	1 tablespoon unsweetened coconut powder
	1 teaspoon black mustard seeds	½ teaspoon chutney powder	
		1 teaspoon minced ginger root	

1. Heat oil in a skillet over medium heat. When oil is hot, but not smoking, add red chili pepper, mustard seeds, and urad dal. Cover and fry briefly until mustard seeds pop and urad dal turns golden brown, about 30 seconds.

2. Add green beans to skillet and mix with the seasonings. Add chutney powder, minced ginger, and salt. Cover and cook over low-medium heat until green beans are tender.

3. Stir in coconut powder. Serve warm.

A simpler version of Green Beans Poriyal I (page 158) flavored with coconut powder.

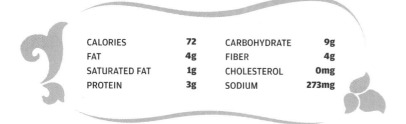

CALORIES	72	CARBOHYDRATE	9g
FAT	4g	FIBER	4g
SATURATED FAT	1g	CHOLESTEROL	0mg
PROTEIN	3g	SODIUM	273mg

beets and green peas poriyal

Serves 4

3 cups peeled and cubed beets

2 teaspoons canola oil

1 whole dried red chili pepper

4 to 6 curry leaves (optional)

1 teaspoon mustard seeds

2 teaspoons urad dal

½ teaspoon chutney powder

½ teaspoon salt

1 tablespoon unsweetened coconut powder

½ cup frozen green peas

This colorful stir-fried dish may be served as an accompaniment to any meal.

1. Steam beets in a steamer basket or in the microwave oven until they are tender. Set aside.

2. Add oil to a warmed skillet. When oil is hot, but not smoking, add chili pepper, curry leaves, mustard seeds, and urad dal. Cover and heat until mustard seeds pop and urad dal is golden brown, about 30 seconds. Note: *You may substitute 1 teaspoon of cumin seeds for the mustard seeds and urad dal if you prefer.*

3. Add steamed beets to skillet along with chutney powder, salt, and coconut powder. Stir well.

4. Add green peas as a final garnish and stir briefly.

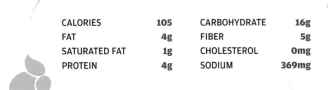

CALORIES	105	CARBOHYDRATE	16g
FAT	4g	FIBER	5g
SATURATED FAT	1g	CHOLESTEROL	0mg
PROTEIN	4g	SODIUM	369mg

SPICE BOX
WITH DRIED WHOLE SPICES

From left (clockwise): Dried red pepper, Urad dal, Cumin seeds, Fenugreek seeds, Fennel seeds, Black mustard seeds, Slivered cinnamon sticks (middle).

SPICE POWDERS

From top (clockwise): Chutney powder, Sambhar powder, Garam masala powder, Coconut powder, Cayenne powder, Black pepper and cumin powder mix, Turmeric powder (middle).

Coriander Chutney

Tomato Chutney

On platter (clockwise from top): Beet Vadais, Samosas, Bondas, Bhajis, Tuna Balls (middle)

Eggplant Chutney

Coconut Chutney

Beet Vadais,
Coriander Chutney

From top (clockwise): Cream of Wheat Uppuma, Coriander Chutney, Idlis, Coconut Chutney, Bell Pepper and Radish Sambhar

Blackeye Peas Sambhar

From top (clockwise):
Vadais, Coconut Chutney,
Coriander Chutney, Plain Dosais,
Green Beans Kulambu

Pooris and Potato Masala

Lemon Rice and
Eggplant Masala

Tamarind Rice

Mixed
Vegetable
Poriyal

Potato Masala and Cabbage Poriyal

Shrimp Masala

Cabbage and Carrot Poriyal

Carrot Poriyal

Basmati Rice
Green Pea

Mushroom Masala

Eggplant
Masala

Chickpea Soondal

Brussels Sprouts
Masala Poriyal

Tuna Masala and Tuna Balls

Okra Masala

Spinach Poriyal

Chettinad Chicken Masala,
Chappatis

Assorted Wraps

bell pepper masala

Serves 4			
	2 tablespoons canola oil	½ cup chopped onion	½ teaspoon salt
	¼ teaspoon asafoetida powder	1 cup chopped tomato	¾ cup tomato sauce
	1 teaspoon black mustard seeds	½ teaspoon turmeric powder	3 cups cubed green bell pepper
	1 teaspoon urad dal	¼ teaspoon cayenne powder	¼ cup unsweetened coconut powder

1. Place oil in a warmed skillet and heat over medium heat. When oil is hot, but not smoking, add asafoetida powder, mustard seeds, and urad dal. Cover and fry until mustard seeds pop and urad dal is golden brown, about 30 seconds.

2. Add onion and tomato to skillet and stir-fry for 2 to 3 minutes over medium heat.

3. Add turmeric powder, cayenne powder, and salt. Mix well to distribute spices evenly. Add tomato sauce and stir well.

4. Add bell peppers and blend well with sauce. Cover and reduce heat to low. Continue cooking until bell peppers are just tender, stirring occasionally.

5. Add coconut powder to skillet at end of cooking and stir gently.

Bell peppers with onions and tomatoes make a delicious accompaniment to any meal.

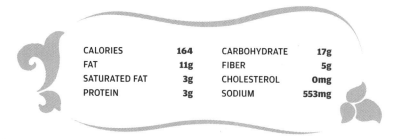

CALORIES	164	CARBOHYDRATE	17g
FAT	11g	FIBER	5g
SATURATED FAT	3g	CHOLESTEROL	0mg
PROTEIN	3g	SODIUM	553mg

bell pepper and tomato pachadi

Serves 6	¼ cup yellow split peas or moong dal	4 to 6 curry leaves	¾ cup chopped tomato	1 teaspoon salt
	½ teaspoon turmeric powder	¼ teaspoon asafoetida powder	2 cups diced green bell pepper	¼ teaspoon tamarind paste
	2 tablespoons canola oil	1 teaspoon black mustard seeds	½ teaspoon cayenne powder	¼ cup tomato sauce
	1 whole dried red chili pepper	1 teaspoon urad dal	½ teaspoon cumin powder	¼ cup chopped fresh coriander (cilantro) leaves
		¼ cup chopped onion		

A delicious combination of vegetables cooked with dal in tamarind paste, this dish is perfect served with rice, chappatis, or pooris.

1. Bring about 2 cups of water to a boil in a saucepan. Add yellow split peas or moong dal and ¼ teaspoon turmeric powder and cook for about 20 minutes over medium heat, uncovered, until split peas or moong dal are semi-soft. Set aside.

2. Heat oil in a saucepan over medium heat. When oil is hot, but not smoking, add red chili pepper, curry leaves, asafoetida powder, mustard seeds, and urad dal. Cover and fry over medium heat until mustard seeds pop and urad dal is golden brown, about 30 seconds.

3. Add onion, tomato, and remaining ¼ teaspoon turmeric powder and stir for a few minutes.

4. Add green bell pepper, cayenne powder, cumin powder, salt, and tamarind paste. Stir well.

5. Add split peas, tomato sauce, and about ¼ cup of water. When the mixture begins to boil, add coriander. Stir well.

6. Cover and cook over medium heat until green pepper is tender.

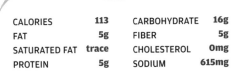

CALORIES	113	CARBOHYDRATE	16g
FAT	5g	FIBER	5g
SATURATED FAT	trace	CHOLESTEROL	0mg
PROTEIN	5g	SODIUM	615mg

bell pepper and potato masala

Serves 4

1 tablespoon canola oil

2 or 3 slivers cinnamon stick

1 teaspoon black mustard seeds

1 teaspoon urad dal

¼ cup chopped onion

½ cup chopped tomato

1 cup cubed, peeled Idaho potato

½ teaspoon turmeric powder

1½ cups chopped green bell pepper

½ teaspoon cayenne powder

¼ teaspoon salt

¼ cup tomato sauce

1. Add oil to a warm skillet. When oil is hot, but not smoking, add cinnamon sticks, mustard seeds, and urad dal. Cover and fry until mustard seeds pop and urad dal turns golden brown, about 30 seconds.

2. Add chopped onion and tomato. Stir-fry for 1 minute.

3. Add potatoes and turmeric powder. Stir well. Cover and cook potatoes for 2 to 3 minutes.

4. Add bell pepper, cayenne powder, salt, and tomato sauce. Stir well with potatoes. Cook covered over low to medium heat until potatoes are cooked.

This seasoned stir-fry dish cooked in tomato sauce may be served as a side dish with any meal.

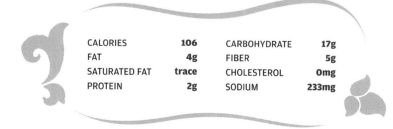

CALORIES	106	CARBOHYDRATE	17g
FAT	4g	FIBER	5g
SATURATED FAT	trace	CHOLESTEROL	0mg
PROTEIN	2g	SODIUM	233mg

blackeye peas masala poriyal

Serves 6	2 tablespoons canola oil	½ cup chopped onion	1 teaspoon salt (more if desired)

Serves 6

2 tablespoons canola oil

3 or 4 slivers cinnamon stick

1 teaspoon black mustard seeds

2 teaspoons urad dal

¼ cup chopped tomato

½ cup chopped onion

¼ teaspoon turmeric powder

¾ cup tomato sauce

½ teaspoon cayenne powder

1 teaspoon salt (more if desired)

1 package (16 ounces) frozen blackeye peas, thawed

2 tablespoons unsweetened coconut powder

A hearty stir-fry dish with coconut, Blackeye Peas Masala Poriyal is excellent served with chappatis or pooris or as an accompaniment to a rice dish, especially Yogurt Rice (page 123).

1. Heat oil in a medium skillet over medium heat. When oil is hot, but not smoking, add cinnamon sticks, mustard seeds, and urad dal. Cover and fry until mustard seeds pop and urad dal is golden brown, about 30 seconds.

2. Add tomato and onion. Stir-fry for 1 to 2 minutes. Add turmeric powder and stir.

3. Add tomato sauce, cayenne powder, and salt. Mix well.

4. Add thawed blackeye peas and blend well with ingredients in skillet. Add 1 cup warm water and cook, covered, over medium-low heat, stirring often, about 10 to 12 minutes.

5. When peas are just tender, add coconut powder. Mix well.

variation   **BUTTER BEAN MASALA PORIYAL**
Frozen butter beans may be substituted for blackeye peas.

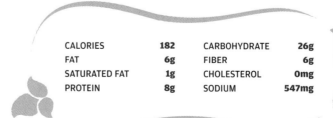

CALORIES	182	CARBOHYDRATE	26g
FAT	6g	FIBER	6g
SATURATED FAT	1g	CHOLESTEROL	0mg
PROTEIN	8g	SODIUM	547mg

broccoli podimas

Serves 6	½ cup yellow split peas	1 teaspoon cumin seeds	1 teaspoon black mustard seeds	1 teaspoon salt (more, if desired)
	2 dried whole red chili peppers (more, if desired)	3 tablespoons canola oil	2 teaspoons urad dal	4 cups finely chopped broccoli (including stems)
	½ teaspoon fennel seeds	4 or 5 curry leaves (optional)	1 cup chopped onion	
			½ teaspoon chutney powder	¼ cup unsweetened coconut powder

1. Soak split peas in enough hot water to cover for 30 minutes. Drain peas and coarsely grind in blender with red chili peppers, fennel seeds, and cumin seeds. **Note:** *It is best to grind the split peas in small batches. Add only enough water to facilitate the grinding process. Ground split peas should have the texture of coarse cornmeal.*

2. Pour coarsely ground mixture into a microwave dish and microwave, uncovered, on high for 3 minutes. (The mixture after cooking in microwave will feel somewhat hard.) Set aside and cool for 5 minutes.

3. Heat oil with curry leaves in a cast-iron skillet over medium heat. When oil is hot, but not smoking, stir in mustard seeds and urad dal. Cover and fry until mustard seeds pop and urad dal is golden brown, about 30 seconds.

4. Add onion to skillet and cook for 30 seconds.

5. Add all of the split pea mixture to ingredients in skillet. Blend well. Fry over medium-low heat stirring frequently until the split peas become golden brown and grainy in texture, 3 to 5 minutes. If split peas begin to stick to bottom of skillet, add a small amount of canola oil as needed to facilitate the process.

6. Stir in chutney powder and salt. Add broccoli and mix well with split pea mixture. Cover and cook over low heat stirring frequently until broccoli becomes tender, about another 7 minutes. Remove from heat.

7. Sprinkle coconut powder over broccoli and stir well. Cover to keep warm until serving.

A satisfying broccoli dish made with split peas and spices coarsely ground and steamed, Broccoli Podimas can be served as a side dish with any meal.

variations   **GREEN BEANS PODIMAS** Instead of broccoli, substitute 3 cups of diced green beans.

CARROT PODIMAS   Use 4 cups of shredded carrots in place of broccoli.

CABBAGE PODIMAS   Use 3 cups of coarsely shredded cabbage in place of broccoli.

CALORIES	162	CARBOHYDRATE	20g
FAT	8g	FIBER	8g
SATURATED FAT	2g	CHOLESTEROL	0mg
PROTEIN	8g	SODIUM	383mg

165

vegetables

HEALTHY SOUTH INDIAN COOKING

broccoli with coconut poriyal

Serves 4 to 6	1 tablespoon canola oil	4 cups coarsely chopped broccoli (including stems)	½ teaspoon chutney powder
	1 teaspoon black mustard seeds	1 green chili pepper, finely chopped	½ cup ground fresh coconut or unsweetened coconut powder
	1 teaspoon urad dal	1 teaspoon salt	
	¾ cup chopped onion		

An easy-to-prepare broccoli stir-fry that makes an excellent side dish at any meal.

1. Heat oil in a large skillet or wok over medium heat. When oil is hot but not smoking, stir in mustard seeds and urad dal. Cover and heat until mustard seeds pop and urad dal is golden brown, about 30 seconds.

2. Add onion and stir-fry for 30 seconds.

3. Add broccoli, green chili pepper, salt, and chutney powder to skillet and stir well. Cook, covered, for 5 to 7 minutes.

4. When the broccoli is tender but still crisp, add the coconut powder and stir well.

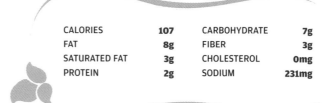

CALORIES	107	CARBOHYDRATE	7g
FAT	8g	FIBER	3g
SATURATED FAT	3g	CHOLESTEROL	0mg
PROTEIN	2g	SODIUM	231mg

brussels sprouts and chickpea poriyal

Serves 6

1 tablespoon canola oil

1 teaspoon black mustard seeds

1 teaspoon urad dal

1 medium onion, chopped

4 cups fresh brussels sprouts, coarsely chopped

½ teaspoon salt

½ teaspoon chutney powder or 1 green chili pepper, chopped

1 can (15 ounces) chickpeas, rinsed and drained

½ cup ground fresh coconut or unsweetened coconut powder

1. Heat oil in a large skillet or wok over medium heat. When oil is hot, but not smoking, stir in mustard seeds and urad dal. Cover and fry until mustard seeds pop and urad dal is golden brown, about 30 seconds.

2. Add onion and stir for 30 seconds.

3. Add brussels sprouts, salt, and chutney powder to skillet and stir well. Cook, covered, for 2 minutes over medium heat. (Be careful not to overcook brussels sprouts.)

4. Add chickpeas and coconut powder. Mix well and cook for an additional minute.

A hearty and fiber-rich stir-fry dish, Brussels Sprouts and Chickpea Poriyal can be served as a side dish with any meal.

variation The same recipe without chickpeas will result in a delicious **BRUSSELS SPROUTS PORIYAL.**

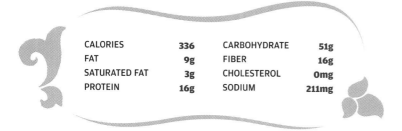

CALORIES	336	CARBOHYDRATE	51g
FAT	9g	FIBER	16g
SATURATED FAT	3g	CHOLESTEROL	0mg
PROTEIN	16g	SODIUM	211mg

brussels sprouts masala poriyal

Serves 4	2 tablespoons canola oil	½ cup chopped onion	½ teaspoon salt
	2 or 3 slivers cinnamon stick	1 cup chopped tomato	½ cup tomato sauce
	½ dry bay leaf, crumbled	¼ teaspoon turmeric powder	2 cups quartered brussels sprouts
	1 teaspoon black mustard seeds	¼ teaspoon cayenne powder (more, if desired)	1 teaspoon unsweetened coconut powder
	1 teaspoon urad dal		

Brussels sprouts cooked using tomatoes and seasonings and blended with coconut makes a favorite accompaniment to any meal.

1. Place oil in a saucepan over medium heat. When oil is hot, but not smoking, add cinnamon sticks, bay leaf, mustard seeds, and urad dal. Cover and fry until mustard seeds pop and urad dal turns golden, about 30 seconds.

2. Add onion, tomato, and turmeric powder and cook until onion is tender.

3. Add cayenne powder and salt and cook for 1 minute. Add tomato sauce. Stir well.

4. Add brussels sprouts and mix sprouts well into seasonings. Add ½ cup of warm water and cook over medium-low heat, covered, until brussels sprouts are tender.

5. Add coconut powder and mix well.

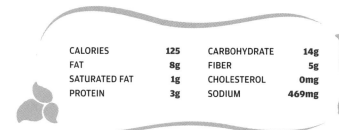

CALORIES	125	CARBOHYDRATE	14g
FAT	8g	FIBER	5g
SATURATED FAT	1g	CHOLESTEROL	0mg
PROTEIN	3g	SODIUM	469mg

caramelized brussels sprouts with cumin

Serves 4	3 cups brussels sprouts	½ teaspoon salt	1 teaspoon cumin powder
	2 or 3 tablespoons olive oil (enough to coat sprouts)	½ teaspoon ground black pepper	

1. Wash brussels sprouts and pat dry with a paper towel. You may cut sprouts in half if they are large in size. Place dried and cut sprouts in a bowl.

2. Add olive oil, salt, pepper, and cumin powder to the bowl. Using your hands, toss the brussels sprouts in the oil and seasonings until the sprouts are evenly coated. Preheat oven to 425 degrees.

3. Spread brussels sprouts on a baking sheet. Make certain that there is space between the sprouts in the baking pan so that sprouts will roast evenly.

4. Place sprouts in preheated oven. Bake, uncovered, about 45 minutes or until sprouts are blackened outside and soft inside. Serve immediately.

A great way to include a high-fiber vegetable in the diet and unique way to enjoy brussels sprouts.

CALORIES	120	CARBOHYDRATE	6g
FAT	10g	FIBER	3g
SATURATED FAT	1g	CHOLESTEROL	0mg
PROTEIN	2g	SODIUM	284mg

cabbage and carrot poriyal

Serves 6	2 tablespoons canola oil	3 cups shredded cabbage	½ teaspoon salt (more, if desired)
	2 to 4 curry leaves (optional)	½ cup shredded carrots	1 tablespoon unsweetened coconut powder
	1 teaspoon black mustard seeds	1 teaspoon chutney powder	
	2 teaspoons urad dal	½ teaspoon minced ginger root	

A colorful combination of vegetables seasoned with coconut.

1. Place oil in a skillet over medium heat. When oil is hot, but not smoking, stir in curry leaves, mustard seeds, and urad dal. Cover and fry until mustard seeds pop and urad dal is golden brown, about 30 seconds.

2. Add cabbage and carrots. Stir well into seasonings and add chutney powder, ginger root, and salt. Cover and cook over low heat until cabbage is tender but still crisp, about 2 to 3 minutes.

3. Add the coconut powder and stir well.

CALORIES	70	CARBOHYDRATE	5g
FAT	5g	FIBER	2g
SATURATED FAT	1g	CHOLESTEROL	0mg
PROTEIN	1g	SODIUM	189mg

cabbage poriyal

Serves 4

2 tablespoons canola oil

4 to 6 curry leaves (optional)

1 teaspoon black mustard seeds

2 teaspoons urad dal

½ cup chopped onion

4 cups shredded cabbage

1 teaspoon minced ginger root

½ green chili pepper, chopped

½ teaspoon salt (more, if desired)

1 tablespoon ground fresh coconut or unsweetened coconut powder

1. Place oil in a wok or skillet over medium heat. When oil is hot, but not smoking, stir in curry leaves, mustard seeds, and urad dal. Cover and fry until mustard seeds pop and urad dal is golden brown, about 30 seconds. Add onion and cook for 1 minute.

2. Add cabbage, ginger root, and green chili pepper. Stir well into seasonings and add salt. Cover and cook over low heat until cabbage is tender but still crisp, about 3 minutes.

3. Add the coconut powder and stir well.

An easy-to-make stir-fry cabbage dish with coconut, Cabbage Poriyal can be served as a side dish with any meal or as an accompaniment to plain rice and sambhar.

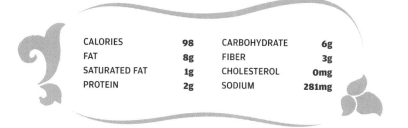

CALORIES	98	CARBOHYDRATE	6g
FAT	8g	FIBER	3g
SATURATED FAT	1g	CHOLESTEROL	0mg
PROTEIN	2g	SODIUM	281mg

cabbage and green peas poriyal

Serves 4

1½ tablespoons canola oil

1 teaspoon mustard seeds

2 teaspoons urad dal

4 to 6 curry leaves (optional)

2 cups coarsely shredded cabbage

½ teaspoon turmeric powder

1 cup frozen green peas

½ green chili pepper, chopped (optional)

1 teaspoon salt

½ teaspoon chutney powder

½ cup ground fresh coconut or unsweetened coconut powder

An easy-to-prepare stir-fry that makes a tasty and unique side dish for any meal.

1. In a saucepan, heat oil over medium heat until hot, but not smoking. Add mustard seeds, urad dal, and curry leaves. Cover and fry until mustard seeds pop and urad dal is golden brown, about 30 seconds.

2. Add cabbage and turmeric powder. Mix well. Continue cooking, uncovered, over medium heat for 1 to 2 minutes, stirring frequently.

3. Add green peas, green chili pepper, salt, and chutney powder. Stir well. Cover and cook over medium heat for 2 minutes.

4. When cabbage and peas are cooked, stir in coconut powder. Do not overcook vegetables.

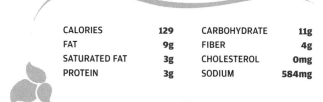

CALORIES	129	CARBOHYDRATE	11g
FAT	9g	FIBER	4g
SATURATED FAT	3g	CHOLESTEROL	0mg
PROTEIN	3g	SODIUM	584mg

cabbage and potato kootu

Serves 6	¾ cup toor dal or moong dal	1 teaspoon urad dal	½ cup shredded Idaho potato (the same size pieces as cabbage)
	½ teaspoon turmeric powder	½ cup chopped onion	
	2 tablespoons canola oil	1 green chili pepper, minced (more, if desired)	2 cups coarsely shredded cabbage
	2 or 3 curry leaves (optional)	1 tablespoon minced ginger root	1 teaspoon cumin powder
	1 teaspoon black mustard seeds		1 teaspoon salt

1. Bring 4 cups of water to a boil in a deep saucepan. Add toor dal and ¼ teaspoon turmeric powder. Reduce heat to medium and cook dal, uncovered, until it becomes creamy, about 30 minutes. If most of the water evaporates before dal becomes creamy add an additional cup of water and continue to cook. It also helps to mash cooked dal in saucepan with a potato masher. Set aside.

2. Heat oil in a saucepan over medium heat. When oil is hot, but not smoking, add curry leaves, mustard seeds, and urad dal. Cover and cook until mustard seeds pop and urad dal is golden brown, about 30 seconds.

3. Add onion, chili pepper, and ginger root. Stir well.

4. Add potato and stir-fry a few minutes and then add the cabbage. Stir-fry about 1 more minute.

5. Add remaining ¼ teaspoon turmeric powder, cumin powder, and salt. Stir well.

6. Immediately add cooked creamy toor dal with about 1 cup of water. Cover and cook over medium heat for 8 to 10 minutes until the vegetables are tender, stirring frequently so that potatoes do not stick to the bottom of the pan.

Kootu is a thick, lightly seasoned vegetable dish cooked with ginger in a creamy dal base. Serve as a side dish with rice.

variation   To make **CABBAGE KOOTU**, just use 3 cups of shredded cabbage and omit the potatoes.

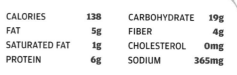

CALORIES	138	CARBOHYDRATE	19g
FAT	5g	FIBER	4g
SATURATED FAT	1g	CHOLESTEROL	0mg
PROTEIN	6g	SODIUM	365mg

vegetables

HEALTHY SOUTH INDIAN COOKING

cabbage with scrambled eggs

Serves 6			
	2 tablespoons canola oil	4 cups coarsely shredded cabbage	1 teaspoon salt
	4 to 6 curry leaves (optional)	1 green chili pepper, chopped (optional)	1 teaspoon chutney powder
	1 teaspoon black mustard seeds	½ teaspoon turmeric powder	2 eggs, beaten
	1 teaspoon urad dal		¾ cup sliced onion (cut lengthwise)

An easy, unique, stir-fry dish with cabbage and eggs that can be served as a side dish with any meal.

1. In a skillet, heat oil over medium heat until hot, but not smoking. Add curry leaves, mustard seeds, and urad dal. Fry, covered, until mustard seeds pop and urad dal is golden brown, about 30 seconds.

2. Add cabbage, green chili pepper, and turmeric powder. Mix well. Continue cooking, covered, over low heat for 1 to 2 minutes, stirring frequently.

3. Add salt and chutney powder. Stir well. Do not overcook cabbage.

4. Pour eggs over cabbage. Scramble until the eggs are cooked. Add the onion slices and stir well.

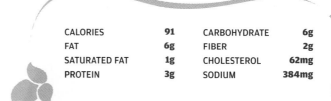

CALORIES	91	CARBOHYDRATE	6g
FAT	6g	FIBER	2g
SATURATED FAT	1g	CHOLESTEROL	62mg
PROTEIN	3g	SODIUM	384mg

carrot pachadi

Serves 4

2 cups peeled and shredded carrots

½ green chili pepper, chopped

2 cups plain yogurt

1 teaspoon canola oil

½ teaspoon asafoetida powder

1 teaspoon black mustard seeds

1 teaspoon urad dal

½ teaspoon salt (more, if desired)

1. In a medium bowl, mix carrots and green chili pepper.

2. Add yogurt to carrot mixture and stir well.

3. Place oil in a small saucepan (such as a butter warmer) and heat over medium heat. When oil is hot, but not smoking, add asafoetida powder, mustard seeds, and urad dal. Cover and fry until mustard seeds pop and urad dal is golden brown, about 30 seconds.

4. Add the fried spices to the yogurt mixture and mix well. Add salt and mix well.

Carrots in yogurt can be served as a great side dish with any meal.

CALORIES	108	CARBOHYDRATE	17g
FAT	1g	FIBER	2g
SATURATED FAT	trace	CHOLESTEROL	2mg
PROTEIN	8g	SODIUM	376mg

carrot poriyal

Serves 4

- 2 cups fresh baby carrots
- 1 tablespoon canola oil
- 4 to 6 curry leaves
- 1 whole dried red chili pepper
- 1 teaspoon black mustard seeds
- 2 teaspoons urad dal
- ¼ teaspoon chutney powder
- ½ teaspoon salt
- 1 teaspoon unsweetened coconut powder

A delightful stir-fry of baby carrots, Carrot Poriyal can be served as a side dish with any meal.

1. Steam or microwave baby carrots in a small amount of water for about 5 minutes.

2. Place oil in a skillet over medium heat. When oil is hot, but not smoking, add curry leaves, red chili pepper, mustard seeds, and urad dal. Cover and fry until mustard seeds pop and urad dal turns golden brown, about 30 seconds.

3. Add carrots to the skillet and stir well into seasonings. Add chutney powder and salt. Mix well.

4. Cook, covered, over medium-low heat until carrots are cooked according to your taste.

5. Mix coconut powder with carrots.

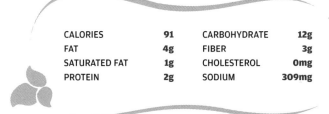

CALORIES	91	CARBOHYDRATE	12g
FAT	4g	FIBER	3g
SATURATED FAT	1g	CHOLESTEROL	0mg
PROTEIN	2g	SODIUM	309mg

cauliflower kootu

Serves 4

- ¾ cup toor dal or moong dal
- ½ teaspoon turmeric powder
- 2 tablespoons canola oil
- ¼ teaspoon asafoetida powder
- 4 to 6 curry leaves
- 1 teaspoon black mustard seeds
- 1 teaspoon urad dal
- ¼ cup chopped onion
- 1 tablespoon finely minced ginger root
- 1 teaspoon finely chopped green chili pepper
- 3 cups cauliflower pieces, cut in 1- to 1½-inch chunks including short stems
- ½ teaspoon cumin powder
- ½ teaspoon salt
- 1 tablespoon unsweetened coconut powder

1. Bring 4 cups of water to a boil in a saucepan. Add toor dal or moong dal and ¼ teaspoon turmeric powder. Reduce heat to medium and cook, uncovered, for about 30 minutes, until dal becomes creamy. If water seems to evaporates during the cooking process, add another cup of water and cook until dal becomes creamy. Set aside.

2. Heat oil in a saucepan over medium heat. When oil is hot, but not smoking, add asafoetida powder, curry leaves, mustard seeds, and urad dal. Cover and cook until mustard seeds pop and urad dal turns golden brown, about 30 seconds.

3. Add onion, ginger root, chili pepper, and remaining ¼ teaspoon turmeric powder. Stir well.

4. Add cauliflower. Mix well with the seasonings in the saucepan.

5. Add creamy toor dal, cumin powder, and salt. Add about ¾ cup warm water. Stir cauliflower well with the dal mixture for a minute or two.

6. Cover and cook over low heat until cauliflower is just tender, about 2 to 4 minutes. Add coconut powder. Stir and cook for an additional minute. Do not overcook cauliflower.

Delightful, seasoned cauliflower cooked with ginger in a creamy dal base, this kootu may be served over plain rice or Yogurt Rice (page 123), or as a side dish with any meal.

CALORIES	200	CARBOHYDRATE	25g
FAT	8g	FIBER	7g
SATURATED FAT	1g	CHOLESTEROL	0mg
PROTEIN	5g	SODIUM	295mg

cauliflower poriyal

Serves 2	2 tablespoons canola oil	1 teaspoon black mustard seeds	3 cups cauliflower pieces, cut in 1-inch chunks including short stems
	1 whole dried red chili pepper	1 teaspoon urad dal	½ teaspoon salt
	4 to 6 curry leaves		1 teaspoon cumin powder

A light, easy-to-prepare stir-fry that enhances any lunch or dinner.

1. Place oil in a skillet over medium heat. When oil is hot, but not smoking, add red chili pepper, curry leaves, mustard seeds, and urad dal. Cover and fry until mustard seeds pop and urad dal turns golden brown, about 30 seconds.

2. Immediately add cauliflower to the skillet and mix well with the seasonings.

3. Add salt and cumin powder and stir well. Add about 2 tablespoons water and cook, covered, over medium-low heat until cauliflower is tender, about 5 minutes. Do not overcook cauliflower.

CALORIES	191	CARBOHYDRATE	13g
FAT	15g	FIBER	5g
SATURATED FAT	2g	CHOLESTEROL	0mg
PROTEIN	5g	SODIUM	583mg

cauliflower masala poriyal

Serves 4	2 tablespoons canola oil	1 small onion, chopped	½ teaspoon cayenne powder (more, if desired)	3 cups cauliflower pieces, cut in 1- to 1½-inch chunks including short stems
	2 or 3 slivers cinnamon stick	1 small tomato, cut in small chunks	½ teaspoon cumin powder	
	2 teaspoons black mustard seeds	½ teaspoon turmeric powder	½ cup tomato sauce	2 teaspoons unsweetened coconut powder (optional)
	2 teaspoons urad dal		1 teaspoon salt	

1. Heat canola oil in a skillet or wok over medium heat. When oil is hot, but not smoking, add cinnamon stick, mustard seeds, and urad dal. Cover and fry until mustard seeds pop and urad dal is golden brown, about 30 seconds.

2. Add onion and tomato. Stir-fry for 1 minute over medium heat.

3. Add turmeric powder, cayenne powder, and cumin powder. Stir well over medium heat for 1 minute. Add tomato sauce and salt. Mix well to obtain a thick paste-like consistency.

4. Add cauliflower chunks and blend carefully with sauce. Cover and cook over medium heat for 2 minutes.

5. Stir in coconut powder, if using. Continue cooking until cauliflower is just tender, stirring occasionally. Be careful not to overcook! **Note:** *If there is too much sauce in skillet, cook uncovered over low heat for few more minutes.*

This cauliflower stir-fry with onions, tomatoes, and spices makes a colorful and tasty side dish.

variation   To make **CAULIFLOWER AND POTATO MASALA PORIYAL**, include 1½ cups of peeled and cubed potatoes (1-inch cubes). Partially cook potatoes in a small saucepan with enough water to cover potatoes. Add ¼ teaspoon turmeric powder and salt to the potatoes. When potatoes are partially cooked, drain and place in a small bowl. Set aside. Follow the recipe for Cauliflower Masala Poriyal. In Step 4, add partially cooked potatoes with the cauliflower chunks and proceed with the recipe.

CALORIES	126	CARBOHYDRATE	14g
FAT	8g	FIBER	5g
SATURATED FAT	1g	CHOLESTEROL	0mg
PROTEIN	3g	SODIUM	749mg

cauliflower paneer masala

Serves 6	4 tablespoons canola oil	1 teaspoon urad dal	½ teaspoon cayenne powder
	1 cup paneer slices	½ cup chopped onion	½ teaspoon cumin powder
	2 or 3 slivers cinnamon stick	½ cup chopped tomato	½ teaspoon salt
	1 dry bay leaf	¼ teaspoon turmeric powder	¼ cup tomato sauce
	1 teaspoon black mustard seeds		3 cups cauliflower florets

Paneer, a type of cheese, is available at Indian groceries. Cauliflower with paneer is a wonderful combination which can be served as a side dish to any meal.

1. Heat a skillet over medium heat and add 3 tablespoons oil. Add the paneer slices and gently fry the paneer to a golden brown. Remove slices from pan and set aside.

2. Add one more tablespoon of oil to the skillet over medium heat. When oil is hot, but not smoking, add cinnamon sticks, bay leaf, mustard seeds, and urad dal. Cover and fry until mustard seeds pop and urad dal is golden brown, about 30 seconds.

3. Add chopped onion and tomato and cook for two minutes. Add turmeric powder and stir.

4. Add cayenne powder, cumin powder, salt, and tomato sauce and stir.

5. Add cauliflower and mix well. When cauliflower is half cooked add the paneer slices and stir gently. Cover and cook until cauliflower is just tender.

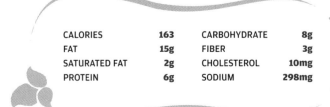

CALORIES	163	CARBOHYDRATE	8g
FAT	15g	FIBER	3g
SATURATED FAT	2g	CHOLESTEROL	10mg
PROTEIN	6g	SODIUM	298mg

cauliflower with potatoes and green peas

Serves 4			
2 tablespoons canola oil	½ cup chopped onion	¼ teaspoon turmeric powder	1 cup cauliflower florets
3 or 4 curry leaves (optional)	1 cup chopped tomato	¼ teaspoon cayenne powder	½ cup frozen green peas
1 teaspoon mustard seeds	1 cup peeled and cubed potato	¼ teaspoon cumin powder	
2 teaspoons urad dal		½ teaspoon salt	

1. Add oil to heated skillet with curry leaves. When oil is hot, but not smoking, add mustard seeds and urad dal. Cover and fry until mustard seeds pop and urad dal turns golden brown, about 30 seconds.

2. Add chopped onion and tomato to skillet and sauté for a few minutes.

3. Add chopped potato and stir well. Add turmeric powder, cayenne powder, cumin powder, and salt. Mix the seasonings with potatoes. Cover and cook over low-medium heat until potatoes are partially cooked.

4. Stir in cauliflower. Cover and continue to cook for a few minutes until cauliflower becomes tender.

5. Stir in frozen peas and steam briefly in covered skillet.

A unique blend of vegetables prepared as a stir-fry.

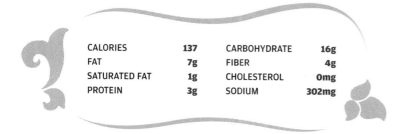

CALORIES	137	CARBOHYDRATE	16g
FAT	7g	FIBER	4g
SATURATED FAT	1g	CHOLESTEROL	0mg
PROTEIN	3g	SODIUM	302mg

chana dal soondal

Serves 4			
½ cup chana dal	1 whole dried red chili pepper	¼ teaspoon asafoetida powder	½ cup ground fresh coconut or unsweetened coconut powder
¼ teaspoon turmeric powder	1 teaspoon mustard seeds	½ teaspoon minced ginger root	
1 teaspoon canola oil	1 teaspoon urad dal		
2 to 4 curry leaves	½ teaspoon salt		

A unique high-fiber dish of chana dal and fresh coconut, Chana Dal Soondal is delicious served as a snack or as a side dish. In South India, soondal is frequently offered as a prasad (offering) during religious ceremonies at home and in temples.

1. Soak chana dal in 1 cup of water for 30 minutes. Drain and set aside.

2. Bring 1 cup of water to a boil in a saucepan. Add chana dal and turmeric powder. Cook dal, uncovered, until it becomes soft, about 15 minutes. Drain water and set aside.

3. Place oil in a skillet and heat over medium heat. When oil is hot, but not smoking, add curry leaves, red chili pepper, mustard seeds, and urad dal. Cover and fry until mustard seeds pop and urad dal turns golden brown, about 30 seconds.

4. Add chana dal and blend well with seasonings in the skillet over low heat.

5. Add salt, asafoetida powder, and ginger root and mix well with chana dal. Add coconut powder and mix well.

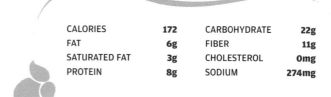

CALORIES	172	CARBOHYDRATE	22g
FAT	6g	FIBER	11g
SATURATED FAT	3g	CHOLESTEROL	0mg
PROTEIN	8g	SODIUM	274mg

chayote squash kootu

Serves 4	½ cup moong dal or toor dal	¼ teaspoon asafoetida powder	2 cups peeled and cubed chayote squash	1 teaspoon cumin powder
	½ teaspoon turmeric powder	4 to 6 curry leaves	1 green chili pepper, chopped (optional)	½ teaspoon salt (more, if desired)
	2 tablespoons canola oil	1 teaspoon black mustard seeds	1 teaspoon minced ginger root	1 tablespoon unsweetened coconut powder
		1 teaspoon urad dal		

1. Bring 4 cups of water to a boil. Add dal of your choice and ¼ teaspoon turmeric powder. Reduce heat to medium-high. Cook, uncovered, for about 30 minutes until dal becomes creamy. If water evaporates during the cooking process, add another cup of water and cook until dal becomes creamy. Set aside.

2. Heat saucepan over medium heat. Add oil. When oil is hot, but not smoking, add asafoetida powder, curry leaves, mustard seeds, and urad dal. Cover and cook until mustard seeds pop and urad dal turns golden brown, about 30 seconds.

3. Add cubed chayote squash, green chili pepper, ginger root, and remaining ¼ teaspoon turmeric powder. Stir the squash well with the seasonings.

4. Add creamy dal, cumin powder, and salt. Add ¾ cup of warm water and stir well.

5. Cover and cook over medium heat until squash is tender, about 7 to 10 minutes. Add coconut powder and stir.

Chayote squash, known as chow chow, is cooked here with ginger, cumin, and creamy lentils for a mild and flavorful accompaniment to a meal. It can also be served with plain rice or Yogurt Rice (page 123).

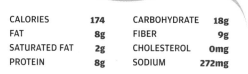

CALORIES	174	CARBOHYDRATE	18g
FAT	8g	FIBER	9g
SATURATED FAT	2g	CHOLESTEROL	0mg
PROTEIN	8g	SODIUM	272mg

chickpea soondal

Serves 2 to 4

1 tablespoon canola oil

1 whole dried red chili pepper

1 teaspoon black mustard seeds

1 teaspoon urad dal

1 can (15 ounces) chickpeas, drained and rinsed

½ teaspoon turmeric powder

½ teaspoon salt

½ teaspoon chutney powder

1 teaspoon minced fresh ginger root

¼ cup ground fresh coconut or unsweetened coconut powder

A delightful combination of chickpeas cooked with ginger and coconut, Chickpea Soondal is often served as a snack during teatime or as a side dish. Like Chana Dal Soondal (page 182), this dish is also served during religious ceremonies.

1. Heat oil in medium skillet or wok over medium heat. When oil is hot, but not smoking, stir in red chili pepper, black mustard seeds, and urad dal. Cover and fry until mustard seeds pop and urad dal is golden brown, about 30 seconds.

2. Immediately add chickpeas, turmeric powder, salt, and chutney powder and mix well. Add ginger root and cook for an additional minute or two. Add coconut powder and stir.

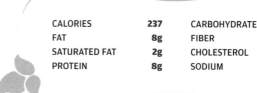

CALORIES	237	CARBOHYDRATE	34g
FAT	8g	FIBER	7g
SATURATED FAT	2g	CHOLESTEROL	0mg
PROTEIN	8g	SODIUM	781mg

chickpea and bell pepper poriyal

Serves 6

2 teaspoons canola oil

5 or 6 slivers cinnamon stick

1 teaspoon black mustard seeds

2 teaspoons urad dal

½ cup chopped onion

½ cup chopped tomato

¼ teaspoon turmeric powder

½ teaspoon cayenne powder (more, if desired)

1 cup tomato sauce (more, if needed)

½ teaspoon salt (more, if desired)

1 can (15 ounces) chickpeas, drained and rinsed

3 cups chopped green bell pepper

1 to 2 teaspoons unsweetened coconut powder

1. Heat oil in a cast-iron skillet or any saucepan over medium heat until hot, but not smoking. Add pieces of cinnamon stick, mustard seeds, and urad dal to the oil. Cover and cook until mustard seeds pop and urad dal is golden brown, about 30 seconds.

2. Add onion and tomato and stir-fry for 1 to 2 minutes over medium heat. Add turmeric powder and stir.

3. Add cayenne powder and mix well. Add 1 cup tomato sauce and salt to skillet. Allow the mixture to boil.

4. Add chickpeas and green peppers. Add more tomato sauce, if needed, to cover chickpeas. Mix well.

5. Cover skillet and cook vegetables over medium heat for about 5 minutes. A small amount of water (1 to 2 tablespoons) may be added to skillet to facilitate the cooking process. Be careful not to overcook the vegetables.

6. Stir in coconut powder and serve.

Vegetables seasoned and cooked in tomato sauce, this dish can be served with rice or bread.

variation   For a delicious variation, you can omit the bell peppers and ½ cup tomato sauce to create CHICKPEA MASALA PORIYAL.

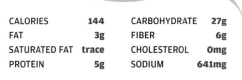

CALORIES	144	CARBOHYDRATE	27g
FAT	3g	FIBER	6g
SATURATED FAT	trace	CHOLESTEROL	0mg
PROTEIN	5g	SODIUM	641mg

chickpea and mango soondal

Serves 4			
	1 tablespoon canola oil	2 (14- to 16-ounce) cans chickpeas, rinsed and drained	1 teaspoon chutney powder
	1 whole dried red chili pepper		½ teaspoon salt
	1 teaspoon black mustard seeds	1 cup chopped fresh mango (unripened)	1 teaspoon minced ginger root
	1½ teaspoons urad dal	¼ teaspoon turmeric powder	1 tablespoon unsweetened coconut powder

An irresistible and healthful snack, which can also be served as a side dish.

1. Heat skillet over medium heat. Add oil. When oil is hot, but not smoking, stir in red chili pepper, mustard seeds, and urad dal. Cover and fry until mustard seeds pop and urad dal is golden brown, about 30 seconds.

2. Immediately add chickpeas, mango, turmeric powder, chutney powder, and salt. Mix well.

3. Add ginger root and cook over low-medium heat for an additional minute or two.

4. Add coconut powder and stir the mixture gently.

CALORIES	314	CARBOHYDRATE	54g
FAT	7g	FIBER	10g
SATURATED FAT	1g	CHOLESTEROL	0mg
PROTEIN	11g	SODIUM	729mg

corn poriyal

Serves 6

- 1 tablespoon canola oil
- 4 to 6 curry leaves
- 1 whole dried red chili pepper
- 1 teaspoon black mustard seeds
- 2 teaspoons urad dal
- 3 cups frozen corn
- ¼ teaspoon chutney powder
- ½ teaspoon salt
- 1 teaspoon unsweetened coconut powder

1. Place oil in a skillet over medium heat. When oil is hot, but not smoking, add curry leaves, red chili pepper, mustard seeds, and urad dal. Cover and fry until mustard seeds pop and urad dal turns golden brown, about 30 seconds.

2. Add frozen corn, chutney powder, and salt. Mix corn well with the seasonings. Add coconut powder and mix well.

A lightly seasoned corn dish, this poriyal can be served as a snack or as a side dish with any meal.

CALORIES	103	CARBOHYDRATE	18g
FAT	3g	FIBER	3g
SATURATED FAT	trace	CHOLESTEROL	0mg
PROTEIN	3g	SODIUM	181mg

cucumber pachadi

Serves 4	2 cups fat-free plain yogurt	1 green chili pepper, chopped	¼ teaspoon asafoetida powder
	2 cups peeled and shredded cucumber	1 teaspoon canola oil	1 teaspoon black mustard seeds
	½ teaspoon salt	1 whole dried red chili pepper	1 teaspoon urad dal

A refreshing dish of cucumber in seasoned yogurt that can be served with baked or grilled chicken or any flavored rice.

1. Put the yogurt in a bowl and beat well until smooth.

2. Add cucumber, salt, and green chili pepper to the yogurt. Mix well.

3. Place oil in a small saucepan and heat over medium heat. When oil is hot, but not smoking, add red chili pepper, asafoetida powder, mustard seeds, and urad dal. Cover and fry until mustard seeds pop and urad dal is golden brown, about 30 seconds. Pour the spices over the yogurt and mix well.

variation   To make POTATO PACHADI, instead of using cucumbers, use 2 cups peeled and sliced boiled potatoes.

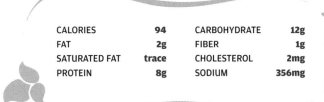

CALORIES	94	CARBOHYDRATE	12g
FAT	2g	FIBER	1g
SATURATED FAT	trace	CHOLESTEROL	2mg
PROTEIN	8g	SODIUM	356mg

eggplant masala

Serves 4				
	3 tablespoons canola oil	1 teaspoon urad dal	½ teaspoon turmeric powder	1 teaspoon cumin powder
	¼ teaspoon asafoetida powder	½ cup sliced onion (cut in small lengthwise pieces)	3 cups unpeeled small oblong pieces eggplant	1 cup tomato sauce
	4 or 5 curry leaves (optional)	½ cup coarsely chopped tomato	¼ teaspoon cayenne powder	½ teaspoon salt
	1 teaspoon black mustard seeds	3 garlic cloves, peeled and quartered		2 teaspoons unsweetened coconut powder

1. Heat oil in a cast-iron skillet over medium heat with asafoetida powder and curry leaves. When oil is hot, but not smoking, stir in mustard seeds and urad dal. Cover and fry until mustard seeds pop and urad dal is golden brown, about 30 seconds.

2. Add onion, tomato, garlic, and turmeric powder. Stir-fry for 2 minutes.

3. Add eggplant and stir well. Cover and simmer over medium-low heat for 2 to 3 minutes.

4. Add cayenne and cumin powders. Add tomato sauce, salt, and 4 tablespoons of water and stir well. Cover and continue to cook, stirring often, over medium-low heat for 12 to 15 minutes or until eggplant becomes tender and sauce is thick.

5. Add coconut powder. Stir briefly for a few minutes.

A delightful, aromatic eggplant dish cooked with tomatoes, onions, and garlic, Eggplant Masala complements many rice and vegetable dishes. As a delicious appetizer, it can be served over cocktail breads and crackers.

variation To make a wonderful EGGPLANT RICE (*Vangibhath*), add 2 cups cooked plain white or basmati rice to the Eggplant Masala. Stir over medium-low heat and blend well. Stir in ¼ cup roasted peanuts and continue to stir well. You may add ½ teaspoon more salt if desired.

CALORIES	158	CARBOHYDRATE	13g
FAT	12g	FIBER	4g
SATURATED FAT	2g	CHOLESTEROL	0mg
PROTEIN	3g	SODIUM	644mg

eggplant and potato masala

Serves 4 to 6	2 medium Idaho potatoes	2 or 3 slivers cinnamon stick	¾ teaspoon turmeric powder	1 cup tomato sauce
	6 baby eggplants or ½ large eggplant	1 teaspoon cumin seeds	½ teaspoon cayenne powder	1 to 2 tablespoons ground fresh coconut or unsweetened coconut powder
	5 tablespoons canola oil	½ cup sliced onion (cut lengthwise)	1 teaspoon salt	
		1 cup diced tomato	¼ teaspoon garam masala powder	

Eggplant and potato cooked in a seasoned tomato sauce, this dish is especially delicious served with any flavored rice.

1. Wash the potatoes but do not peel. Cut into small chunks (approximately 1½ x ½ inches) to make 2 cups.

2. Cut unpeeled eggplant(s) into pieces the same size as the potatoes to make about 2 cups.

3. Place oil in a heavy skillet over medium heat. When oil is hot but not smoking, add cinnamon sticks and cumin seeds. Cover and fry until seeds are golden brown.

4. Add onion and tomato. Stir-fry for a few minutes.

5. Add potatoes and turmeric powder. Mix well and cook over medium heat, stirring often, for 3 to 5 minutes, until potatoes are slightly cooked. Add eggplant and mix well.

6. Add cayenne powder, salt, and garam masala powder. Stir in tomato sauce and mix well. You may add about ¼ cup of water to facilitate the cooking process. Cover and cook over low heat until vegetables are tender.

7. Add coconut powder and mix well.

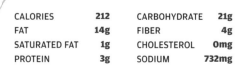

CALORIES	212	CARBOHYDRATE	21g
FAT	14g	FIBER	4g
SATURATED FAT	1g	CHOLESTEROL	0mg
PROTEIN	3g	SODIUM	732mg

eggplant kootu

Serves 4

¾ cup toor dal

½ teaspoon turmeric powder

2 tablespoons canola oil

4 to 6 curry leaves

1 whole dried red chili pepper

1 teaspoon black mustard seeds

1 teaspoon urad dal

½ teaspoon cumin seeds

½ cup chopped onion

2 cups chopped unpeeled eggplant

1 teaspoon salt

1 teaspoon cumin powder

1. Bring 4 cups of water to a boil in a saucepan over medium heat. Add toor dal and ¼ teaspoon turmeric powder. Reduce heat to medium and cook, uncovered, for about 30 minutes, until dal becomes creamy. If water evaporates during the cooking process, add another cup of water and cook until dal becomes creamy. Set aside.

2. Place oil in a saucepan over medium heat. When oil is hot, but not smoking, add curry leaves, chili pepper, mustard seeds, urad dal, and cumin seeds. Cover and fry until mustard seeds pop and urad dal turns golden brown, about 30 seconds.

3. Add onion and eggplant together with remaining ¼ teaspoon turmeric powder. Stir well into seasonings in saucepan.

4. Add creamy toor dal plus 2 cups of warm water to the eggplant mixture. Add salt and cumin powder. Stir well.

5. Cook, covered, over medium heat until eggplant becomes tender, about 5 to 7 minutes.

Mildly seasoned eggplant cooked with creamy dal, this Chettinad delight goes particularly well with plain rice or Yogurt Rice (page 123).

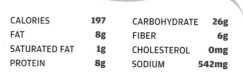

CALORIES	197	CARBOHYDRATE	26g
FAT	8g	FIBER	6g
SATURATED FAT	1g	CHOLESTEROL	0mg
PROTEIN	8g	SODIUM	542mg

chettinad vegetable aviyal

Serves 6

2 cups cubed unpeeled eggplant

1 cup peeled and cubed Idaho potato

1 cup unsweetened coconut powder

½ cup roasted chickpeas or peanuts

1 tablespoon fennel seeds

2 green chili peppers (more, if desired)

1 tablespoon melted butter

1 tablespoon canola oil

3 whole dry bay leaves

½ cup chopped onion

1 cup chopped tomato

½ teaspoon turmeric powder

1 teaspoon salt (more, if desired)

A potato and eggplant dish with a creamy texture, which is delicious served with idlis, dosais, plain rice, or even over pasta.

1. Immerse the cut vegetables separately in water to prevent vegetables darkening until they are ready to be cooked. Set aside.

2. Place in a blender coconut powder, chickpeas, fennel seeds, and green chili peppers together with 2 cups of hot water and grind the ingredients to a smooth paste.

3. Place melted butter and oil in a wide-bottomed sauce-pan. Heat over medium heat. When the oil is hot, but not smoking, add bay leaves. Heat until bay leaves become aromatic.

4. Add chopped onion and tomato and cook until onion becomes translucent. Add turmeric powder.

5. Drain potatoes and eggplant and add to ingredients in saucepan.

6. Add ground mixture from the blender together with 3 cups of water. Stir well. Add 1 teaspoon salt and stir. Cook over medium heat until potatoes and eggplant are tender.

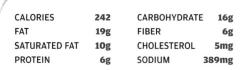

CALORIES	242	CARBOHYDRATE	16g
FAT	19g	FIBER	6g
SATURATED FAT	10g	CHOLESTEROL	5mg
PROTEIN	6g	SODIUM	389mg

green peas poriyal

Serves 2 to 4	1 package (10 to 16 ounces) frozen green peas	1 teaspoon urad dal	1 teaspoon chutney powder (optional)
	2 teaspoons canola oil	½ green chili pepper or 1 dried red chili pepper, chopped	1 tablespoon ground fresh coconut or unsweetened coconut powder
	2 or 3 curry leaves (optional)		
	1 teaspoon black mustard seeds	½ teaspoon salt (more, if desired)	

1. Cook green peas according to package directions. Set aside.

2. In a skillet, heat oil over medium heat. When oil is hot, but not smoking, add curry leaves, mustard seeds, and urad dal. Cover and fry until mustard seeds pop and urad dal is golden brown, about 30 seconds.

3. Add peas and chili pepper. Stir-fry for 1 minute.

4. Add salt and chutney powder and stir gently, being careful not to mash the peas.

5. Add the coconut powder and stir gently.

A green pea stir-fry that is a versatile side dish.

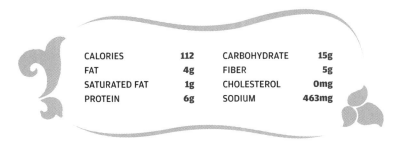

CALORIES	112	CARBOHYDRATE	15g
FAT	4g	FIBER	5g
SATURATED FAT	1g	CHOLESTEROL	0mg
PROTEIN	6g	SODIUM	463mg

lima beans masala

Serves 6

1 package (16 ounces) frozen baby lima beans (about 2 cups)

½ teaspoon turmeric powder

1 teaspoon salt

2 tablespoons canola oil

2 or 3 slivers cinnamon stick

1 teaspoon black mustard seeds

2 teaspoons urad dal

½ cup chopped onion

1 cup chopped tomato

½ teaspoon cayenne powder

½ teaspoon cumin powder

1 cup tomato sauce

2 tablespoons unsweetened coconut powder

Lima beans cooked with seasonings in tomato sauce are delicious served with any flavored rice dish, in particular Yogurt Rice (page 123). It also may be enjoyed as a sandwich filling for pita bread.

1. Cook lima beans in a saucepan with 1 cup of water, ¼ teaspoon turmeric powder, and ½ teaspoon salt until almost tender, approximately 3 minutes. Set aside but do not drain.

2. Place oil in a skillet over medium heat. When oil is hot, but not smoking, add pieces of cinnamon stick, mustard seeds, and urad dal. Cover and cook over medium heat until mustard seeds pop and urad dal is golden brown, about 30 seconds.

3. Add onion and tomato and stir for a few minutes. Add remaining ¼ teaspoon turmeric powder and stir well over medium heat.

4. Add cayenne and cumin powders and remaining ½ teaspoon salt and stir well. Add tomato sauce.

5. When mixture begins to boil, add undrained cooked lima beans and stir well. Cover and cook over medium heat until lima beans are tender.

6. Add coconut powder and stir well.

CALORIES	178	CARBOHYDRATE	27g
FAT	6g	FIBER	5g
SATURATED FAT	1g	CHOLESTEROL	0mg
PROTEIN	7g	SODIUM	645mg

lima beans poriyal

Serves 4 to 6	1 package (10 to 16 ounces) frozen baby or Fordhook (large) lima beans	4 to 6 curry leaves (optional)	1 teaspoon urad dal
	1 teaspoon salt	1 whole dried red chili pepper	1 teaspoon chutney powder
	1 teaspoon turmeric powder	1 teaspoon black mustard seeds	1 tablespoon unsweetened coconut powder
	2 tablespoons canola oil		

1. Bring 1 cup of water to a boil. Add frozen lima beans, ½ teaspoon salt, and ½ teaspoon turmeric powder. Reduce heat and cook gently until tender, 10 to 12 minutes. Drain. (You may also cook lima beans in microwave according to package directions.)

2. Place oil in a skillet over medium heat. When oil is hot, but not smoking, stir in curry leaves, red chili pepper, mustard seeds, and urad dal. Cover and fry until mustard seeds pop and urad dal is golden brown, about 30 seconds.

3. Add drained lima beans and remaining ½ teaspoon turmeric powder and mix well over medium heat.

4. Add remaining ½ teaspoon salt and chutney powder and stir. Add coconut powder and blend the seasonings well with lima beans.

An easy-to-prepare lima beans stir-fry, Lima Beans Poriyal can be served as a side dish for lunch or dinner.

variations   In the last step, you may add 1 cup of shredded carrots to make LIMA BEANS WITH CARROTS PORIYAL.

You may enhance the taste of Lima Beans Poriyal by adding ½ cup chopped fresh mango.

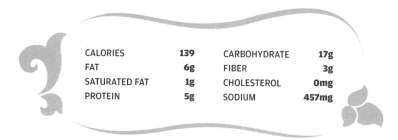

CALORIES	139	CARBOHYDRATE	17g
FAT	6g	FIBER	3g
SATURATED FAT	1g	CHOLESTEROL	0mg
PROTEIN	5g	SODIUM	457mg

mushroom and onion fry

Serves 4	2 cups fresh mushrooms (caps and stems)	1 cup sliced onion (cut lengthwise)	¼ teaspoon black pepper and cumin powder mixture (more, if desired)
	2 tablespoons canola oil	1 tablespoon minced garlic cloves	½ teaspoon salt
	1 teaspoon cumin seeds		

An innovative and easy-to-prepare stir-fry dish that complements any meal.

1. Wash mushrooms thoroughly. Cut into chunks of uniform size (halves or quarters).

2. Heat oil in a skillet over medium heat. When oil is hot, but not smoking, add cumin seeds. Fry until seeds are golden brown.

3. Add onion slices and garlic and mix well with ingredients in skillet.

4. Add mushrooms and toss with onions. Cook, uncovered, for a few minutes over medium-high heat until mushrooms are cooked.

5. Add black pepper and cumin powder and salt. Blend well with the ingredients in skillet.

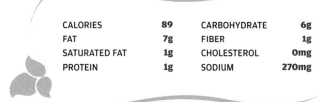

CALORIES	89	CARBOHYDRATE	6g
FAT	7g	FIBER	1g
SATURATED FAT	1g	CHOLESTEROL	0mg
PROTEIN	1g	SODIUM	270mg

mushroom masala

Serves 4

1 teaspoon canola oil

1 sliver cinnamon stick

1 dry bay leaf, crumbled

½ teaspoon cumin seeds

½ cup chopped onion

¼ cup chopped tomato

¼ cup tomato sauce

¼ teaspoon cayenne powder

½ teaspoon cumin powder

½ teaspoon salt

2 cups (8 ounces) fresh mushrooms, quartered

¼ cup chopped fresh coriander (cilantro) leaves

1. Place oil in a wok or iron skillet over medium heat. When oil is hot, but not smoking, add cinnamon, bay leaf, and cumin seeds. Immediately add the onion and tomato.

2. Stir-fry for a few minutes, then add tomato sauce, cayenne powder, cumin powder, and salt. When the mixture thickens, add mushrooms and stir well.

3. Cook mushrooms, uncovered, on low heat for 3 minutes. Add coriander, stir and serve.

Lightly seasoned mushrooms cooked in tomato sauce make a delicious side dish.

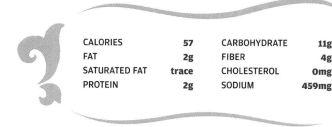
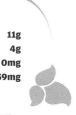

CALORIES	57	CARBOHYDRATE	11g
FAT	2g	FIBER	4g
SATURATED FAT	trace	CHOLESTEROL	0mg
PROTEIN	2g	SODIUM	459mg

okra masala

Serves 4	2 tablespoons canola oil	½ cup chopped onion	½ teaspoon cayenne powder (more, if desired)	2 cups sliced fresh or frozen okra
	¼ teaspoon asafoetida powder	½ cup chopped tomato	½ teaspoon cumin powder	1 tablespoon unsweetened coconut powder
	1 teaspoon black mustard seeds	½ teaspoon turmeric powder	½ cup tomato sauce	
	2 teaspoons urad dal		1 teaspoon salt	

Okra lightly seasoned and cooked with tomatoes, Okra Masala goes well with any flavored or plain rice dish.

1. Place oil in skillet over medium heat. When oil is hot, but not smoking, add asafoetida powder, mustard seeds, and urad dal. Cover and fry until mustard seeds pop and urad dal turns golden brown, about 30 seconds.

2. Add onion and tomato. Stir-fry for 1 minute. Add turmeric powder, cayenne powder, cumin powder, tomato sauce, and salt. Cook the seasonings with onion mixture for a minute or two.

3. Add okra and stir for a minute or two. Cover and cook over low heat until okra is tender.

4. Add coconut powder and cook for 1 more minute.

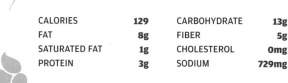

CALORIES	129	CARBOHYDRATE	13g
FAT	8g	FIBER	5g
SATURATED FAT	1g	CHOLESTEROL	0mg
PROTEIN	3g	SODIUM	729mg

okra pan-fried

Serves 4	3 cups fresh okra	1 teaspoon salt	1 teaspoon mustard seeds
	½ teaspoon turmeric powder	4 tablespoons canola oil	1 teaspoon urad dal
	1 teaspoon cayenne powder	½ teaspoon asafoetida powder	½ cup sliced onion (cut lengthwise)
	1 teaspoon cumin powder	4 to 6 curry leaves	½ cup chopped tomato

1. Wash okra, remove ends, and cut lengthwise. In a bowl, combine okra with turmeric powder, cayenne powder, cumin powder, and salt. Mix to coat well.

2. Heat oil in a skillet. When oil is hot, but not smoking, add asafoetida powder, curry leaves, mustard seeds, and urad dal. Cover and fry until mustard seeds pop and urad dal turns golden brown, about 30 seconds.

3. Add onion slices and tomato. Stir-fry for 1 minute.

4. Add coated okra. Cook over medium heat, stirring often, until okra is cooked, 5 to 6 minutes.

Lightly seasoned and pan-fried, this authentic okra specialty enhances any vegetarian meal.

CALORIES	170	CARBOHYDRATE	10g
FAT	14g	FIBER	4g
SATURATED FAT	2g	CHOLESTEROL	0mg
PROTEIN	2g	SODIUM	543mg

okra and potato fry

Serves 4	3 tablespoons canola oil	1 cup peeled and cubed potato	½ teaspoon cumin powder
	2 cups sliced okra	½ teaspoon cayenne powder	¼ teaspoon salt
	½ teaspoon turmeric powder		

This lightly seasoned and pan-fried combination of okra and potatoes can be served as a side dish with any meal.

1. Heat a skillet over medium heat. Add 2 tablespoons oil. When oil is hot but not smoking, add okra and ¼ teaspoon turmeric powder and pan-fry until desired crispness. Remove okra from skillet and set aside.

2. In the same skillet add another tablespoon oil and pan-fry potatoes with ¼ teaspoon turmeric powder to desired crispness.

3. When potatoes are cooked, add the okra to the pan. Add cayenne powder, cumin powder, and salt. Toss the seasonings well with potato and okra mixture.

CALORIES	142	CARBOHYDRATE	11g
FAT	11g	FIBER	2g
SATURATED FAT	1g	CHOLESTEROL	0mg
PROTEIN	2g	SODIUM	138mg

potato, okra and blackeye pea mundi

Serves 6

2 tablespoons canola oil

¼ teaspoon asafoetida powder

1 whole dried red chili pepper

4 to 6 curry leaves

1 teaspoon black mustard seeds

2 teaspoons urad dal

½ cup chopped onion

¼ cup peeled and quartered garlic cloves

¼ teaspoon turmeric powder

1 cup peeled and cubed Idaho potato

1 cup frozen blackeye peas

1 cup fresh or frozen sliced okra

½ cup chopped tomato

¼ teaspoon cayenne powder

½ teaspoon cumin powder

1 teaspoon tamarind paste

½ cup tomato sauce

½ teaspoon salt

1. Place oil in a saucepan and heat over medium heat. When oil is hot, but not smoking, add asafoetida powder, red chili pepper, curry leaves, mustard seeds, and urad dal. Cover and fry until mustard seeds pop and urad dal turns golden brown, about 30 seconds.

2. Add onion and garlic. Saute for a few minutes. Add turmeric powder and stir well.

3. Add potato, blackeye peas, okra, and tomato and stir well with the seasonings.

4. Add cayenne powder and cumin powder and mix well with vegetables over medium heat.

5. Mix tamarind paste with 2 cups of warm water and add to the potato mixture along with tomato sauce and salt. Stir well. Cover and cook over medium heat until all vegetables are tender.

A Chettinad specialty—blackeye peas, okra, and potatoes are cooked in an aromatic tamarind sauce.

NOTE   If the mixture thickens and the vegetables are not cooked, add another ½ cup of warm water. Stir and cook until vegetables are tender.

CALORIES	146	CARBOHYDRATE	21g
FAT	6g	FIBER	4g
SATURATED FAT	trace	CHOLESTEROL	0mg
PROTEIN	5g	SODIUM	309mg

madras potato poriyal

Serves 4

3 cups peeled and cubed Idaho potato

½ teaspoon turmeric powder

2 tablespoons canola oil

2 or 3 slivers cinnamon stick

1 dry bay leaf

1 teaspoon black mustard seeds

1 teaspoon urad dal

¾ cup sliced onion (cut lengthwise)

½ cup chopped tomato

¼ teaspoon cayenne powder

½ teaspoon cumin powder

½ cup tomato sauce

½ teaspoon salt (more, if desired)

¼ cup chopped fresh coriander (cilantro) leaves

An exquisitely seasoned dish, this culinary classic from Tamil Nadu is a wonderful accompaniment to any meal.

1. In a saucepan over medium heat, parboil cubed potatoes, uncovered, in 1½ cups water with ¼ teaspoon turmeric powder. When potatoes are half cooked, remove from heat and set aside. Do not drain any remaining water.

2. Place oil in a cast-iron skillet and heat over medium heat until oil is hot but not smoking. Add cinnamon sticks, bay leaf, mustard seeds, and urad dal. Cover and fry until mustard seeds pop and urad dal turns golden brown, about 30 seconds.

3. Add onion and tomato and sauté for a few minutes, stirring frequently.

4. Add remaining ¼ teaspoon turmeric powder, cayenne powder, cumin powder, and tomato sauce. Stir well.

5. Add potatoes with cooking water and gently stir into mixture in skillet.

6. Add salt and cook, covered, over medium heat until potatoes absorb tomato sauce and become thoroughly cooked. Add 1 to 2 tablespoons of water if the potatoes need to cook more and the mixture becomes too thick.

7. Add coriander and stir gently.

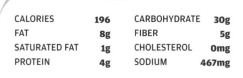

CALORIES	196	CARBOHYDRATE	30g
FAT	8g	FIBER	5g
SATURATED FAT	1g	CHOLESTEROL	0mg
PROTEIN	4g	SODIUM	467mg

potato curry for pooris

Serves 6

4 cups quartered Idaho potatoes

1½ teaspoons salt

1 teaspoon turmeric powder

2 tablespoons canola oil

1 dry bay leaf

2 or 3 slivers cinnamon stick

1 teaspoon black mustard seeds

1 teaspoon urad dal

1½ cups sliced onion (cut lengthwise)

½ cup chopped tomato

2 green chili peppers, finely chopped

1 tablespoon chopped ginger root

1 teaspoon curry powder

1 teaspoon lemon juice (optional)

¼ cup fresh coriander (cilantro) leaves

1. In a covered saucepan, boil potatoes in water just to cover with ½ teaspoon salt and ½ teaspoon turmeric powder for about ½ hour or until tender. Drain, peel, and mash potatoes. (Do not add milk). Set aside and keep warm. (Potatoes may also be cooked in a pressure cooker.)

2. Heat oil in skillet over medium heat. When oil is hot, but not smoking, crumble bay leaf and stick cinnamon into oil. Stir in mustard seeds and urad dal. Cover and fry until mustard seeds pop and urad dal is golden brown, about 30 seconds.

3. Immediately add onion slices, tomato, chili peppers, and ginger root. Cook, stirring, about 1 minute.

4. Stir in remaining ½ teaspoon turmeric powder. Add mashed potatoes and curry powder. Stir in about ¾ cup of water, remaining 1 teaspoon salt, and lemon juice. Add coriander and mix well. Cook over low to medium heat for 2 to 4 minutes.

5. Taste and add additional seasonings if desired.

Potatoes cooked with onions, tomatoes, and ginger, this dish is delicious served with pooris or chappatis.

NOTE   Potato curry may also be made thicker by eliminating water added in Step 4 and may then be used as a sandwich filling or with pita bread.

CALORIES	149	CARBOHYDRATE	25g
FAT	5g	FIBER	5g
SATURATED FAT	1g	CHOLESTEROL	0mg
PROTEIN	3g	SODIUM	546mg

potato kurma

Serves 6

½ cup ground fresh coconut or unsweetened coconut powder

3 green chili peppers (more, if desired)

10 raw almonds

1 tablespoon white poppy seeds (optional)

2 teaspoons cumin seeds

1 teaspoon fennel seeds

2 thick slices ginger root

1 tablespoon roasted chickpeas

2 tablespoons canola oil

4 to 6 curry leaves

1 dry bay leaf

3 or 4 slivers cinnamon stick

1 cup coarsely chopped onion

½ cup chopped tomato

4 cups peeled and cubed Idaho potato

½ teaspoon turmeric powder

1 teaspoon curry powder

1 teaspoon salt (more, if desired)

½ cup chopped fresh coriander (cilantro) leaves

Cooked in a delectable coconut-based sauce, Potato Kurma can be served over plain rice, Bell Pepper and Tomato Rice (page 109), Vegetable Biriyani Rice (page 121), and Tomato Rice (page 119), or with pooris and any other Indian breads.

variation To enhance the flavor of Potato Kurma, add 1 tablespoon of canola oil and 1 tablespoon of melted clarified butter (ghee) in Step 2.

1. In a blender put coconut powder, green chili peppers, almonds, white poppy seeds, 1 teaspoon cumin seeds, ½ teaspoon fennel seeds, ginger, and roasted chickpeas and grind with 2 cups hot water into a smooth paste.

2. Place oil in a wide-bottomed saucepan over medium heat. When canola oil is hot but not smoking, add curry leaves, bay leaf, cinnamon sticks, remaining 1 teaspoon cumin seeds and ½ teaspoon fennel seeds. Stir-fry to a golden brown.

3. Add onion and ¼ cup chopped tomato to saucepan and stir-fry for a few minutes.

4. Add potatoes and turmeric powder and stir well for 1 minute. Add curry powder. Blend the seasonings well with potatoes for a couple of minutes.

5. Add the ground spices from the blender to the potato mixture. Add salt and 2 cups of warm water and mix thoroughly.

6. When mixture begins to boil, reduce the heat to low. Add the remaining ¼ cup tomato and the coriander. Cover and cook until potatoes are tender.

CALORIES	101	CARBOHYDRATE	23g
FAT	trace	FIBER	4g
SATURATED FAT	trace	CHOLESTEROL	0mg
PROTEIN	3g	SODIUM	365mg

VARIATION WITH CANOLA OIL AND GHEE

CALORIES	137	CARBOHYDRATE	23g
FAT	5g	FIBER	4g
SATURATED FAT	3g	CHOLESTEROL	11mg
PROTEIN	3g	SODIUM	385mg

potato moong dal pachadi

Serves 4

½ cup moong dal

½ teaspoon turmeric powder

2 tablespoons canola oil

4 to 6 curry leaves

1 whole dried red chili pepper

¼ teaspoon asafoetida powder

1 teaspoon black mustard seeds

1 teaspoon urad dal

1 cup peeled and chopped potato

½ cup chopped tomato

½ teaspoon cayenne powder

½ teaspoon cumin powder

½ teaspoon salt

¼ cup chopped fresh coriander (cilantro) leaves

1. Bring 2 cups of water to a boil in a saucepan. Reduce heat to medium and add moong dal and ¼ teaspoon turmeric powder. Cook, uncovered, for 20 minutes until moong dal become soft. Do not drain. Set aside.

2. Place oil in a small saucepan over medium heat. When oil is hot, but not smoking, add curry leaves, red chili pepper, asafoetida powder, mustard seeds, and urad dal. Cover and fry over medium heat until mustard seeds pop and urad dal turns golden brown, about 30 seconds.

3. Immediately add potato and tomato. Stir well with the seasonings.

4. Add remaining ¼ teaspoon turmeric powder, cayenne powder, cumin powder, and salt, and mix well with vegetables.

5. Add cooked moong dal with 2 cups of warm water to the mixture and stir well. When the mixture begins to bubble, add coriander and let simmer until potatoes are cooked.

Potatoes and tomatoes cooked in moong dal and simmered with fresh coriander, this pachadi is delicious served over plain rice, or as an accompaniment to most Indian vegetables, rice dishes, and breads.

CALORIES	207	CARBOHYDRATE	29g
FAT	7g	FIBER	6g
SATURATED FAT	1g	CHOLESTEROL	0mg
PROTEIN	8g	SODIUM	280mg

potato masala

Serves 4 to 6	2 medium to large Idaho potatoes with skins, cut in half	¼ teaspoon asafoetida powder	1 cup chopped onion	¼ teaspoon cayenne powder (more, if desired)
	½ teaspoon turmeric powder	3 or 4 curry leaves (optional)	½ cup chopped tomato	¼ cup minced fresh coriander (cilantro) leaves
	1 teaspoon salt	1 teaspoon black mustard seeds	1 green chili pepper, chopped	
	2 tablespoons canola oil	1½ teaspoons urad dal	1 tablespoon minced fresh ginger root	

A seasoned stir-fry dish, Potato Masala makes a delicious filling for samosas, bondas, and Masala Dosais. It may also be served with pooris or chappatis, or as a side dish with any type of rice.

1. Cook potatoes in sufficient water to cover in a covered saucepan over medium heat with ¼ teaspoon turmeric and ½ teaspoon salt for approximately 20 minutes or until potatoes become soft. Drain, peel, and coarsely chop potatoes; set aside.

2. In a cast-iron skillet, heat oil over medium heat. When oil is hot, but not smoking, add asafoetida powder, curry leaves, mustard seeds, and urad dal. Cover and fry until mustard seeds pop and urad dal is golden brown, about 30 seconds.

3. Add onion, tomato, green chili pepper, and ginger root. Stir-fry for 1 minute. Add the remaining ¼ teaspoon turmeric powder, ½ teaspoon salt, and cayenne powder. Stir well.

4. Add potatoes and stir gently with ingredients in skillet. Cover and cook over medium heat for 2 to 3 minutes, so flavors will blend well. Taste for seasonings and add more salt, if desired. Add coriander and mix well.

CALORIES	122	CARBOHYDRATE	16g
FAT	6g	FIBER	2g
SATURATED FAT	1g	CHOLESTEROL	0mg
PROTEIN	3g	SODIUM	437mg

potatoes roasted with garlic and tomatoes

Serves 4	2 Idaho potatoes	¾ teaspoon cayenne powder	4 or 5 curry leaves (optional)	2 peeled garlic cloves, chopped
	½ teaspoon turmeric powder	4 tablespoons canola oil	1 teaspoon black mustard seeds	2 tablespoons unsweetened coconut powder
	½ teaspoon salt (more, if desired)	½ teaspoon asafoetida powder	2 teaspoons urad dal	
			1 tomato, chopped	

1. Thoroughly wash raw potatoes. Cut each potato in half with skin on. Then cut each half into quarters and next cut quarters into slices approximately ¼-inch thick.

2. Place potato pieces in a large bowl. Sprinkle with turmeric powder, salt, and cayenne powder. Toss potato pieces in bowl to cover evenly with spices.

3. Pour oil into a cast-iron skillet over medium heat. When oil is hot, but not smoking, add asafoetida powder, curry leaves, mustard seeds, and urad dal. Stir briefly and cover. Fry until mustard seeds pop and the urad dal is golden brown, about 30 seconds.

4. Add the seasoned potato pieces to skillet. Cook, covered, over low-medium heat for a few minutes. Add tomato and garlic to the potatoes and cover and cook over medium-low heat until potatoes are tender. Be certain to stir the potatoes every few minutes to prevent sticking.

5. Uncover skillet when potatoes are tender and continue to fry over low heat until potatoes become crisp, stirring frequently. Add coconut powder and stir gently.

Pan-fried with garlic and tomatoes, these potatoes are an excellent accompaniment to any flavored rice or vegetable dishes.

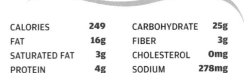

CALORIES	249	CARBOHYDRATE	25g
FAT	16g	FIBER	3g
SATURATED FAT	3g	CHOLESTEROL	0mg
PROTEIN	4g	SODIUM	278mg

seasoned roasted potatoes

Serves 4	2 cups peeled and cubed Idaho potato (1-inch cubes)	½ teaspoon cayenne powder (more, if desired)	4 or 5 curry leaves
	¼ teaspoon turmeric powder	½ teaspoon cumin powder	¼ teaspoon asafoetida powder
	½ teaspoon salt	3 tablespoons canola oil	

Lightly seasoned and pan-fried, these potatoes are particularly delicious served with any flavored rice dish.

1. Place potatoes in a small saucepan. Add water just to cover potatoes and bring to a boil. Do not cover saucepan. After the water begins to boil, reduce heat and add turmeric powder and salt to the potatoes. Parboil until potatoes are half-cooked. Be careful not to overcook them. Drain and place in a small bowl.

2. Sprinkle cayenne powder and cumin powder over potatoes and shake bowl to coat them evenly.

3. Place oil in a cast-iron skillet over medium heat. When oil is hot, but not smoking, add curry leaves and asafoetida powder.

4. Add seasoned potatoes to skillet and spread evenly. Cook over low heat until golden brown, turning frequently.

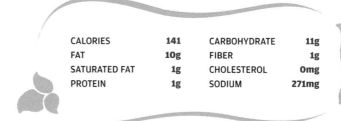

CALORIES	141	CARBOHYDRATE	11g
FAT	10g	FIBER	1g
SATURATED FAT	1g	CHOLESTEROL	0mg
PROTEIN	1g	SODIUM	271mg

sweet potato masiyal

Serves 2	1 sweet potato, peeled and sliced (about 1 cup)	¼ teaspoon turmeric powder	¼ cup chopped fresh coriander (cilantro) leaves
	2 teaspoons canola oil	¼ teaspoon garam masala powder	
	1 teaspoon cumin seeds	¼ teaspoon salt (more, if desired)	
	¼ cup chopped onion		

1. Boil sweet potato in a saucepan with enough water to cover until tender. (You may also cook sweet potato in a microwave oven with about ½ cup of water for 5 to 6 minutes.) When potato is tender, drain and mash with a masher or with a fork.

2. Heat saucepan over medium heat and add oil. When oil is hot, but not smoking, add cumin seeds and stir-fry until brown. Add onion and sauté for a few minutes.

3. Add mashed sweet potato and turmeric powder and stir well.

4. Add garam masala powder and salt and stir well for a few minutes.

5. Add chopped coriander. Stir briefly and serve.

Mashed sweet potatoes, delicately seasoned, are delicious as a side dish with any meal.

NOTE Yams may be substituted for the sweet potatoes in this recipe. The taste will be similar to that of the sweet potatoes, but the nutritional value will be somewhat reduced.

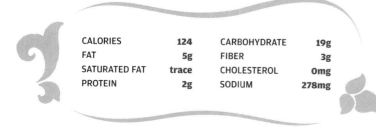

CALORIES	124	CARBOHYDRATE	19g
FAT	5g	FIBER	3g
SATURATED FAT	trace	CHOLESTEROL	0mg
PROTEIN	2g	SODIUM	278mg

sweet potato poriyal

Serves 4

2 cups peeled and sliced sweet potato (¼ inch thick)

1 tablespoon canola oil

1 whole dried red chili pepper

1 teaspoon black mustard seeds

1½ teaspoons urad dal

¼ teaspoon turmeric powder

1 teaspoon chutney powder

½ teaspoon salt

1 tablespoon coconut powder

¼ cup roasted walnut halves for garnish (optional)

Sweet potatoes lightly seasoned and garnished with coconut is a delicious easy dish that can be served as a side dish.

1. Put sweet potato slices in a heat-proof bowl and cover them with ½ cup water. Microwave on high heat for 5 minutes or until tender. (You can also cook the potatoes by boiling.) Drain.

2. Add oil to a skillet and heat over medium heat. When oil is hot, but not smoking, add red chili pepper, mustard seeds, and urad dal. Cover and heat until mustard seeds pop and urad dal turns golden brown, about 30 seconds.

3. Add cooked sweet potato slices, together with turmeric powder and chutney powder. Mix gently with ingredients in the skillet.

4. Add salt and stir well. Garnish with coconut powder and (if desired) roasted walnut halves.

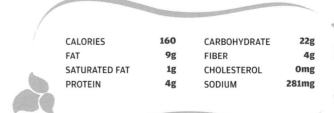

CALORIES	160	CARBOHYDRATE	22g
FAT	9g	FIBER	4g
SATURATED FAT	1g	CHOLESTEROL	0mg
PROTEIN	4g	SODIUM	281mg

seasoned fresh spinach in yogurt

Serves 4

1 teaspoon canola oil

1 teaspoon cumin seeds

½ cup chopped onion

½ green chili pepper, chopped (more, if desired)

1 tablespoon minced garlic clove

6 ounces baby spinach (field fresh in ready to use package), chopped

1 teaspoon cumin powder

¼ teaspoon salt

1 cup nonfat plain yogurt

1. In a skillet or wok, heat oil over medium heat. When oil is hot, but not smoking, add cumin seeds and stir until they become light brown.

2. Add onion, chili pepper, and garlic. Stir-fry for a minute or two.

3. Add chopped spinach and mix well with seasonings. Add cumin powder and salt. Cook spinach until it is slightly wilted. Transfer the spinach mixture to a bowl. Let it cool.

4. Add yogurt to the spinach and mix well. Refrigerate until ready to use.

This spinach dish can be served as a dip with appetizers, or as a side dish with a main meal, or with any bread.

variation You may add 1 tablespoon unsweetened coconut powder for a delicious variation.

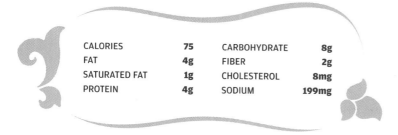

CALORIES	75	CARBOHYDRATE	8g
FAT	4g	FIBER	2g
SATURATED FAT	1g	CHOLESTEROL	8mg
PROTEIN	4g	SODIUM	199mg

spinach kootu

Serves 6	½ cup yellow split-peas or moong dal	1 whole dried red chili pepper	4 garlic cloves, finely chopped	1 teaspoon cumin powder
	¼ teaspoon turmeric powder	1 teaspoon black mustard seeds	1 package (10 ounces) frozen chopped spinach, thawed	1 teaspoon salt
	2 tablespoons canola oil	1 teaspoon urad dal		1 green chili pepper, chopped (optional)
		¼ cup chopped onion		

Spinach blended with creamy split peas, garlic, and cumin, Spinach Kootu is delicious served over plain rice. Its mild, delicate taste will enhance any meal.

NOTE   To make Spinach Kootu with a creamier consistency increase yellow split peas or moong dal in the above recipe to ¾ cup and cook with an additional ½ cup of water.

variation   For a hearty enhancement, you may add ½ cup frozen baby lima beans (uncooked) to the spinach in Step 4 to create SPINACH AND LIMA BEAN KOOTU. You may also add an additional ½ cup water and ½ teaspoon cumin powder if desired.

1. Bring 4 cups of water to a boil. Add yellow split peas and turmeric powder. Reduce heat to medium high and cook, uncovered, for about 30 minutes until split peas become creamy. If water evaporates during the cooking process, add another cup of water and cook until split peas become creamy. Set aside.

2. Heat oil in a saucepan over medium heat. When oil is hot, but not smoking, stir in red chili pepper, mustard seeds, and urad dal. Cover and fry until mustard seeds pop and urad dal is golden brown, about 30 seconds.

3. Add onion and garlic. Stir-fry for about 1 minute.

4. Stir in thawed spinach. Add cooked split pea mixture and 1 cup of warm water and stir.

5. Add cumin powder, salt, and green chili pepper, if desired, to spinach mixture. Blend well with ingredients in saucepan.

6. Cover and cook over low heat for another 5 to 7 minutes, until spinach is cooked and all ingredients are thoroughly blended.

CALORIES	113	CARBOHYDRATE	16g
FAT	5g	FIBER	7g
SATURATED FAT	1g	CHOLESTEROL	0mg
PROTEIN	7g	SODIUM	403mg

spinach poriyal

Serves 4

½ cup dry yellow split peas or moong dal	1 whole dried red chili pepper	1 package (10 ounces) frozen chopped spinach
¼ teaspoon turmeric powder	1 teaspoon black mustard seeds	1 teaspoon salt
2 tablespoons canola oil	1 teaspoon urad dal	2 tablespoons ground fresh coconut or unsweetened coconut powder (optional)
	1 cup chopped onion	

1. Bring about 2 cups of water to a boil in a saucepan. Add yellow split peas or moong dal and turmeric powder and cook, uncovered, for about 20 minutes over medium heat, until split peas are semi-soft. If water evaporates before split peas or dal become tender, add an additional ¼ cup of water. When split peas are tender, drain and set aside.

2. Heat oil with whole red chili pepper in a skillet over medium heat. When oil is hot, but not smoking, stir in mustard seeds and urad dal. Cover and fry until mustard seeds pop and urad dal is golden brown, about 30 seconds.

3. Add onion and stir for 1 minute.

4. Add frozen spinach and ½ cup water. Blend well with mixture in skillet. Add salt. Cover and cook over medium heat approximately 5 minutes until spinach is tender, stirring occasionally.

5. Add drained split peas to spinach mixture and blend thoroughly.

6. Sprinkle with coconut powder. Stir briefly and serve.

Spinach stir-fried with split peas and coconut, Spinach Poriyal is excellent served with rice or chappatis. You may also use it to stuff mushrooms (see page 46) or as a unique topping for crackers.

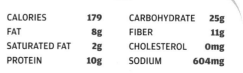

CALORIES	179	CARBOHYDRATE	25g
FAT	8g	FIBER	11g
SATURATED FAT	2g	CHOLESTEROL	0mg
PROTEIN	10g	SODIUM	604mg

sugar snap peas poriyal

Serves 4

2 cups sugar snap pea pods

1 tablespoon canola oil

1 teaspoon black mustard seeds

2 teaspoons urad dal

½ teaspoon chutney powder

½ teaspoon salt

¾ cup sliced onion (cut lengthwise)

2 tablespoons ground fresh coconut or unsweetened coconut powder

An innovative easy-to-prepare stir-fry, Sugar Snap Peas Poriyal goes well with most dishes.

1. Remove ends of pea pods and peel off strings. Wash thoroughly.

2. Add oil to a saucepan and heat over medium heat. When oil is hot, but not smoking, add mustard seeds and urad dal. Cover and heat until mustard seeds pop and urad dal is golden brown, about 30 seconds.

3. Reduce heat to low and add snap pea pods. Add chutney powder and salt and stir well. Cover and cook over low heat until just tender, about 3 minutes.

4. Add onion slices and coconut powder. Cook for a few more minutes. Onion slices should remain crisp. Stir well and serve with rice or bread.

variation Cooked moong dal will enhance the taste of the above recipe: Cook ¼ cup of moong dal in 1 cup of water with ¼ teaspoon turmeric powder for about 10 minutes until dal becomes tender. Add cooked moong dal to the recipe in Step 5.

CALORIES	75	CARBOHYDRATE	7g
FAT	5g	FIBER	2g
SATURATED FAT	1g	CHOLESTEROL	0mg
PROTEIN	2g	SODIUM	269mg

tomato moong dal pachadi

Serves 4	¼ cup moong dal	1 whole dried red chili pepper	1 teaspoon urad dal	½ teaspoon cumin powder
	½ teaspoon turmeric powder	¼ teaspoon asafoetida powder	1 cup chopped tomato	½ teaspoon salt
	2 tablespoons canola oil	1 teaspoon black mustard seeds	¼ teaspoon cayenne powder or ½ green chili pepper, chopped	¼ cup chopped fresh coriander (cilantro) leaves
	2 to 4 curry leaves			

1. Bring 2 cups of water to a boil in a saucepan. Reduce heat to medium and add moong dal with ¼ teaspoon turmeric powder. Cook, uncovered, for about 20 minutes until moong dal becomes soft. Set aside.

2. In a small saucepan heat oil over medium heat. When oil is hot, but not smoking, add curry leaves, red chili pepper, asafoetida powder, mustard seeds, and urad dal. Cover and fry over medium heat until mustard seeds pop and urad dal turns golden brown, about 30 seconds.

3. Immediately add tomato and stir well with the seasonings. Add remaining ¼ teaspoon turmeric powder, cayenne powder, cumin powder, and salt. Mix well.

4. Add cooked moong dal with 2 cups of warm water to the above mixture and let it simmer over low heat for about 2 minutes. Add coriander and let simmer for a few additional minutes.

Tomatoes and coriander simmered with moong dal, this versatile pachadi goes well with plain rice, Yogurt Rice (page 123), or any Indian breads.

215

vegetables

HEALTHY SOUTH INDIAN COOKING

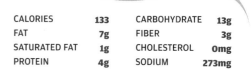

CALORIES	133	CARBOHYDRATE	13g
FAT	7g	FIBER	3g
SATURATED FAT	1g	CHOLESTEROL	0mg
PROTEIN	4g	SODIUM	273mg

vegetable kurma

Serves 6	½ cup ground fresh coconut or unsweetened coconut powder	1 teaspoon fennel seeds	3 or 4 slivers cinnamon sticks	1 teaspoon American curry powder
		2 thick slices ginger root	1 cup chopped onion	½ cup green peas (fresh or frozen)
	1 green chili pepper (more, if desired)	1 tablespoon roasted chickpeas	1 cup chopped tomato	1 cup cauliflower florets
	12 raw almonds	2 tablespoons canola oil	2 cups peeled and cubed Idaho potato	½ teaspoon salt (more, if desired)
	1 tablespoon white poppy seeds, optional	6 to 8 curry leaves	½ cup peeled and thinly sliced carrots	½ cup chopped fresh coriander (cilantro) leaves
	2 teaspoons cumin seeds	1 dry bay leaf	½ teaspoon turmeric powder	

Vegetables cooked in a coconut almond sauce is a lavish Chettinad specialty! Serve with any rice or bread.

1. In a blender put coconut powder, green chili pepper, almonds, white poppy seeds, 1 teaspoon cumin seeds, ½ teaspoon fennel seeds, ginger root slices, and chickpeas. Add 2 cups of hot water and grind the ingredients to a smooth paste.

2. Heat oil in a wide-bottom saucepan over medium heat. When oil is hot, but not smoking, add curry leaves, bay leaf, cinnamon sticks, remaining 1 teaspoon cumin seeds, and remaining ½ teaspoon fennel seeds. Cover and fry to a golden brown.

3. Add onion and ½ cup of the chopped tomato to saucepan and stir-fry for a few minutes until onion is lightly translucent.

4. Add potato and carrots to saucepan. Add turmeric powder and stir well.

5. Add curry powder and stir-fry for a minute or two.

6. Add peas and cauliflower to mixture and stir-fry for a couple of minutes.

7. Add ground spices from the blender to vegetable mixture in saucepan plus 2 cups of warm water. Mix thoroughly.

8. When the mixture begins to boil, reduce heat. Add remaining ½ cup chopped tomato, salt, and coriander. Cover and cook about 10 minutes or until potatoes are tender.

CALORIES	197	CARBOHYDRATE	25g
FAT	10g	FIBER	7g
SATURATED FAT	5g	CHOLESTEROL	0mg
PROTEIN	5g	SODIUM	205mg

madras vegetable medley

Serves 6	1 package (16 ounces) frozen lima beans (2 cups)	1 teaspoon black mustard seeds	1 teaspoon chutney powder (more, if desired)
	2 tablespoons canola oil	2 teaspoons urad dal	1 cup cauliflower florets
	4 to 6 curry leaves	1 cup peeled and thinly sliced beets	2 tablespoons ground fresh coconut or unsweetened coconut powder
	2 to 4 slivers cinnamon sticks	½ teaspoon salt (more, if desired)	

An innovative and colorful stir-fry of beets, cauliflower, and lima beans, Madras Vegetable Medley is easy to make and is a delightful accompaniment to any meal.

1. Cook frozen lima beans according to package directions, about 10 minutes. Set aside.

2. Place oil in a wok or cast-iron skillet over medium heat. When oil is hot, but not smoking, add curry leaves, cinnamon sticks, mustard seeds, and urad dal. Cover and fry until mustard seeds pop and urad dal is golden brown, about 30 seconds.

3. Add beets and lima beans together with salt and chutney powder. Blend well and cook, covered, over medium heat for a few minutes.

4. Add cauliflower and continue cooking, covered, for a few more minutes until vegetables are tender.

5. Add coconut powder and stir well.

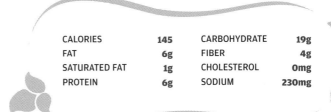

CALORIES	145	CARBOHYDRATE	19g
FAT	6g	FIBER	4g
SATURATED FAT	1g	CHOLESTEROL	0mg
PROTEIN	6g	SODIUM	230mg

mixed vegetable poriyal

Serves 4

- 3 tablespoons canola oil
- 2 or 3 slivers cinnamon stick
- 1 dry bay leaf, crumbled
- 1 teaspoon black mustard seeds
- 2 teaspoons urad dal
- ½ cup chopped onion
- ½ cup finely chopped tomato
- ¼ teaspoon turmeric powder
- 1 cup peeled and cubed Idaho potato (1-inch cubes)
- 1 package (16 ounces) frozen baby lima beans (2 cups)
- 1 cup tomato sauce
- ¼ cup peeled and thinly sliced beets
- ¼ cup brussels sprouts, quartered
- ½ teaspoon cayenne powder
- 1 teaspoon cumin powder
- 1 teaspoon salt
- 2 tablespoons unsweetened coconut powder

1. Heat oil in a cast-iron skillet over medium heat. When oil is hot, but not smoking, add cinnamon sticks, bay leaf, mustard seeds, and urad dal. Cover and heat until mustard seeds pop and urad dal is golden brown, about 30 seconds.

2. Add onion and tomato. Stir and cook briefly. Add turmeric powder and mix well.

3. Add potato and lima beans and stir well with seasonings for few minutes. Stir in tomato sauce.

4. Add beets and brussels sprouts. Stir well.

5. Add cayenne powder, cumin powder, and salt. Blend the seasonings well with the vegetables. Cook, covered, over medium heat until vegetables are tender.

6. Add about 1 cup of warm water so that the vegetables cook without sticking to the bottom of the skillet. Blend carefully. **Note:** *Be certain not to overcook or mash the vegetables.*

7. Add coconut powder. Stir briefly and immediately remove from heat.

This colorful stir-fry dish is made with potatoes, beets, brussels sprouts, and lima beans lightly seasoned and cooked in tomato sauce. It can be served as a side dish with any meal or used to make vegetable wraps.

NOTE Leftovers can be refrigerated and may be used to make vegetable wraps with any type of tortillas or pita bread. Serve them for lunch.

CALORIES	201	CARBOHYDRATE	27g
FAT	9g	FIBER	5g
SATURATED FAT	2g	CHOLESTEROL	0mg
PROTEIN	6g	SODIUM	641mg

kerala aviyal

Serves 4

2 cups peeled and cubed Idaho potato (1½ x ½ inch cubes)

½ cup peeled and cubed carrots (cut same size as potato)

½ cup green beans, cut in half same length as potato

1 cup Fordhook (large) lima beans

½ teaspoon turmeric powder

1 teaspoon salt (more, if desired)

1 green bell pepper

¼ cup ground fresh coconut or unsweetened coconut powder

2 teaspoons cumin seeds

1½ tablespoons minced fresh ginger root

3 green chili peppers (more, if desired)

¾ cup buttermilk

¼ cup fat-free yogurt

1 tablespoon coconut oil

4 to 6 curry leaves

Mixed vegetables cooked with coconut and spices are a Kerala specialty.

1. In a large saucepan place potato, carrots, green beans, and lima beans with enough water to cover vegetables. Stir in turmeric powder and salt. Cook vegetables, covered, over medium heat until tender, about 10 minutes. Add more water if needed. (Be careful not to overcook the vegetables.) Drain and set aside.

2. Cut bell pepper lengthwise into strips the same size as the potato and set aside.

3. Place coconut powder, cumin seeds, ginger root, and chili peppers in blender with buttermilk. Grind to a coarse consistency and pour over vegetables in saucepan. Stir gently.

4. Add bell pepper and cook over low heat until ingredients are cooked through. Remove saucepan from heat.

5. Add yogurt and stir gently.

6. Heat coconut oil in a butter warmer. When oil is hot, but not smoking, add curry leaves and pour over the vegetables, then gently stir.

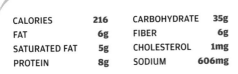

CALORIES	216	CARBOHYDRATE	35g
FAT	6g	FIBER	6g
SATURATED FAT	5g	CHOLESTEROL	1mg
PROTEIN	8g	SODIUM	606mg

zucchini kootu

Serves 4	½ cup toor dal	1 teaspoon black mustard seeds	1 teaspoon minced fresh ginger root
	½ teaspoon turmeric powder	1 teaspoon urad dal	1 teaspoon cumin powder
	2 tablespoons canola oil	¼ cup chopped onion	1 teaspoon salt
	¼ teaspoon asafoetida powder	1 green chili pepper, chopped	1 tablespoon unsweetened coconut powder
	4 to 6 curry leaves (optional)	3 cups peeled and cubed zucchini	

1. Bring 4 cups of water to a boil. Add toor dal and ¼ teaspoon turmeric powder. Reduce heat to medium high. Cook, uncovered, for about 30 minutes until dal becomes creamy. If water evaporates during the cooking process, add another cup of water and cook until dal becomes creamy. Set aside.

2. Heat oil in a saucepan over medium heat. When oil is hot, but not smoking, add asafoetida powder, curry leaves, mustard seeds, and urad dal. Cover and cook until mustard seeds pop and urad dal turns golden brown, about 30 seconds.

3. Add onion, chili pepper, and remaining ¼ teaspoon turmeric powder. Add zucchini and ginger root and blend well.

4. Add creamy toor dal, cumin powder, and salt. Add ¾ cup of warm water. Stir well for 1 to 2 minutes.

5. Cover and simmer until zucchini is tender, about 5 minutes. Add coconut powder. Stir and cook for an additional minute.

As with other kootus cooked with creamy lentils, Zucchini Kootu is a mild and flavorful accompaniment to any meal.

variation You may also use moong dal instead of toor dal.

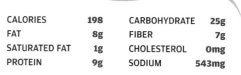

CALORIES	198	CARBOHYDRATE	25g
FAT	8g	FIBER	7g
SATURATED FAT	1g	CHOLESTEROL	0mg
PROTEIN	9g	SODIUM	543mg

nonvegetarian dishes

chicken biriyani rice

Serves 6

1 recipe Garlic and Pepper Chicken (page 232)

3 tablespoons butter

2 or 3 slivers cinnamon stick

1 dry bay leaf

3 or 4 curry leaves (optional)

2 cups basmati rice, rinsed and drained

¼ teaspoon turmeric powder

4 to 6 whole cloves

1 teaspoon cardamom powder

1 tablespoon minced fresh ginger root

¼ teaspoon garam masala powder

2 or 3 saffron threads

1 teaspoon salt (more, if desired)

¼ cup chopped fresh coriander (cilantro) leaves

½ cup sliced red onion (cut lengthwise)

½ cup roasted cashew pieces

Biriyani is a highly aromatic and elaborate basmati rice dish that can be either vegetarian or nonvegetarian. Chicken Biriyani Rice is a delicious accompaniment to Chettinad Chicken Kurma (page 228), Egg Masala (page 235), and any of the yogurt salads.

1. Prepare Garlic and Pepper Chicken and set aside. Preheat oven to 350 degrees.

2. Melt butter in a large nonstick, wide-bottomed saucepan over medium heat. Add cinnamon sticks, bay leaf, and curry leaves. Add basmati rice. Stir-fry for 4 to 5 minutes, until rice becomes slightly toasted.

3. Add turmeric powder, whole cloves, ½ teaspoon cardamom powder, ginger root, and 4 cups of hot water.

4. Reduce heat to low. Immediately add garam masala powder, saffron threads, salt, and coriander. Stir well. Heat, uncovered, until mixture reaches the boiling point.

5. Cover saucepan and continue cooking over low heat until all liquid evaporates and rice is tender. When rice is cooked, set aside to cool for a few minutes.

6. Add prepared chicken to rice and fluff the rice gently.

7. Add remaining cardamom and red onion and fluff the rice gently. Taste to see if the seasonings are right.

8. To complete the biriyani rice, transfer the rice with chicken into a rectangular baking dish. Sprinkle top with cashew pieces. Cover the dish with aluminum foil. Place in oven for about 30 minutes to heat through and to maximize the aromatic flavor of rice.

CALORIES	349	CARBOHYDRATE	52g
FAT	13g	FIBER	3g
SATURATED FAT	5g	CHOLESTEROL	16mg
PROTEIN	8g	SODIUM	471mg

chettinad chicken chops

Serves 4	1 pound (or 6 pieces) boneless, skinless chicken thighs	¼ cup chopped tomato	2 teaspoons cumin powder	EGG BATTER
	1 tablespoon canola oil	1 tablespoon finely minced garlic clove	½ teaspoon salt	2 eggs
	⅓ cup finely chopped onion	¼ teaspoon turmeric powder	½ cup tomato sauce	½ teaspoon salt
		½ teaspoon cayenne powder	oil for frying	½ teaspoon turmeric powder

1. Cut each thigh in half. Wash chicken pieces, drain, and set aside.

2. Add oil to a cast-iron skillet over medium heat. When oil is hot, but not smoking, add onion, tomato, and garlic and sauté for a few minutes until the vegetables become tender.

3. Add chicken pieces and brown.

4. Add turmeric powder and stir well. Add cayenne powder, cumin powder, and salt.

5. Add tomato sauce with 2 tablespoons of water. Continue to cook chicken in sauce over medium heat, covered, stirring frequently, being careful to spoon sauce over chicken as it cooks. When chicken is cooked, remove from sauce and place on a platter.

6. The sauce remaining in skillet can be transferred to a small serving bowl and served over rice or pasta. Garnish with fresh coriander for extra flavor.

7. Set a platter, lined with paper towels, beside the stove to hold fried chicken chops.

8. Beat eggs with salt and turmeric powder. Dip chicken pieces in egg batter. Heat oil in a skillet or wok and fry a few pieces at a time. When pieces are fried thoroughly, about 1 minute each side, set aside on the platter. Serve warm.

Boneless, skinless chicken thighs simmered in a seasoned tomato sauce and lightly fried, chicken chops are a distinctly satisfying accompaniment to any rice and vegetable dish.

CALORIES	340	CARBOHYDRATE	5g
FAT	22g	FIBER	1g
SATURATED FAT	3g	CHOLESTEROL	160mg
PROTEIN	30g	SODIUM	771mg

chettinad chicken kulambu

Serves 4

3 tablespoons canola oil

2 or 3 slivers cinnamon stick

1 dry bay leaf, crumbled

¼ teaspoon fennel seeds

½ teaspoon cumin seeds

½ cup chopped onion

¼ cup chopped tomato

3 garlic cloves, peeled and quartered

1 tablespoon minced ginger root

¼ teaspoon turmeric powder

2 pounds boneless, skinless chicken breasts or thighs

2 teaspoons curry powder

1 teaspoon cayenne powder

1 teaspoon garam masala powder

1 cup tomato sauce

½ teaspoon black pepper and cumin powder mixture

1 teaspoon salt

¼ cup chopped fresh coriander (cilantro) leaves

Slow-cooked in an aromatic sauce seasoned with garlic and ginger, Chicken Kulambu is delicious served over plain rice or accompanied by chappatis. This South Indian specialty is comparable to the well-known Vindaloo Chicken dish.

variations You may also use bone-in chicken thighs or breasts to make Chicken Kulambu.

You may substitute cornish hen for the chicken to make CORNISH HEN KULAMBU. Cut the cornish hen into 4 to 6 small pieces and proceed with the recipe.

1. Heat oil in a wide saucepan over medium heat. When oil is hot, but not smoking, add cinnamon sticks, bay leaf, fennel seeds, and cumin seeds.

2. Add onion, tomato, garlic, and ginger and sauté for a few minutes. Add turmeric powder.

3. Cut chicken into small stew-size pieces. Add chicken pieces to saucepan and continue to sauté for several minutes until chicken turns opaque.

4. Add curry powder, cayenne powder, garam masala powder, and tomato sauce. Stir in black pepper and cumin powder. Add salt, cover, and continue cooking over medium-low heat for several minutes, stirring often.

5. Add coriander. Reduce heat to low. Cover and cook, stirring often, until chicken is tender, about 20 minutes. If the sauce becomes too thick, you may add small amounts of both water and tomato sauce as desired.

CALORIES	305	CARBOHYDRATE	13g
FAT	17g	FIBER	4g
SATURATED FAT	2g	CHOLESTEROL	108mg
PROTEIN	28g	SODIUM	1060mg

chettinad chicken masala

Serves 4

2 pounds chicken pieces (about 6 thighs or halved breasts)

4 tablespoons canola oil

4 to 6 curry leaves (optional)

2 to 4 slivers cinnamon stick

1 dry bay leaf

¼ teaspoon whole black peppercorns

¼ teaspoon fennel seeds

½ teaspoon cumin seeds

1 cup chopped onion

¼ cup chopped tomato

6 garlic cloves, chopped

1 heaping tablespoon minced ginger root

½ teaspoon turmeric powder

1½ teaspoons curry powder

¾ teaspoon cayenne powder

1 teaspoon salt

¾ teaspoon black pepper and cumin powder mixture

1 cup tomato sauce

1. Wash chicken thoroughly and remove skin. Chicken parts may be used whole or cut into smaller pieces. Set aside.

2. Place oil in a wide-bottomed iron skillet and heat over medium heat. When oil is hot, but not smoking, add curry leaves, cinnamon sticks, bay leaf, and peppercorns. Cover and heat until peppercorns pop.

3. Add fennel and cumin seeds. Fry until cumin seeds become brown.

4. Add onion, tomato, garlic, ginger root, and turmeric powder and stir well. Stir-fry until onions are tender.

5. Add chicken pieces. Brown well and cook on high heat until chicken become opaque (partially cooked). Reduce heat.

6. Add curry powder, cayenne powder, salt, and black pepper and cumin powder. Stir well. Add tomato sauce and stir.

7. Cook, covered, over medium-low heat until chicken becomes tender and has absorbed the flavors of the sauce, 30 to 45 minutes.

Note: *During the cooking process, check often and stir frequently to prevent the chicken from sticking to skillet. Add ¼ cup of water at intervals to enable the thorough cooking of the chicken without it sticking to the skillet.*

Tender pieces of chicken simmered in a ginger and garlic sauce, Chettinad Chicken Masala can be served with plain rice, lemon rice, or any other flavored rice.

NOTE   You may also use boneless chicken thighs and breasts in this recipe. If chicken thighs and breasts are cut into small pieces cooking time will be less in Step 7.

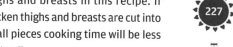

CALORIES	438	CARBOHYDRATE	15g
FAT	18g	FIBER	5g
SATURATED FAT	3g	CHOLESTEROL	132mg
PROTEIN	55g	SODIUM	1063mg

chettinad chicken kurma

Serves 4	2 pounds skinned chicken pieces (about 6 thighs or breasts)	12 raw almonds	¾ cup sliced onion (cut lengthwise)
	¾ cup ground fresh coconut or unsweetened coconut powder	3 teaspoons cumin seeds	½ cup chopped tomato
		2 tablespoons white poppy seeds	½ teaspoon turmeric powder
	4 small slices ginger root	1 teaspoon fennel seeds	2 teaspoons salt
	2 garlic cloves, peeled	4 to 6 slivers cinnamon stick	1 teaspoon curry powder
	2 green chili peppers or 2 to 4 whole dried red chili peppers (more, if desired)	1 tablespoon butter	¾ teaspoon cardamom powder
		2 tablespoons canola oil	⅓ cup minced fresh coriander (cilantro) leaves
	¼ cup roasted chickpeas	1½ dry bay leaves	
		8 to 10 curry leaves	

Tender pieces of chicken in an exquisite coconut-based sauce, Chicken Kurma can be served over plain rice, Vegetable (page 121) or Chicken Biriyani Rice (page 224) or Basmati Rice with Green Peas (page 108), or can accompany any Indian breads.

1. Cut chicken thighs and breasts into small pieces. Wash the chicken pieces, drain, and set aside.

2. In an electric blender, grind together coconut powder, ginger root, garlic, chili peppers, roasted chickpeas, almonds, 1½ teaspoons cumin seeds, white poppy seeds, ½ teaspoon fennel seeds, and 2 or 3 slivers of cinnamon stick. Add 3 cups of hot water to facilitate the grinding process. (Water must be hot for coconut to blend properly.) Process on high for at least 5 minutes until mixture has a creamy, liquid consistency. Set kurma sauce aside.

3. Heat butter and oil in a large saucepan over medium heat. When the oil is hot, but not smoking, add bay leaves, curry leaves, remaining 2 or 3 slivers of cinnamon stick, remaining 1½ teaspoons cumin seeds, and remaining ½ teaspoon fennel seeds. Stir-fry until seeds are golden.

4. Immediately add onion and tomato and cook for a few minutes. Add turmeric powder and mix well.

5. Add the chicken pieces to saucepan. Stir well and cook, uncovered, over medium-high heat for 3 to 5 minutes, until chicken becomes opaque and slightly brown.

6. Pour kurma sauce over chicken mixture. Add salt, curry powder, and 1 cup warm water. Mix well. Add cardamom powder. Cook, covered, over low heat, until chicken becomes tender, about 20 minutes, stirring occasionally.

7. Add coriander and continue cooking over low heat for a few more minutes.

NOTE If you find kurma sauce to be too spicy, add ¼ cup tomato sauce and stir well at low heat. You may also use boneless chicken thighs to make chicken kurma in order to reduce the cooking time.

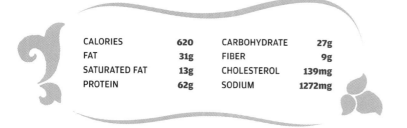

CALORIES	620	CARBOHYDRATE	27g
FAT	31g	FIBER	9g
SATURATED FAT	13g	CHOLESTEROL	139mg
PROTEIN	62g	SODIUM	1272mg

madras chicken curry in a hurry

Serves 4	5 tablespoons canola oil	¼ cup peeled and quartered garlic cloves	¼ teaspoon turmeric powder	1 teaspoon cumin powder
	3 dry bay leaves	1 tablespoon minced ginger root	½ teaspoon cayenne powder	1 teaspoon salt
	1 cinnamon stick, broken in half	3 pounds skinned chicken pieces with bones (about 6 to 8 pieces)	1 teaspoon American curry powder or garam masala powder	1 cup tomato sauce
	1 cup chopped onion			
	1 cup chopped tomato			

This simpler version of Chettinad Chicken Masala (page 227) can be served over rice or with any Indian breads such as chappatis.

variation For **CHICKEN CURRY WITH POTATOES** in step 3 add 2 lbs. boneless, skinless chicken thighs and 2 cups peeled and cubed Idaho potato in place of just the chicken, and brown both. Then follow the rest of the recipe to make this delicious dish.

1. In a heavy wide saucepan heat oil over medium heat. When oil is hot, but not smoking, add bay leaves and cinnamon stick.

2. Add onion, tomato, garlic, and ginger root. Stir-fry for a couple of minutes.

3. Add chicken and cook until browned.

4. Add turmeric powder, cayenne powder, curry powder, cumin powder, and salt. Blend the powders well with the chicken seasonings.

5. Add tomato sauce and slow cook over medium low heat until chicken is cooked.

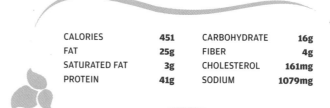

CALORIES	451	CARBOHYDRATE	16g
FAT	25g	FIBER	4g
SATURATED FAT	3g	CHOLESTEROL	161mg
PROTEIN	41g	SODIUM	1079mg

roasted cornish hens

Serves 4	2 Cornish hens	2 tablespoons whole black peppercorns	4 whole dried red chili peppers	½ cup olive oil
	4 tablespoons dried yellow split peas	2 tablespoons cumin seeds	1 teaspoon minced garlic clove	

1. Wash Cornish hens thoroughly and pat-dry. Cut them in half. Set aside.

2. Dry roast the split peas, black peppercorns, cumin seeds, and red chili peppers in a skillet over medium heat for about 3 to 5 minutes, stirring until the spices are aromatic.

3. Grind roasted spices in a blender until coarsely ground. Place the ground mixture in a bowl. Add minced garlic and olive oil. Using your hand, blend the mixture into a paste.

4. Rub the spice mixture well into all sides of the Cornish hens.

5. Line a baking pan with aluminum foil. Place Cornish hens in the baking pan and roast, uncovered, in a 350° F oven for 45 minutes to an hour, until skin is brown and crisp. Check for doneness.

Spice-rubbed oven-roasted Cornish hens make a wonderful main dish.

variation You may use several cut-up chicken pieces (about 6 to 8 pieces) with skin in place of the Cornish hens.

CALORIES	653	CARBOHYDRATE	15g
FAT	52g	FIBER	6g
SATURATED FAT	10g	CHOLESTEROL	170mg
PROTEIN	33g	SODIUM	114mg

garlic and pepper chicken

Serves 4 to 6	2 pounds boneless, skinless chicken thighs (see note below)	2 whole dried red chili peppers	10 garlic cloves, peeled and cut in half	1½ teaspoons salt

Serves 4 to 6

2 pounds boneless, skinless chicken thighs (see note below)

3 tablespoons canola oil

4 or 5 slivers cinnamon stick

1 dry bay leaf

2 whole dried red chili peppers

1 teaspoon cumin seeds

½ teaspoon fennel seeds

1 teaspoon urad dal

½ cup chopped onion

10 garlic cloves, peeled and cut in half

½ teaspoon turmeric powder

1 tablespoon minced ginger root

1½ teaspoons ground black pepper and cumin powder mixture

1½ teaspoons salt

1 teaspoon curry powder (more, if desired)

¾ teaspoon cayenne powder

¼ cup tomato sauce

¼ cup chopped red onion (optional)

Chicken stir-fried with garlic and pepper, this dish goes particularly well with plain rice or any flavored rice dish. It's also delicious as a filling for pita bread.

Note Boneless skinless chicken breasts may be used in place of chicken thighs, but more water (½ to 1 cup) will have to be added in Step 5 to maintain moistness. Adjust other seasonings according to taste.

CALORIES	343	CARBOHYDRATE	10g
FAT	16g	FIBER	3g
SATURATED FAT	3g	CHOLESTEROL	145mg
PROTEIN	38g	SODIUM	801mg

1. Cut chicken into medium-size pieces. Rinse, drain, and set aside.

2. Heat oil in a cast-iron skillet over medium heat. When oil is hot, but not smoking, add cinnamon sticks, bay leaf, red chili peppers, cumin seeds, fennel seeds, and urad dal.

3. Add onion and garlic. Sauté for few minutes. Stir in turmeric powder.

4. Add chicken and ginger root to skillet. Cook, covered, over low heat until the chicken is partially cooked.

5. Add black pepper and cumin powder, salt, curry powder, and cayenne powder. Stir well to coat the chicken with spices. Add tomato sauce and about 2 tablespoons water. Stir and cook chicken, covered, over medium heat for 12 to 15 minutes. During the cooking process, check often and stir frequently to prevent chicken from sticking to the skillet.

6. To enhance flavor or to increase tenderness of chicken, add red onions over the chicken and continue cooking. Simmer until the onions are cooked to preferred degree of doneness.

ground turkey with split peas and coconut

Serves 4	½ cup dry yellow split peas	2 to 4 slivers cinnamon stick	2 to 4 garlic cloves, finely chopped	½ teaspoon cayenne powder
	1 teaspoon turmeric powder	1 teaspoon cumin seeds	1 green chili pepper (more, if desired)	½ teaspoon cumin powder
	2 tablespoons canola oil	½ teaspoon fennel seeds	1 pound ground turkey	1 teaspoon salt
	1 dry bay leaf	1 cup chopped onion	2 teaspoons curry powder	¼ cup ground fresh coconut or unsweetened coconut powder

1. Bring 2 cups of water to a boil in a saucepan. Add split peas and ¼ teaspoon turmeric powder. Reduce heat to medium and cook, uncovered, about 15 minutes until split peas are tender and water is absorbed. (Add an additional ½ cup of water, if water is absorbed before split peas are tender.) Drain any remaining water and set aside.

2. Heat oil in a large skillet over medium heat. When oil is hot, but not smoking, add bay leaf and cinnamon sticks into oil. Add cumin and fennel seeds.

3. Immediately add onion, garlic, chili pepper, and the remaining ¾ teaspoon turmeric powder. Cook, stirring, for about 1 minute, until onions are tender. Add ground turkey and pan-fry for about 3 minutes until browned, stirring and breaking up meat as it cooks.

4. Stir in curry powder, cayenne powder, and cumin powder. Cover and cook 2 minutes. Stir in salt, cover, and cook another 5 minutes.

5. Stir in cooked split peas. Cover and cook another 2 minutes. Add coconut powder and stir well. Taste and add additional seasonings if desired.

This is a particularly easy-to-make stir-fry using split peas and coconut. You may, in fact, use any ground meat to make this delicious dish. For example, in the Chettinand region, Mutton Podimas is made by using ground lamb or goat meat.

NOTE   If the turkey becomes dry during the cooking process, beat one egg with a pinch of turmeric powder. Add the beaten egg to the turkey mixture. Stir until egg is cooked. This process will moisten the resulting dish.

nonvegetarian dishes

HEALTHY SOUTH INDIAN COOKING

CALORIES	361	CARBOHYDRATE	28g
FAT	19g	FIBER	11g
SATURATED FAT	5g	CHOLESTEROL	90mg
PROTEIN	29g	SODIUM	663mg

chettinad egg kulambu

Serves 4

4 large eggs

3 tablespoons canola oil

2 or 3 slivers cinnamon stick

1 dry bay leaf

4 to 6 curry leaves (optional)

¼ teaspoon fenugreek seeds

¼ teaspoon cumin seeds

¼ teaspoon fennel seeds

½ teaspoon urad dal

½ cup chopped onion

¼ cup chopped tomato

6 to 8 garlic cloves, chopped

½ green chili pepper, chopped

¼ teaspoon turmeric powder

1 teaspoon curry powder

½ teaspoon cayenne powder

½ teaspoon tamarind paste

1 teaspoon black pepper and cumin powder mixture

1 teaspoon salt

1 cup tomato sauce

¼ cup finely chopped fresh coriander (cilantro) leaves

Boiled eggs cooked with spices in an aromatic tamarind sauce can be served over plain rice or as an accompaniment to idlis, dosais, and chappatis.

nonvegetarian dishes

HEALTHY SOUTH INDIAN COOKING

NOTE   You may add an additional ½ cup of tomato sauce for a milder taste.

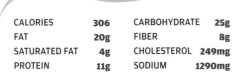

CALORIES	306	CARBOHYDRATE	25g
FAT	20g	FIBER	8g
SATURATED FAT	4g	CHOLESTEROL	249mg
PROTEIN	11g	SODIUM	1290mg

1. Hard-boil the eggs. Peel them and set aside.

2. Heat oil in a saucepan over medium heat. When oil is hot, but not smoking, add cinnamon stick, bay leaf, curry leaves, fenugreek seeds, cumin seeds, fennel seeds, and urad dal. Stir gently. Cover and cook until seeds pop and urad dal is golden brown, about 30 seconds.

3. Immediately add onion, tomato, garlic, and chili pepper to saucepan. Stir and add turmeric powder.

4. When onion is tender, add curry powder, cayenne powder, tamarind paste, and black pepper and cumin powder. Add salt, tomato sauce, and 1 cup of water. Mix well and allow the mixture to boil for about 2 minutes. Add coriander.

5. When the mixture starts to boil, reduce the heat and allow to simmer over low heat for about 2 minutes.

6. Score boiled eggs with cross marks on each end and add the eggs to the simmering sauce so that they will absorb the flavor of the sauce.

7. Spoon the sauce over the eggs. Remove from heat. Cover and let the eggs soak in the sauce until served.

egg masala 1

Serves 4			
	4 eggs	2 garlic cloves, coarsely chopped	¼ teaspoon cumin powder
	1 teaspoon canola oil	¼ cup finely chopped fresh coriander (cilantro) leaves	½ teaspoon black pepper and cumin powder mixture
	¼ teaspoon cumin seeds		¼ teaspoon tamarind paste
	½ teaspoon urad dal	¼ teaspoon turmeric powder	½ teaspoon salt
	½ cup chopped onion	¼ teaspoon cayenne powder	¼ cup tomato sauce
	½ cup chopped tomato		

1. Hard-boil the eggs. Peel them and set aside.

2. Heat the oil in a small cast-iron skillet over medium heat. When oil is hot, but not smoking, add the cumin seeds and urad dal. Cover and heat until urad dal is golden brown, about 30 seconds.

3. Immediately add the onion, tomato, garlic, and coriander to skillet. Add turmeric powder and stir briefly.

4. When onion is tender, add cayenne powder, cumin powder, and black pepper and cumin powder mixture. Add tamarind paste, salt, and tomato sauce. Stir well to blend all the ingredients.

5. Cook, uncovered, over medium heat for 3 to 4 minutes. Lower the heat.

6. Cut eggs in half lengthwise. Add eggs to the sauce. Spoon sauce over the eggs. Stir eggs gently with mixture. Remove from heat and cover. Allow eggs to stay in the sauce for several minutes before serving.

Boiled eggs simmered in a rich sauce, Egg Masala may accompany any lunch or dinner entree.

CALORIES	101	CARBOHYDRATE	5g
FAT	6g	FIBER	1g
SATURATED FAT	2g	CHOLESTEROL	187mg
PROTEIN	6g	SODIUM	418mg

egg masala II

Serves 4	4 large eggs	½ cup chopped onion	¼ teaspoon garam masala powder
	1 teaspoon minced ginger root	½ cup chopped tomato	½ teaspoon salt
	2 garlic cloves, peeled	¼ teaspoon cayenne powder	¼ cup tomato sauce
	1 teaspoon unsweetened coconut powder	½ teaspoon black pepper and cumin powder mixture	¼ cup minced fresh coriander (cilantro) leaves

A unique version of boiled eggs simmered in an oil-free sauce, Egg Masala II is a welcome accompaniment to any meal.

1. Hard-boil the eggs. Peel them and set aside.

2. Place ginger, garlic, and coconut powder with ¼ cup of water in a blender and grind to a smooth paste.

3. Sauté onion in a small skillet without oil for 2 to 3 minutes over medium heat. Add tomato and cook until soft.

4. Add ground paste to skillet and blend with other ingredients. Stir in cayenne powder, black pepper and cumin powder, garam masala powder, and salt. Cook for a few minutes.

5. Add tomato sauce and blend with ingredients in skillet. Stir in coriander.

6. Add hard-boiled eggs to sauce. Eggs may be served whole or cut in half. The sauce should be scooped over the eggs.

236

nonvegetarian dishes

HEALTHY SOUTH INDIAN COOKING

CALORIES	166	CARBOHYDRATE	6g
FAT	10g	FIBER	1g
SATURATED FAT	3g	CHOLESTEROL	399mg
PROTEIN	13g	SODIUM	480mg

seasoned scrambled eggs

Serves 4			
	4 large eggs	2 to 4 curry leaves (optional)	½ green chili pepper, finely chopped
	¼ teaspoon turmeric powder	1 teaspoon black mustard seeds	2 tablespoons dry roasted cashew halves (optional)
	½ teaspoon salt	1 teaspoon urad dal	
	2 tablespoons canola oil	½ cup finely chopped onion	

1. In a small bowl, beat the eggs with turmeric powder and salt. Set aside.

2. Place oil in a skillet over medium heat. When oil is hot, but not smoking, add curry leaves, mustard seeds, and urad dal. Cover and fry until mustard seeds pop and urad dal turns golden brown, about 30 seconds.

3. Immediately add onion and chili pepper. Cook for 1 minute.

4. Add the beaten eggs to the skillet. Fry until well done. You may add cashew halves after the eggs are cooked. Toss and serve.

South Indian-style scrambled eggs can be served for breakfast, lunch, or dinner.

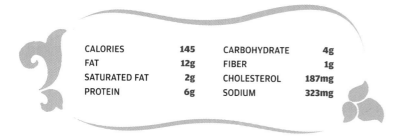

CALORIES	145	CARBOHYDRATE	4g
FAT	12g	FIBER	1g
SATURATED FAT	2g	CHOLESTEROL	187mg
PROTEIN	6g	SODIUM	323mg

chettinad lamb kulambu

Serves 4	1 pound lamb chops or leg of lamb or goat meat	¼ teaspoon fenugreek seeds	4 garlic cloves, chopped	½ teaspoon cayenne powder (more, if desired)
	2 tablespoons canola oil	1 teaspoon cumin seeds	1 tablespoon minced ginger root	½ teaspoon black pepper and cumin powder mixture
	1 dry bay leaf	¼ teaspoon fennel seeds	½ cup chopped tomato	½ cup tomato sauce
	2 to 4 slivers cinnamon stick	1 teaspoon urad dal	½ teaspoon turmeric powder	1 teaspoon salt
	2 to 4 curry leaves (optional)	½ cup chopped onion	2 teaspoons curry powder	¼ cup chopped fresh coriander (cilantro) leaves

Lamb Kulambu is another Chettinad specialty that is delicious served over plain rice or with idlis and dosais.

1. Cut lamb or goat into small pieces as if for a stew. Remove fat. Rinse the meat under cold water several times. Drain and set aside.

2. Heat oil in a saucepan or pressure cooker over medium heat. When oil is hot, but not smoking, add bay leaf, cinnamon stick, curry leaves, fenugreek seeds, cumin seeds, fennel seeds, and urad dal. Cover and fry until seeds pop and urad dal turns golden brown, about 30 seconds.

3. Immediately add onion, garlic, ginger root, tomato and turmeric powder and cook until onions are tender.

4. Increase heat to medium high. Add lamb and stir-fry for 3 to 5 minutes until lamb is coated with turmeric mixture and begins to turn pink.

5. Add curry powder, cayenne powder, black pepper and cumin powder. Stir and mix the powders well into meat.

6. Add tomato sauce and salt. Cook and stir for another 2 minutes. Add 2 cups of water. When mixture begins to boil, add coriander and reduce heat to medium-low.

7. If cooking in a saucepan, cover and cook about 45 minutes, stirring often, until meat is tender. Additional tomato sauce and water can be added, about ¼ cup at a time, if the sauce becomes too thick or if the meat is not yet tender. If cooking in a pressure cooker, cover and cook for 10 to 15 minutes, until meat is tender and the kulambu sauce has thickened.

variation   For **LAMB PORIYAL**, transfer the cooked lamb with sauce to a cast-iron skillet, stir-fry the mixture over medium-high heat until the sauce thickens and is absorbed by the meat.

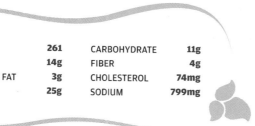

CALORIES	261	CARBOHYDRATE	11g
FAT	14g	FIBER	4g
SATURATED FAT	3g	CHOLESTEROL	74mg
PROTEIN	25g	SODIUM	799mg

fish kulambu

Serves 6				
	3 tablespoons canola oil	1 cup chopped onion	¼ teaspoon cayenne powder	½ teaspoon tamarind paste
	4 to 6 curry leaves (optional)	¼ cup peeled and quartered garlic cloves	2 teaspoons curry powder	1 pound firm-fleshed fish, cut into 1-inch thick steaks or fillets
	½ teaspoon fenugreek seeds	1 green chili pepper, cut lengthwise	1 teaspoon black pepper and cumin powder mixture	½ cup chopped fresh coriander (cilantro) leaves
	½ teaspoon fennel seeds	¼ cup chopped tomato	1 teaspoon salt	
	½ teaspoon cumin seeds	½ teaspoon turmeric powder	2 cups tomato sauce	
	½ teaspoon urad dal		2 tablespoons minced ginger root	

Cooked in a thick, aromatic tamarind sauce, this Chettinad specialty is particularly tasty when prepared several hours prior to serving because the fish will absorb the flavor of the sauce. Serve Fish Kulambu over white rice or as an accompaniment to idlis, dosais, or chappatis.

1. Place oil in a large saucepan over medium heat. When oil is hot, but not smoking, add curry leaves, fenugreek seeds, fennel seeds, cumin seeds, and urad dal. Cover and fry until seeds pop and urad dal is golden brown, about 30 seconds.

2. Add onion, garlic, chili pepper, and tomato. Stir-fry for about 1 minute. Blend in turmeric powder and cook for another minute.

3. Add cayenne powder, curry powder, black pepper and cumin powder, and salt, and stir and cook for another minute.

4. Add tomato sauce, ginger root, and tamarind paste. Blend well into mixture. Add about 1 to 2 cups of warm water. Stir well and allow mixture to simmer, uncovered, for a few minutes over medium-low heat.

5. When mixture begins to boil, add fish pieces and spoon sauce carefully over fish. Add coriander. Continue cooking over low heat, covered, for 5 to 7 minutes until fish is opaque and flaky. **Note:** *Sauce should be stirred gently during the cooking process and more tomato sauce can be added, if necessary. Use the handles of the saucepan to swirl the sauce, rather than risk breaking the fish steaks with a spoon.*

6. When fish is cooked, remove saucepan from heat. Cover and let it remain at room temperature until serving. If fish is not served immediately, reheat only briefly before serving.

The best fish to buy for this recipe are tilapia, cod, halibut, haddock, whitefish, pomfret (an Indian favorite also known as pompano), and sierra (also known as king fish). Have the fish cut into steaks or small fillets, as you desire.

CALORIES	282	CARBOHYDRATE	15g
FAT	13g	FIBER	3g
SATURATED FAT	2g	CHOLESTEROL	36mg
PROTEIN	26g	SODIUM	971mg

fish varuval

Serves 4

1 pound tilapia or other fish fillets without skin

1 teaspoon tamarind paste or lemon juice

½ teaspoon turmeric powder

½ teaspoon cayenne powder

1 teaspoon cumin powder

½ teaspoon salt

4 tablespoons canola oil

3 or 4 curry leaves (optional)

For Fish Varuval, a traditional Chettinad specialty, the fish is first marinated, and then pan-fried. Possible fish to buy for this recipe are tilapia, cod, halibut, haddock, whitefish, pomfret (an Indian favorite also known as pompano), and sierra (also known as king fish). This dish can be served as an accompaniment to any meal that includes plain white rice.

1. Wash fish fillets in water. Pat dry with paper towels and set aside.

2. Place tamarind paste, turmeric powder, cayenne powder, cumin powder, and salt in a small bowl. Add two tablespoons of water and blend together with hands into a smooth paste.

3. Rub the paste well into both sides of fish fillets and place fish in a covered dish in refrigerator. Allow fish to marinate in spice paste for at least 30 minutes.

4. Add oil to a heated non-stick skillet. Add curry leaves. (You may wish to use a splatter screen to minimize oil splatters.)

5. Add fish fillets. Do not crowd skillet with fish fillets, as this will cause fish to steam instead of pan-fry. You may wish to fry fish slices in several batches. Pan-fry fish, turning frequently, until fish becomes golden brown and crusty.

6. Set a plate lined with paper towels beside the stove to hold fried fish. Serve immediately.

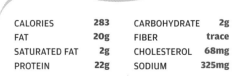

CALORIES	283	CARBOHYDRATE	2g
FAT	20g	FIBER	trace
SATURATED FAT	2g	CHOLESTEROL	68mg
PROTEIN	22g	SODIUM	325mg

shrimp in eggplant sauce

Serves 6	2 tablespoons canola oil	½ cup chopped onion	½ teaspoon cayenne powder (more, if desired)	1 teaspoon salt
	2 to 4 curry leaves (optional)	½ cup chopped tomato	1 teaspoon cumin powder	½ pound (about 20) raw or pre-boiled medium shrimp, shells removed
	1 teaspoon cumin seeds	2 cups cubed unpeeled eggplant	1 cup tomato sauce	
	½ teaspoon fenugreek seeds	¼ teaspoon turmeric powder	½ teaspoon tamarind paste	

1. Heat oil in a saucepan over medium heat. When oil is hot, but not smoking, add curry leaves, cumin seeds, and fenugreek seeds.

2. Immediately add onion and tomato and cook for a few minutes. Add eggplant to saucepan and allow to cook with the seasonings for a few minutes.

3. Add turmeric powder, cayenne powder, and cumin powder. Stir and add tomato sauce, tamarind paste, salt, and 1½ cups of warm water. Let eggplant slow cook over low heat, covered, until soft and the sauce has thickened.

4. When the eggplant is cooked and the mixture begins to thicken, add the shrimp. Cook for about 5 minutes. If the sauce is too thick, add an additional ½ cup to 1 cup of warm water and let it simmer for a few additional minutes.

Shrimp in Eggplant Sauce, served over plain rice or Yogurt Rice (page 123), has a unique and enticing combination of flavors.

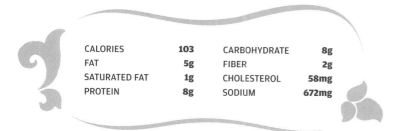

CALORIES	103	CARBOHYDRATE	8g
FAT	5g	FIBER	2g
SATURATED FAT	1g	CHOLESTEROL	58mg
PROTEIN	8g	SODIUM	672mg

shrimp masala

Serves 4	1 tablespoon canola oil	¼ cup chopped tomato	½ teaspoon curry powder	1 teaspoon black pepper and cumin powder mixture
	2 or 3 slivers cinnamon stick	4 or 5 garlic cloves, chopped	¼ cup tomato sauce	1 pound fresh shrimp, peeled and washed
	1 teaspoon cumin seeds	2 tablespoons minced ginger root	½ teaspoon cayenne powder	
	¾ cup chopped onion	½ teaspoon turmeric powder	1 teaspoon salt	¼ cup chopped fresh coriander (cilantro) leaves

Shrimp pan-fried with ginger, garlic, and other seasonings, Shrimp Masala can accompany many flavored rice dishes and chappatis or pooris.

1. Place oil in an iron skillet over medium heat. When oil is hot, but not smoking, add cinnamon stick and cumin seeds. Stir-fry until spices are golden brown.

2. Add onion, tomato, garlic, and ginger root. Stir-fry for a few minutes.

3. Stir in turmeric powder and curry powder.

4. Add tomato sauce, cayenne powder, salt, and black pepper and cumin powder. Blend the seasonings well and simmer for a few minutes.

5. Add shrimp and mix with the seasonings. Cook until shrimp turns pink.

6. Add coriander and stir-fry, uncovered, for an additional few minutes. (Shrimp is delicious when allowed to absorb the flavor of the seasoned sauce while stir-frying over low heat.)

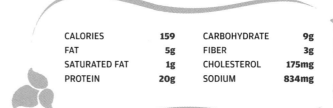

CALORIES	159	CARBOHYDRATE	9g
FAT	5g	FIBER	3g
SATURATED FAT	1g	CHOLESTEROL	175mg
PROTEIN	20g	SODIUM	834mg

shrimp pasta

Serves 6

1 cup pasta shells (preferably whole wheat)

1 tablespoon olive oil

½ teaspoon cumin seeds

1 cup chopped onion

¼ cup chopped tomato

2 or 3 garlic cloves, minced (more, if desired)

½ teaspoon garam masala powder

1 pound raw shrimp, shelled and deveined

¼ cup Cajun (or spicy) dry bread crumbs

½ teaspoon salt (more, if desired)

½ cup chopped fresh coriander (cilantro) leaves

1. Boil pasta until just tender. Drain and set aside.

2. Place olive oil in a wok or large skillet. Heat over medium heat until oil is hot, but not smoking.

3. Add cumin seeds to oil. Brown for a few seconds. Add onion, tomato, and garlic and stir-fry for a few minutes. Add garam masala powder and mix well.

4. Add shrimp to skillet and cook until shrimp turns pink. Be careful not to overcook shrimp.

5. Add cooked pasta shells, bread crumbs, and salt. Stir well with shrimp and seasonings.

6. Add chopped coriander to pasta. Stir for an additional minute and serve.

Shrimp Pasta is an innovative dish combining Indian and Western flavors.

CALORIES	169	CARBOHYDRATE	19g
FAT	3g	FIBER	2g
SATURATED FAT	1g	CHOLESTEROL	117mg
PROTEIN	16g	SODIUM	447mg

beverages & desserts

buttermilk Drink

| Serves 6 | 2 cups reduced-fat cultured buttermilk

4 cups cold water | ¼ teaspoon asafoetida powder (optional)

1 teaspoon cumin powder

¼ teaspoon salt | 2 to 4 chopped curry leaves or ¼ cup minced fresh coriander (cilantro) leaves (optional) |

A refreshing beverage that cools your body, this drink is made from reduced-fat cultured buttermilk. It is an excellent source of vitamins A and D and calcium. In South India, people sometimes drink buttermilk instead of coffee and soft drinks. The buttermilk drink can be kept in the refrigerator for a long time. Always stir before serving. Buttermilk is also delicious served with ice.

1. Mix buttermilk with water in a tall pitcher.

2. Add asafoetida powder, cumin powder, and salt. Stir well.

3. Add curry leaves or coriander, if using, and stir well.

4. Refrigerate. Stir before serving.

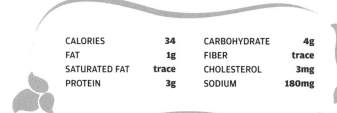

CALORIES	34	CARBOHYDRATE	4g
FAT	1g	FIBER	trace
SATURATED FAT	trace	CHOLESTEROL	3mg
PROTEIN	3g	SODIUM	180mg

madras coffee

Serves 1	½ cup 2% milk	1 teaspoon instant coffee powder	1 teaspoon sugar
	½ cup water		

1. In a cup mix milk and water. Transfer the mixture into a small saucepan. Let the mixture come to a full boil. As the milk rises to the top (comes to a boil), remove from stove.

2. In another cup mix coffee powder and sugar. Pour the milk over coffee and sugar.

3. Transfer the contents from one cup to another a few times until a froth develops.

4. Pour the coffee into a cup and serve.

Traditional Madras Coffee, also known as Mysore Coffee, is made with coffee beans that are carefully selected, blended, and roasted. The coffee is brewed in a special vessel called a decoction container.

For a great tasting and easy-to-make version of Madras Coffee, you may use any premium instant coffee powder. Madras Coffee may also be prepared from any brewed coffee, provided it is brewed in a concentrated, espresso-style.

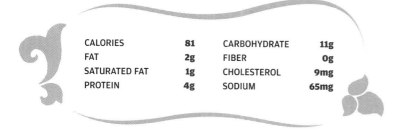

CALORIES	81	CARBOHYDRATE	11g
FAT	2g	FIBER	0g
SATURATED FAT	1g	CHOLESTEROL	9mg
PROTEIN	4g	SODIUM	65mg

indian tea 1

Serves 1	¾ cup water	1 or 2 strong tea bags or 1 to	¼ teaspoon crushed
		2 teaspoons loose black tea	cardamom or cardamom
	¼ cup 2% milk		powder

Cardamom-flavored hot tea with milk (also known as Chai) is a perfect drink to relax with!

1. Mix water and milk in a cup. Pour the mixture into a small saucepan and bring just to a boil.

2. Immerse the teabag or loose tea in the boiling milk. Add the cardamom.

3. When the mixture boils to the top of the pan (begins to boil), remove from stove.

4. Either remove the tea bag or strain the tea and crushed cardamom. Pour the tea into a cup. Add sugar to taste. Stir and serve.

CALORIES	37	CARBOHYDRATE	4g
FAT	1g	FIBER	trace
SATURATED FAT	1g	CHOLESTEROL	5mg
PROTEIN	2g	SODIUM	39mg

indian tea II

Serves 2	2 cups water	½ teaspoon crushed cardamom or cardamom powder	1 or 2 strong tea bags or 1 to 2 teaspoons loose black tea
			¼ cup 2% milk

1. Bring water to a boil in a small saucepan. Add cardamom to the boiling water.

2. Immerse the tea bag or add loose tea to the boiling water. Remove from heat and cover. Let tea stand in hot water for a few minutes. Strain tea and cardamom. Transfer the tea essence to a teapot with lid.

3. Boil milk in a small saucepan or in microwave.

4. Pour tea and milk into a cup according to your taste. Add sugar to taste. Stir and serve.

You may also want to try this variation of Indian Tea (Chai) in which the tea is steeped in a more traditional way.

CALORIES	19	CARBOHYDRATE	2g
FAT	1g	FIBER	trace
SATURATED FAT	trace	CHOLESTEROL	2mg
PROTEIN	1g	SODIUM	24mg

moong dal payasam

Serves 4	¼ cup yellow moong dal	2 cups 2% milk	½ cup packed dark brown sugar
	¼ cup cashews	¼ teaspoon cardamom powder	2 to 4 saffron threads
	1 tablespoon butter or ghee (clarified butter)		

Payasam is a sweet-flavored milk drink that serves as a dessert in South India. This particular payasam is also used in religious ceremonies in South India, and is enjoyed by devotees after prayers.

1. Bring 3 cups of water to a boil in a saucepan. Add moong dal. Cook for 15 to 20 minutes, uncovered, until moong dal becomes soft. At the final stage of cooking, remove moong dal from heat and mash it with masher to a creamy consistency. Add an additional 2 cups of water to dilute the dal mixture. Set aside.

2. Fry cashews in butter until golden brown and set aside.

3. Heat milk to boiling point in a saucepan.

4. Mix creamy dal with milk in the saucepan and cook over medium heat for 3 to 5 minutes, stirring frequently.

5. Add cashews, cardamom powder, brown sugar, and saffron. Cook an additional few minutes over medium to low heat.

NOTE This payasam can be served hot or cold. If you prefer to serve it cold, refrigerate for 2 to 3 hours before serving. Serve payasam in a cup.

beverages & desserts

HEALTHY SOUTH INDIAN COOKING

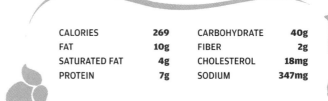

CALORIES	269	CARBOHYDRATE	40g
FAT	10g	FIBER	2g
SATURATED FAT	4g	CHOLESTEROL	18mg
PROTEIN	7g	SODIUM	347mg

pala payasam

Serves 6	½ cup skinned almonds	1 teaspoon cardamom powder	Pinch of kesari powder or yellow food coloring
	4 cups 2% milk	1 teaspoon saffron threads	1 can (10 ounces) mixed fruit cocktail
	1 cup sugar (more, if desired)		

1. In a blender, grind almonds with milk. Pour into a heavy-bottomed saucepan and heat the mixture over medium-low heat until it begins to boil.

2. Add sugar, cardamom powder, saffron, and kesari powder to the mixture and stir frequently until it begins to boil. After the mixture boils, set it aside and let cool.

3. Pour the fruit cocktail along with the syrup into the cooled milk mixture. Stir gently. Leave payasam in refrigerator until it is time to serve.

A flavored sweet milk drink featuring almonds, saffron, and fruits, served as a dessert.

NOTE Pala Payasam may thicken after refrigeration. Before serving, if payasam seems too thick, you may add an additional 1 cup of skim milk to dilute it. Stir and serve.

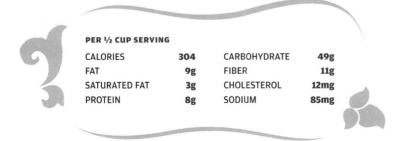

PER ½ CUP SERVING

CALORIES	304	CARBOHYDRATE	49g
FAT	9g	FIBER	11g
SATURATED FAT	3g	CHOLESTEROL	12mg
PROTEIN	8g	SODIUM	85mg

carrot halva

Serves 8	10 raw cashew halves	2 cups grated carrots	½ teaspoon cardamom powder
	1 tablespoon melted butter	½ cup sugar	
	1 cup whole milk		4 to 6 saffron threads

Carrots cooked in milk with sugar, cardamom, and saffron make a tempting treat!

1. In a small skillet, fry cashew halves in butter. Set aside.

2. In a heavy-bottomed saucepan, bring milk just to a boil over medium heat.

3. When the milk comes to a boil, reduce heat to medium-low. Add grated carrots and sugar. Simmer carrots over medium-low heat until tender, stirring often.

4. Add cardamom powder, saffron, and roasted cashews. Mix well and stir until the mixture thickens.

5. Pour mixture into a glass plate or bowl and let cool before serving.

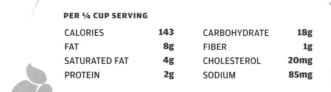

PER ¼ CUP SERVING

CALORIES	143	CARBOHYDRATE	18g
FAT	8g	FIBER	1g
SATURATED FAT	4g	CHOLESTEROL	20mg
PROTEIN	2g	SODIUM	85mg

kesari

Serves 4	3 tablespoons butter	1 cup sugar	Pinch of kesari powder or yellow food coloring
	1/4 cup raw cashews	10 raisins	
	1/2 cup regular uncooked cream of wheat	1/4 teaspoon cardamom powder	Pinch of crystalline camphor (optional)
	1 cup 2% milk		

1. In a small nonstick skillet, melt 1 tablespoon butter. Fry cashews in butter until golden brown. Remove cashews from skillet and set aside.

2. Add cream of wheat to the same skillet and cook for a few minutes.

3. Add 1 cup of warm water and the milk. Stir into the mixture gently.

4. Add sugar, raisins, cardamom powder, kesari powder, and camphor to cream of wheat and blend well over medium heat. Add the remaining 2 tablespoons butter and cook, stirring frequently, until cream of wheat is cooked.

5. Add fried cashews to cream of wheat and serve.

A popular sweet dish made with cream of wheat, sugar, raisins, and cardamom powder, Kesari is served during breakfast or for tea.

CALORIES	441	CARBOHYDRATE	75g
FAT	14g	FIBER	2g
SATURATED FAT	7g	CHOLESTEROL	28mg
PROTEIN	6g	SODIUM	122mg

ricotta cheese dessert

Serves 8	1 pound regular or low-fat ricotta cheese	1 teaspoon rose essence	¼ cup almond halves
		1 cup white sugar	

An innovative and easy-to-prepare dessert made from ricotta cheese and almonds flavored with rose essence.

1. Preheat oven to 350° F. Blend ricotta cheese and rose essence thoroughly in a mixing bowl. Add sugar and stir well.

2. Spread cheese mixture in a greased shallow baking pan. Bake for 20 to 30 minutes until golden brown.

3. Garnish with almond halves. Cool for 30 to 45 minutes. Cut into slices and serve.

CALORIES	202	CARBOHYDRATE	29g
FAT	7g	FIBER	trace
SATURATED FAT	3g	CHOLESTEROL	17mg
PROTEIN	7g	SODIUM	72mg

tapioca payasam

Serves 4	¼ cup raw cashew halves	Pinch of kesari powder or yellow food coloring	2 very small pieces cystalline camphor (optional)
	1 tablespoon butter	¼ teaspoon cardamom powder	½ cup sugar (more, if desired)
	½ cup tapioca (not quick-cooking)	4 to 6 saffron threads	¼ cup raisins (optional)
	3 cups 2% milk or whole milk, as desired		

1. Fry cashew halves in ½ tablespoon butter in a small skillet or butter warmer over medium heat until evenly cooked. Remove cashews from skillet and set aside.

2. Melt another ½ tablespoon butter in a deep saucepan. Add tapioca and cook for a few minutes in butter, stirring constantly.

3. Add milk slowly in 1 cup increments, stirring all the while, over medium to low heat, until tapioca cooks, about 15 minutes. When tapioca is cooked it will increase in size and will become softer.

4. Add kesari powder, cardamom powder, saffron threads, crystalline camphor, and sugar. Stir well over low heat.

5. Add cashew halves and raisins, if desired.

6. Serve in custard cups or sherbert glasses. You may serve payasam at room temperature or as a cold dessert (see Note).

Tapioca cooked in milk is delicious flavored with saffron and cardamom.

NOTE If room temperature serving is preferred, remove Tapioca Payasam from heat and cover it. Leave at room temperature until time of serving. Even at room temperature, it thickens. Add additional warm milk and sugar as desired before serving.

If you prefer to serve payasam cold, leave it in the refrigerator where it will thicken. Stir well and add additional cold milk until payasam reaches the desired consistency. You may also add additional sugar as desired.

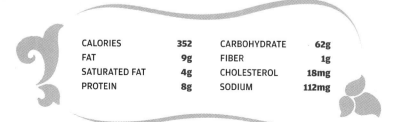

CALORIES	352	CARBOHYDRATE	62g
FAT	9g	FIBER	1g
SATURATED FAT	4g	CHOLESTEROL	18mg
PROTEIN	8g	SODIUM	112mg

vermicelli payasam

Serves 4	¼ cup raw cashew halves	2 cups 2% milk or whole milk, as desired	4 to 6 saffron threads
	1 tablespoon butter	¼ teaspoon cardamom powder	½ cup sugar (more, if desired)
	½ cup broken vermicelli pasta		¼ cup raisins (optional)

This exquisite dessert features vermicelli cooked in milk with saffron and cardamom.

NOTE If room temperature serving is preferred, remove Vermicelli Payasam from heat and cover. Leave at room temperature until time of serving. Even at room temperature, it will thicken. Add additional warm milk and sugar as desired before serving.

If you prefer to serve payasam cold, place it in the refrigerator where it will thicken. Stir gently and add additional cold milk until payasam reaches the desired consistency. You may also add additional sugar as desired.

1. Fry cashew halves in ½ tablespoon butter in a small skillet or butter warmer over medium heat until evenly cooked. Remove cashews from skillet and set aside.

2. Melt another ½ tablespoon butter in a small saucepan. Add vermicelli. Fry vermicelli for a few minutes in butter over low-medium heat, stirring constantly.

3. Add milk slowly in 1 cup increments, stirring all the while, over medium to low heat until vermicelli cooks, 5 to 7 minutes. (When vermicelli cooks it becomes softer.)

4. Add cardamom powder, saffron threads, and sugar. Stir and cook over low heat for a few minutes. Add cashew halves and raisins, if desired.

5. Serve in custard cups or sherbet glasses. You may serve vermicelli payasam at a room temperature or as a cold dessert (see Note).

CALORIES	298	CARBOHYDRATE	52g
FAT	8g	FIBER	1g
SATURATED FAT	3g	CHOLESTEROL	13mg
PROTEIN	7g	SODIUM	81mg

homemade yogurt

Makes 1 cup	1 cup 2% milk	1 teaspoon cultured buttermilk or fat-free plain yogurt

1. Place milk in a small saucepan. Heat over medium heat until milk just approaches the boiling point and begins to rise to top of saucepan. Remove from heat.

2. Transfer milk to a small dish and allow to cool slightly until just warm to touch, about 30 minutes.

3. Add 1 teaspoon cultured buttermilk or yogurt to milk. Stir well.

4. Cover the dish and set aside at room temperature for 6 to 8 hours until the yogurt is formed.

5. Store the homemade yogurt in the refrigerator until serving.

Yogurt (sometimes called "curd") is often served over plain rice as a last course in a meal because it is soothing and aids in digestion. Homemade yogurt (thayir) can be made without a yogurt maker using this recipe.

NOTE For richer homemade yogurt, you may use whole milk instead of 2% milk.

variation **HOMEMADE YOGURT WITH SKIM MILK** Pour desired amount of skim milk into a glass dish. Microwave, uncovered, 3 to 4 minutes until milk approaches the boiling point and begins to rise to top of dish. Remove dish from microwave and place on counter. Allow to cool slightly until just warm to touch, about 30 minutes. Continue with step 3 as above.

259

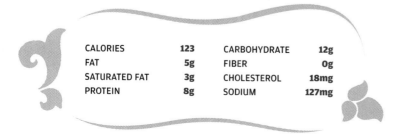

CALORIES	123	CARBOHYDRATE	12g
FAT	5g	FIBER	0g
SATURATED FAT	3g	CHOLESTEROL	18mg
PROTEIN	8g	SODIUM	127mg

SUGGESTED RECIPES FOR BEGINNERS

Most of the recipes in this book are very easy to follow even for novice cooks. Nevertheless, we list a sample of selected recipes that are particularly good starter recipes to follow.

SUGGESTED MENUS

The abundance of similar seasonings and spices in South Indian dishes makes them very complementary in taste to each other. Certain dishes, however, are particularly well suited to being served together and enhance the enjoyment of the other. Impressions gained from preparing recipes in this book and your own taste preferences will soon guide you in selecting appropriate combinations of dishes for a meal. Meanwhile, we can suggest the following groupings. But consider the groupings as suggestions only. Pappadums are excellent accompaniments to these meals. You may also add any item from the dessert section if you desire.

Suggested Vegetarian Menus For Main Meals

Plain Rice
Blackeye Peas Sambhar
Cabbage with Coconut Poriyal
Yogurt Rice

Lemon Rice
Potatoes Roasted with Garlic and Tomatoes
Lima Beans Masala or Eggplant Masala
Yogurt Salad

Coconut Rice
Cauliflower Masala Por iyal or
  Green Beans Poriyal
Acorn Squash Masala Poriyal

Plain Rice
Carrot Sambhar
Tomato Rasam
Seasoned Roasted Potatoes
Zucchini Kootu
Yogurt Rice

Bell Pepper and Tomato Rice with Cashews
Cauliflower Poriyal
Potato Masala
Tomato Pachadi

Vegetable Biriyani Rice
Potato Kurma
Brussels Sprouts Masala Poriyal
Yogurt Salad

Black Pepper Rice with Cashews
Carrot Poriyal
Cucumber Pachadi
Chickpea Soondal

Yogurt Rice
Lima Beans Masala
Bell Pepper and Tomato Pachadi
Paruppu Thuvaiyal

Plain Rice
Bell Pepper and Radish Sambhar
Spinach Kootu
Cabbage with Coconut Poriyal

Tamarind Rice
Coconut Thuvaiyal
Lima Beans Poriyal or Madras Potato Poriyal

Plain Rice
Masoor Dal Vegetable Sambhar
Green Peas Poriyal
Cauliflower Kootu
Yogurt Rice

Suggested Nonvegetarian Menus

Lemon Rice
Chettinad Chicken Poriyal
Yogurt Salad
Potatoes Roasted with Garlic and Tomatoes

Plain Rice
Chettinad Chicken Kulambu
Green Beans Poriyal
Spinach Kootu

Chicken Biriyani Rice
Chettinad Chicken Kurma or Potato Kurma

Yogurt Salad
Egg Masala (I or II)
Acorn Squash Masala Poriyal

Plain Rice
Fish Kulambu
Cabbage and Green Peas Poriyal
Potatoes Roasted with Garlic and Tomatoes

Plain Rice
Shrimp in Eggplant Sauce
Brussels Sprouts and Chickpea Poriyal
Lima Beans Poriyal

Plain Rice
Chettinad Lamb Kulambu
Cauliflower Poriyal
Broccoli Podimas

Suggested Breakfast, Tea, or Snack Menus

Uppuma (Cream of Wheat or Cracked Wheat
  or Soji)
Potato Sambhar or any chutney

Idiyappam
Kosamalli or Potato Moong Dal Pachadi

Dosais
Any sambhar or chutney
Onion and Potato Kose

Pooris
Potato Curry for Pooris

Chappatis
Potato Kurma

Idlis
Any sambhar or chutney

Adais
Kosamalli

Urad Dal Vadais
Any chutney

fUSION COMBINING SOUTH INDIAN AND WESTERN fOODS

Incorporating individual South Indian dishes into a typically Western meal can result in a delicious blending of tastes. The culinary term for the blending of dishes from different cuisines is "fusion," very much a characteristic of the current world of food preparation with its increasingly cosmopolitan orientation. Many individual South Indian dishes "fuse" beautifully with Western favorites. The rich complexity of flavors and seasonings inherent in South Indian dishes blends especially well with simple mainstays of the Western menu, such as grilled chicken and fish. You only have to use your imagination to come up with your own creative and delicious combinations. We offer a few suggestions below:

A. With Grilled, Roasted, or Baked Chicken

Any one flavored rice dish:

Bell Pepper and Tomato Rice with Cashews
Coconut Rice
Lemon Rice
Spinach Rice
Tamarind Rice
Tomato Rice with Cashews

One or more vegetable dishes:

Broccoli with Coconut Poriyal or Broccoli Podimas
Cabbage and Peas Poriyal
Cauliflower Poriyal
Carrot Poriyal
Eggplant Masala or Eggplant and Potato Masala
Green Beans Poriyal
Green Peas Poriyal
Lima Beans Masala or Lima Beans Poriyal
Sugar Snap Pea Pods Poriyal
Potato Masala or Potatoes Roasted with Garlic and Tomatoes
Spinach Poriyal
Acorn Squash Masala Poriyal
Tomato Pachadi
Yogurt Salad

B. With Roasted Turkey

Any one flavored rice dish:

Bell Pepper Tomato Rice with Cashews
Cauliflower Rice
Savory Mushroom Rice
Vegetable Biriyani Rice

One or more vegetable dishes:

Green Beans Poriyal
Green Peas Poriyal
Potatoes Roasted with Garlic and Tomatoes
Acorn Squash Masala Poriyal

C. With Grilled Fish or Shrimp

Any one flavored rice dish:

Coconut Rice
Lemon Rice
Black Pepper Rice with Cashews
Tamarind Rice

One or more vegetable dishes:

Cabbage with Coconut Poriyal
Potato Masala
Yogurt Salad

D. Vegetable Wraps and Sandwiches

You can make any vegetable poriyal or masala dish from our vegetable section, such as **Spinach Poriyal**, **Potato Masala**, or **Cabbage and Peas Poriyal**, and use the vegetable as a filling for a vegetable wrap. Pita bread or wheat or flour tortillas can be used as a wrap. One can also make delicious vegetarian sandwiches using any of the vegetable poriyal or masala recipes. One can also make chutney sandwiches as a unique variation of the tea-time cucumber sandwich, using any of the South Indian chutneys as a spread.

E. Nonvegetarian Wraps

Tuna Masala, **Chettinad Chicken Poriyal** (boneless), or **Ground Turkey with Split Peas and Coconut** can be served as a delicious sandwich filling with pita bread, wheat or flour tortillas, or regular sliced whole grain bread.

F. Vegetable Pastas

Make a vegetable from the vegetable section, such as **Mixed Vegetable Poriyal**, **Mixed Vegetable Kurma**, or **Broccoli Poriyal**, and serve over angel hair pasta or any type of pasta you prefer.

G. Nonvegetarian Pastas

Boneless **Chettinad Chicken Kurma** or **Chettinad Chicken Poriyal** can be served over your choice of pasta for a hearty meal.

H. Novel Appetizers and Snack Ideas

Tuna Masala on cocktail rye or French bread

Eggplant Chutney on French bread or crackers

Tomato or Coriander Chutney with tortilla chips

Tomato Pachadi over baked potato

Any chutney with French fried potatoes

Any chutney, sambhar, or kulambu with tortillas, toasted bread, buttermilk pancakes

fusion Thanksgiving Dinner
A UNIQUE BLEND Of EAST AND WEST

suggested menu

SPICE-RUBBED ROASTED TURKEY *(recipe follows)*

CURRIED STUFFING *(recipe follows)*

PAN GRAVY *(recipe follows)*

BELL PEPPER AND TOMATO RICE WITH CASHEWS

SWEET POTATO MASIYAL

GREEN BEANS PORIYAL

CARMELIZED BRUSSELS SPROUTS

CRANBERRY FRUIT SALAD *(recipe follows)*

DINNER ROLLS WITH BUTTER

MANGO LASSI WITH HONEY

PUMPKIN OR PECAN PIE WITH ICE CREAM

INDIAN TEA WITH CARDAMOM

spice-rubbed roasted turkey with curried stuffing

Serves 8 to 10	10 to 12 lb. Butterball turkey, fresh or frozen	CURRIED STUFFING	¾ teaspoon turmeric powder
	SPICE RUB	4 tablespoons unsalted butter	1 teaspoon salt
	2 teaspoons garam masala powder	2 cups stuffing croutons, preferably onion sage flavor	1 teaspoon black pepper powder
	¾ teaspoon cayenne powder	1½ cups diced celery	
	1 teaspoon turmeric powder	1 cup chopped walnuts	
	3 teaspoons garlic powder	1½ cups chopped onions	
	1 teaspoon salt	6 to 8 garlic cloves, minced	
	½ cup canola oil	2 teaspoons curry powder	

1. If turkey is frozen, follow directions for thawing turkey. Instructions are often enclosed in the outer wrapping of the turkey. After turkey is thawed, remove all the packaging from inside the cavity of turkey. Rinse turkey thoroughly and pat dry inside and out with paper towels.

2. Place turkey in roasting pan. **Note:** *You may wish to purchase a disposable aluminum-foil roasting pan in grocery store.*

3. In a small bowl, blend all spice rub ingredients. Rub the spiced-oil mixture all over the turkey, inside and out.

4. **FOR CURRIED STUFFING** Melt butter in a large saucepan. Add all of the stuffing ingredients including seasonings to the melted butter over medium-low heat. Toss stuffing ingredients for a few minutes to blend evenly and coat with butter. Allow stuffing to cool.

5. Fill cavity of turkey with stuffing, being careful not to pack too tightly. **Note:** *It is advisable to stuff turkey just before roasting.*

6. Truss (tie up) stuffed turkey with string according to package directions. Follow package instructions for roasting.

CONTINUED

american style pan gravy *(Optional Step)*

1. After removing turkey from oven, remove it from the roasting pan and set aside covered with aluminum foil to keep warm.

2. Pour off excess fat from roasting pan, leaving only about ½ cup of drippings in roasting pan. Heat the drippings for a few minutes over medium-low heat, while loosening turkey bits from bottom of roasting pan with a spoon. Add 2 cups of water to roasting pan. Season moderately with salt and pepper.

3. Place 1 tablespoon of cornstarch or flour in a small cup and blend thoroughly with 2 tablespoons of water to make a paste. Add ½ cup more water to paste and stir into drippings in the roasting pan. This will thicken the gravy.

4. Continue stirring gravy about 7 minutes, until desired thickness. Taste and adjust seasonings. You may add a few drops, if desired, of a browning and seasoning sauce called "Kitchen Bouquet" which is readily available in all grocery stores.

cranberry fruit salad

2 (12 oz.) bags fresh cranberries	2 (10 oz.) cans crushed pineapple in juice	2 cups miniature marshmallows
2 cups sugar, more if desired	2 cups chopped walnuts	2 pints whipping cream

1. Rinse and drain cranberries. Chop cranberries in blender coarsely.

2. Mix cranberries and sugar in a bowl and set aside.

3. Open and drain canned pineapple. Add the crushed pineapple to cranberries.

4. Add walnuts and marshmallows to cranberry mixture and blend well.

5. Whip cream to a firm consistency. **Note:** *It is helpful to cool the bowl and blades of the electric beater for at least 30 minutes before whipping. This will quicken the whipping process.*

6. Carefully fold whipped cream into cranberry mixture. Refrigerate cranberry salad in bowl until serving.

mango lassi with honey

1 can (about 30 oz) mango pulp	Sugar and honey as desired
Lowfat cultured buttermilk, same quantity as mango pulp	2 tablespoons rose essence (optional)
	Rum to taste (optional)

Blend all of the above ingredients in a large punch bowl. Whisk ingredients until well blended. Adjust level of sweetness. Refrigerate and serve cold with crushed ice.

Happy Thanksgiving!

Although the preceding ideas of food combinations are unusual from a purely South Indian culinary perspective, you may find them truly enjoyable. Now, you can use your own creativity!

index

HEALTHY SOUTH INDIAN COOKING

HEALTHY SOUTH INDIAN COOKING   index